Loners

Loners describes a unique group of solitary children who were unable to adapt to the social and educational demands of school life. All were seen in a child psychiatric setting over a twenty-year period. Some of these children were gifted; most coped better once they had left school.

Sula Wolff brings together the results of a number of studies of these 'schizoid' children and illustrates the findings with detailed case histories. The condition of the children is thought to represent a constitutional deviation of personality development. It is discussed in relation to Asperger's original description of autistic psychopathy of childhood and in relation to current diagnostic practices in child and adult psychiatry.

Loners makes the case for the clinical recognition of such children although they are on the whole not nearly as impaired as those children who are currently given a diagnosis of Asperger's syndrome. Even when mildly affected, they and their parents need a treatment approach which differs from that for children with disorders due to adverse life experiences.

Loners will help psychiatrists and other professionals towards a realistic approach to the treatment and education of people with this condition, both children and adults.

Sula Wolff, a child psychiatrist, formerly at the Royal Hospital for Sick Children, Edinburgh, is Honorary Fellow at the University of Edinburgh Department of Psychiatry. She is the author of *Children under Stress* (1968; 2nd edn 1981) and *Childhood and Human Nature: The Development of Personality* (1989).

Loners

The Life Path of Unusual Children

Sula Wolff

London and New York

First published 1995
by Routledge
11 New Fetter Lane, London EC4P 4EE

Simultaneously published in the USA and Canada
by Routledge
29 West 35th Street, New York, NY 10001

© 1995 Sula Wolff

Typeset in Times by Michael Mepham, Frome, Somerset
Printed and bound in Great Britain by
Biddles Ltd, Guildford and King's Lynn

British Library Cataloguing in Publication Data
A catalogue record for this book is available from the British Library

Library of Congress Cataloguing in Publication Data
A catalogue record for this book has been requested

ISBN 0–415–06504–6 (hbk)
ISBN 0–415–06665–4 (pbk)

Contents

Illustrations

Foreword

Loners is destined to be a clinical classic. Sula Wolff has described a group of youngsters with socially isolated personalities and unusual interest patterns who do not fit criteria for other established clinical entities. Her analysis is based on remarkably broad personal experience, not only with the initial evaluation of such youngsters, but with the course of their development into young adulthood. The syndrome she has described is important because the clinical management of youngsters with this personality pattern is distinctly different from that appropriate for others. Customary approaches based on psychodynamic investigations and therapies aimed at altering intrafamilial relationships are contraindicated. Parents need to be helped to understand that the prognosis, for the most part, is relatively good; that these youngsters need support at school and at home to cultivate the assets they have; and that pressure for socialization by joining clubs and groups is likely to be counterproductive.

The last chapter of this book is no less fascinating than the rest. In particular, Dr Wolff suggests that Ludwig Wittgenstein may well have been such a loner. I, for one, am persuaded by the evidence she presents, though, of course, it suffers from being limited to a retrospective search for data. Not many loners will grow up to be Wittgensteins, though I would not be surprised to find his counterparts among mathematicians, philosophers, lighthouse keepers and forest rangers – individuals who have chosen careers which usually limit their social interactions. Let me at once confess that I do not know, either socially or professionally, any lighthouse keepers or forest rangers; I do know academics who fit the pattern!

In the Preface to his *Tractatus Logico-Philosophicus* Wittgenstein (1922) wrote that the whole meaning of his book could be summed up in the following words:

> What can be said at all can be said clearly; and whereof one cannot speak, thereof one must be silent.

Wittgenstein does not seem to me to have lived by his aphorism; the *Tractatus* is not always clear and it was not always persuasive even to Bertrand Russell, his mentor. Sula Wolff, on the other hand has observed his injunction with great fidelity. What she says, she says clearly. Her style is simple and direct. And whereof she cannot speak, such as the causes of the syndrome, she is silent as all must be until these are uncovered.

In the more than forty years I have been an academic child psychiatrist, I have emphasized to trainees the importance of clinical descriptive and phenomenological research. Most demur on the grounds that 'everything has already been described'. *Loners* proves them wrong. The task of separating out new clinical syndromes is not easy. It takes a good clinical eye; it requires being willing to stick by families and support them even though one is frankly puzzled about the best tack to take and uncertain about outcome; it takes a mind that is not hobbled by conventional modes of thought. The notion that children may differ in personality for reasons which are not experiential is no longer radical. It was very much so when Sula Wolff began her clinical work. Psychodynamic *furor therapeuticus* was ubiquitous. Watchful waiting has never been easy for doctors; it is, however, the only safeguard against iatrogenic disease when uncertainty abounds.

I wish I had had *Loners* to read when I began my career. I would have avoided clinical errors I made and only remedied after reading Dr Wolff's earlier papers on the subject. I commend this book to all those starting out on their mental health careers as an insightful portrait of an important condition and as a standard of clarity and brevity for their own research and writing. I commend it as well to mature clinicians whose understanding will be sharpened by studying its contents. This monograph demonstrates the importance of careful clinical longitudinal observation and incisive thought for the provision of appropriate psychiatric care for children and their families.

Leon Eisenberg, MD
Harvard Medical School
Boston, MA

REFERENCE

Wittgenstein, L. (1922/1981) *Tractatus Logico-Philosophicus.* Translated by C. K. Ogden. London: Routledge and Kegan Paul Ltd.

Acknowledgements

The researches summarized in this book were supported by grants from the Scottish Home and Health Department and from the McGhie Fund for Research into Mental and Nervous Disorders.

My special gratitude goes to a number of colleagues who actively participated in the work: Jonathan Chick, Ralph McGuire, Anne Barlow, Ann Cull, Lorraine Waterhouse and Douglas Blackwood. I want to thank Rose Townshend, who did most of the research interviews, and Andy Ginsborg, Barbara Moyes, David Weekes, Eunice Urquart and Louise Mountford, who also took part in the studies.

Most of all, I want to thank the many former child patients and their parents who told us about themselves and their lives and often made us welcome in their homes. Their readiness to keep in touch, sometimes for very many years, helped us to gain a new understanding of important aspects of personality development.

Lionel Hersov and Henry Walton read an earlier draft of this book. Their critical comments but also their encouragement were invaluable.

Permissions were kindly given by the Association for Child Psychology and Psychiatry to quote from an article by Wolff and Barlow and by Oxford University Press to quote from *Ludwig Wittgenstein: A Memoir*. Copyright on Miss Whiteley's works is held by the University of London Library and permission to quote from her Diary is acknowledged. The quotation from articles by Princesse de Bourbon-Orleans (Opal Whiteley) are reprinted from *Queen* magazine, courtesy of the National Magazine Company.

Author's note

All names of the participants of the studies are fictitious, and the case histories have been somewhat disguised in order to preserve anonymity. But what the children, the children grown-up and their parents actually said has been quoted verbatim, because no secondary account can ever do justice to the vividness with which people communicate about their life experiences.

Wenn wir einen Chinesen hören, so sind wir geneigt, sein Sprechen für ein unartikuliertes Gurgeln zu halten. Einer der Chinesisch versteht, wird darin die *Sprache* erkennen. So kann ich oft nicht die *Menschen* im Menschen erkennen.

(If we listen to a Chinese, we are inclined to regard his speech as inarticulate gurgling. Someone who understands Chinese will recognize it as *language*. In the same way I can often not recognize *the humanity* of another human being.)
(Wittgenstein, 1991, p. 18)

Introduction

IAN had serious behaviour problems at school from the age of 9, and at 14 he was referred to a child psychiatrist. He did not share the interests of the other boys, who found him snobbish and 'precious'; he was temperamental, aggressive and sullen, annoying other children until they retaliated; then he would lose control, screaming and holding his head. He had only one friend, and got on better with adults, conversing with them at a level beyond his years and his just average intelligence.

Ian could not tolerate quite ordinary stresses, running away at the prospect of an immunization and weeping when put into the second instead of the first of two music groups. He had only a single friend. Once, when his school books were torn up by other children, he simply threw them away on his way home from school. Ian's abiding interest was music, and his favourite composers were Benjamin Britten and Shostakovich. He played percussion in the school orchestra and had just started to learn the piano. His school work was adequate, except for maths. His total preoccupation with musical interests and his special musical gift were insufficiently valued at school.

In an essay about his life, Ian wrote: 'I like classical music which I regard as a serious art. . . . (one) of the periods which I dread most is PE. I am never very good at it. I have tried to play but if I am playing tennis or badminton I usually miss the ball. . . . Most of the people in my class do not have the same interests as me; they usually scorn and laugh. . . . I would really like to create some kind of friendship with my contemporaries in my class. I have difficulty in communicating with them because they either talk about sport or what they did last night. I definitely think that they can see that I have not a very good sense of humour. I have tried to change my way before but I seem to be falling into the same old rut again. . . . I seem to get on better with adults than I do with people of my own age.'

Ian had been a healthy but irritable baby, born by Caesarean section because of his mother's ill health. His general development was normal, but he had always been solitary, a poor mixer, rigid in his views and unable to adapt to the wishes of others. As a little boy he often lost his temper. He needed little sleep, contentedly lying awake at night, thinking or reading. He had enjoyed play group, but never fitted in at school. From the age of 3 he listened to modern composers, such as Gustav Holst, with passionate interest. Ian's father, a withdrawn and uncommunicative man, taught music, and two of his grandparents had also been musical. The mother, warm and affectionate, did her best to smooth Ian's path.

In his mid-teens Ian joined a youth orchestra, but fell out with the instructor and was asked not to come back. He was thought to be arrogant. He said: 'I was wanting to move forward more and they thought it was big-headed. If a point wasn't right, I'd explain it to the instructor.' The instructor, in turn, thought the boy was undermining him, and said: 'If Ian comes back, I'll retire.' His music tutor was more tolerant, merely smiling when Ian stamped his feet or said 'you can't teach me anything', so that the lessons continued.

In his final school year, Ian was chosen from among 400 candidates to join a prestigious youth orchestra. He went to music college and ended his course with distinction. It is remarkable that in later years he seemed to get on better in foreign countries, where a language barrier may have disguised his persisting difficulties in making emotional contact with other people. For his post-graduate studies he went to Europe and now, at the age of 28, after a period of real difficulty in finding work, he teaches orchestra to children in the Middle East.

On reading an account of the study to be reported in this book, he wrote that he 'recognized the observations contained therein only too clearly' and would like 'younger people at school [to] avoid the situation that the other participants and myself experienced during our time spent at school.'

All teachers but few parents know that some children are loners. These children cannot fit in, especially at school and, while sometimes gifted, their odd and eccentric behaviour creates trouble for themselves and others. The causes of these difficulties are often misunderstood. Parents may be blamed for failing to discipline or even for emotionally harming their offspring. This is especially so if, as often happens, the parents themselves have some of their children's personality traits.

This book sets out to give an account of a group of eccentric loners who were disturbed enough to be referred to a child psychiatric clinic, and who were followed up into adult life. Throughout, comparisons will be made with a control group of other referred children also reassessed in later years.

Some of the affected children were gifted and established successful working and family lives for themselves. Some, if also intellectually impaired, tended to remain solitary and dependent on their families. A few had a delinquent development, especially when exposed to social demands beyond their competence, and a very few became mentally ill.

This book has two aims: one practical, the other more speculative. The practical aim is to help parents, teachers and young people themselves to identify this particular personality constellation, which can make for major difficulties, especially at school. A degree of conformity is called for at school that is not experienced within the family or nursery group in the early years and will rarely be experienced again later, when most people can chose and structure their social and working lives to fit in with their personality make-up. Loners, often exquisitely sensitive, find the school years of gregarious conformity painful; noisy rough-and-tumble, competitive games and a prescribed syllabus are not for them. It is essential to identify such children so that their school life can be structured to meet their special needs; secondary emotional and behavioural disorders can be avoided; and the children helped to make the best use of their intelligence, interests and gifts.

The second aim of this book is to set out what is known about the nature of the condition. A number of aspects will be considered. These include: the range of severity of the disorder, from serious abnormality through mild eccentricity to a normal variety of personality functioning; its sex incidence and the manifestations in boys and girls; its frequent association in childhood with specific learning difficulties; the occasional association with both high intelligence and special giftedness; the numerically very slight risk of developing a mental illness in later life; its association with delinquency; and its possible genetic basis.

The descriptions of the childhood picture and of outcome in later life are based on clinical experience and on research findings. Most of these have been published and will be presented in summary form, with references to the fuller research reports. In the absence, at present, of systematic studies of the effects of different treatment interventions and of the educational needs of affected children, discussions of these topics can only rely on clinical experience.

1 Early observations

THE FIRST ELEVEN CASES

Some thirty years ago, as a child psychiatrist working in a children's hospital, I noticed that out of my first just over two hundred consecutively referred children, eleven had a particularly puzzling clinical picture. Many of their behavioural difficulties were exactly the same as those of other children attending the child psychiatry department, but the child's life history and family circumstances did not, as they usually do, reveal the explanations for the disorders. Most psychiatrically disturbed children have suffered from traumatic life events or chronic social, family or educational adversity, often from both, and their parents are only too aware of what the causes of the trouble might be. In a very few children disturbed behaviour is clearly due to some organic brain impairment; but these eleven children were physically healthy and only a few of them had been exposed to adverse circumstances.

All these children were boys; they ranged in age from 7 to 14 years; they were of normal, some of superior, intelligence; and nine had fathers in professional or higher managerial occupations. Ten of the eleven were referred because of marked difficulty in social adjustment at school, and eight of these were also failing educationally. The one child referred because of difficulties at home – stealing from his mother – had been solitary at school.

All the parents described their children as finding it hard to make friends and join in with group activities. School entrance precipitated the difficulties of one child; return to school after an illness those of another; a change of school those of a third; and going to boarding school was the trigger for those of two others. All these children found school life stressful, but coped with it in different ways. Two of the younger children refused to talk in class – in one case, if the teacher wanted a response, she would get the boy to write it down. A third boy, now older, had not talked in school throughout his first year there. These children had suffered from what is called 'elective mutism': they talked at home but not at school. Three children attempted to avoid going to school altogether and, if pressed, developed aches and pains: they presented with the syndrome of 'school refusal'. Another would stand by the school gate, refusing to enter until the janitor rang the bell. One boy, then 13, avoided gym and all school games, becoming panicky to the point of tears if urged to take part, so that finally the school made other arrangements for him during periods of gym and sports. Altogether seven of the eleven boys said they hated school games.

The mothers of all these children described difficulties as having existed since the pre-school years, but as not severe enough for them to have sought help. When 2 years old, one boy refused to wear a blazer, 'because if you wear a blazer, you grow up and if you grow up your parents leave you'. His mother then put his teddy bear in a blazer, and gradually her son too accepted this garment. Ten of the mothers were puzzled by their sons, concerned because they found they did not really understand them. One said: 'I don't know him as I should.' Other parents described their children as 'remote', 'lacking in feeling', 'solitary'. One mother said: 'He never lets his feelings go although he looks as if he'd like to'; another: 'He finds it difficult to show affection. Questions only result in a closing up'; and a third: 'There's a strangeness about him'.

A second characteristic reported by seven mothers was their children's difficulty in adapting to new circumstances and negativism or obstinacy over particular issues for reasons the child never made clear; if pressed to conform, temper outbursts occurred. Among other difficulties mentioned were: extreme modesty, despite the absence of parental prudishness, in three of the children; compulsive motor habits in three; and difficulty in falling asleep at night, also in three of the eleven.

One of the children, DAVID, had had two brief paranoid illnesses in which he thought a hidden tape recorder was recording him and that people were after him. To avoid this, he had to 'pay penalties' in the form of whistling and singing to the imagined tape recorder. At school he felt other people looked at him, 'because I invented this hymn'. He said: 'The main idea of the tape-recording thing was the year was not 1960 but two centuries later, and the experiment was to find out what a man was like now, and I was chosen and this was mixed up with the idea . . . I hummed songs to myself and I imagined little tape recorders all over the place. I didn't see them. I got a few theories of a whole model town . . . '

In the families of the children the most striking feature was that in five cases one of the parents, and in two other cases a more distant relative, was withdrawn and unsociable and made poor emotional contact with other people; and that in three other families one of the parents was found to talk all too freely, to have an impaired sense of what was socially appropriate, to show a mood state not apparently congruous with what was being discussed, and to have some unusual, metaphorical ways of expressing him- or herself in words. Although coping well with their work and family commitments, these three parents found tidiness and punctuality difficult to achieve.

One mother described a transient delusional experience following her last pregnancy: she found herself wandering out of the house along a country lane in a changed mood state, longing for her husband to fetch her back and feeling that if a cliff had been near, she would have thrown herself into the sea. She then heard a radio discussion and suddenly felt that the broadcaster could help her. She wrote to him, and to his response she attributed her subsequent recovery.

Four parents spontaneously likened their children to themselves or to an affected relative. One father said: 'He demonstrates a number of things which are personality characteristics of my own, I'm afraid', and went on to describe how a minor professional disagreement with a colleague had led him to give up a better paid job in order to devote five years of his life to a research project designed to prove his point; which he achieved. Of his son he said: 'His approach has been to bang his head against a brick wall. I've a sympathy for him, but his mother says she can't understand him.' One mother, who likened her son to her father, described the latter as 'brilliant but odd and impossible to live with. He couldn't make contact with other people and preferred to live alone.' Another mother felt her son resembled her brother: 'a spitfire as a child and a lone wolf who never made friends and isolated himself with his books'.

The family life of nine of the children was harmonious, and six of these had not experienced major *stressful life events* either. Two children had parents in discordant (including one disrupted) marriages; and three others had been exposed to major traumata associated with physical illness (namely, the mother's repeated stillbirths; the mother's increasing incapacity because of disseminated sclerosis; the child's own cancer and its treatment).

Like their unusual relatives, the children themselves fell into two groups: four were withdrawn and uncommunicative; seven outgoing and communicative.

The *withdrawn, uncommunicative children* engaged in the most limited conversation and play. Three of the four were extremely shy. The fourth lacked affect, discussing his stealing, for example, with detachment, and reporting one day: 'The conductor never took my bus fare today and I spent the money on sweets. . . . I had that happen before.'

Among the *communicative, outgoing* children, all of whom were of superior intelligence, two were hostile and paranoid. Faced with a family move and change of school, one boy said: 'People tell you you have to make friends and then when you do, you have to move and they want to get rid of you.' This boy preferred animals to people: 'Animals can't talk back. You don't really get to know animals and don't notice when they go away. I can't put up with other human beings. They're a nuisance more or less.' He was drawing two dinosaurs and I commented that even his dinosaur had a mate. He replied: 'Not a mate, but a sworn enemy. Would you like it if a certain animal wanted you for food?' The other somewhat paranoid boy also said: 'I prefer animals to human beings. They don't pick fights with you unless you bother them.' These two were the most rigid and obstinate of the seven communicative children, reacting with rage to demands for conformity. The remaining five were communicative and sensitive, revealing symbolic thought content unusually freely. Their conversation was characterized by emotional detachment, literalness and much use of metaphor.

One boy, in anticipation of coming to the hospital, thought: 'They're going to make a human being of me'; and after his first interview he said: 'It's as if I've been very, very sick and we've cleared up all the sick . . . [and] the smell.'

All the children said they felt different from other people. The oldest, then 14, put this most clearly: 'I'm an odd person, different from most people. I have different tastes. I like being by myself. It's my nature. I'm more fond of things than people. I see a lot of people with each other and I can't fit in. They have interests like fishing and pop records and I'm a square. I don't mind it, it's other people who object. They're nasty to me and I have to put up with it. I don't like fighting back much. I'm not a destructive type of person.'

This sense of being different and a preference for being alone was expressed by the children in different ways. One said: 'I'm different from the rest. I was called "posh one"'. Another boy said: 'I just can't make friends. . . . I'd like to be on my own and look at my coin collection. . . . I've got a hamster at home. That's enough company for me . . . I can play by myself. I don't need other people.' Another put it this way: '[I make friends] at school but not with people in the street. They like Cowboys and Indians and football and I don't. . . . I like to get away from people. . . . . I watch my mice.' A fourth boy said: 'I just don't think I'm like any of them [his mother, his father and his brother] . . . My friends are not like me. I don't talk very much. I prefer to be by myself.'

Both the withdrawn and the outgoing children had a number of *specific interests* which they pursued with unusual single-mindedness: stamp and coin collecting; music; reading; pet animals. The communicative children in addition had areas of extraordinary competence compared with their often poor school performance. The two paranoid children were very well informed and had strong views about politics. Two of the boys were exceptional at mechanical constructions, although their products were sometimes very odd. Another was expert at electronics and had made several radio and television sets. This boy also had a vivid fantasy life, which had preoccupied him for years and was to form an important part of his inner self well into his adult years. From the age of 5 he had had 'a dreamed-up island, square and on wheels on the ocean bed', which he described in a never-ending series of stories and cartoon strips.

EARLY ATTEMPTS AT TREATMENT

Seven of the children were initially diagnosed as having a psychogenic disorder, that is, their symptoms were thought to be due to adverse life experiences. A psychotherapeutic approach, however, failed to increase the therapist's, the patients' or the parents' understanding of what had brought the difficulties about. After four months of regular encounters with the 13 year old who had a phobic avoidance of gym at school, the significance of this symptom remained as obscure as before, although he was a talkative and forthcoming boy. After three months, a non-communicative 7-year-old boy was as quiet as ever, always played with his back to the room, whispered his sparse verbal responses, but told his mother that he loved coming. No change whatever had occurred in his behaviour at home, at school or in the clinic.

Attempts to urge the children to reveal their feelings more freely, or to explain to them that their symptoms might have an underlying meaning (for example, that the delusional experiences of one of the boys might reflect his worries about his mother's health) sometimes led to transient disorganization of behaviour. In one case a sudden outburst of anger – 'get away with you!' – unacknowledged even seconds later, followed such an intervention; in another case there were sudden tears and a paranoid feeling that the therapist's smile meant she was 'trying to get the better of' him.

So long as the treatment staff conveyed to the families that the child's difficulties were environmentally produced, that change in the child was expected and that the onus was on the families, with help, to bring this about, understanding between treatment staff and families remained limited. Children and parents continued to be as anxious as ever and no progress was made. But as soon as the child's symptoms were recognized as springing from his particular and inherent personality make-up, unusual but not unheard of, and certainly not caused by faulty parenting, poor teaching or ill will on the part of the boy, an understanding between treatment staff and families was established, and the child's own perceptions and those of his parents were confirmed. This brought relief to everyone, including the teachers, especially when a new spirit of hope could be introduced as well.

This hope relied on two quite specific therapeutic interventions. The first was to convey to the families and the education authorities that the children's basic personality characteristics could not be expected to change; and that the parents and the schools would need to make allowances for what the children could and could not manage, in order to help them adapt to school life. Often this meant that the child was officially allowed to avoid particularly stressful settings, like school games or a noisy playground. Sometimes education in smaller, more flexible classes was called for, and teachers were encouraged to build on the children's special interests and abilities in their educational endeavours. The second intervention engendering hope was to indicate to everyone that the child's future outlook was likely to be good. This was thought to be justified even at that time, when no systematic follow-up studies were yet available, because many of the children resembled other family members in their personality features, and these relatives had in general managed their adult lives well. Moreover, it was thought even then that, once out of school, free to avoid noisy social groups and free also to pursue their own interests and ambitions, these children might find life a good deal easier than during the regimented years of school.

WHAT SHOULD WE CALL THIS CONDITION?

Because the characteristics shared by the eleven children described above resembled those found in the older and also in the then current psychiatric literature under the term 'schizoid personality', this was the initial diagnostic label chosen for the children's condition (Wolff, 1964). It was recognized even then that this term might be misunderstood and could convey unintended prognostic gloom, because schizoid personality traits had been found to excess in the past histories of schizophrenic patients and in the biological relatives of such patients. The point needs to be made right away that, even if this is so, this tells one nothing about the frequency with which people with schizoid traits can be expected to develop this serious psychotic illness. In fact, as we shall see later, the risk is likely to be very small. What is essential is not to call a clinical syndrome, which resembles a well-known condition in adult life, by a different name merely because it occurs in childhood. In clinical practice what was important was to ascribe the difficulties that brought the children to attention to their 'personality make-up', and this formulation of their troubles seemed to be acceptable both to the children and to their parents.

Three courses of action followed the recognition of these first eleven children as 'schizoid':

1 a determination to look out for other such children in the course of ordinary clinical practice;
2 to try to define more accurately what the precise difficulties of the children are, as a basis for long-term, systematic follow-up studies because, if indeed the affected children have a particular personality constellation or disorder, then their characteristics should endure well into adult life;
3 to search the literature for accounts in childhood and adult life of people with the same or similar difficulties.

In the next chapter we shall examine the descriptions found in the literature of this puzzling condition and of related disorders, and will discuss the problem of diagnostic labelling. Much of the rest of this book will deal with the follow-up studies carried out in Edinburgh of 'schizoid' children seen in child psychiatric practice. Here we shall summarize the children's clinical features as they appeared to us in the early years, and describe a study of their psychological functioning.

THE CLINICAL FEATURES

After some years it became possible to describe the clinical features of these children more definitively. They formed about 4 per cent of new clinic referrals. Girls too could be affected, but the condition was commoner in boys, with a sex ratio of about 3.5:1. The children were almost all referred during their school years, usually because of social difficulties at school. In addition, many were failing educationally despite average or superior intelligence, and some had specific developmental delays, such as a lag in language development; reading, writing or spelling difficulties at school; or excessive clumsiness. A very small number had evidence of organic brain impairment and/or were of below average intelligence. Intelligence tests often revealed large discrepancies between different areas of functioning, for example, between verbal and non-verbal intelligence subscales. These children were described as *solitary* and as finding group activities, especially rough-and-tumble games, stressful; when pressed to conform, outbursts of rage or tears ensued. They *lacked empathy*, finding it difficult to imagine what other people felt and thought, and were unusually detached and objective when describing other people and also themselves. While often very *sensitive* themselves, sometimes even suspicious, they lacked sensitivity for the feelings of others, were poor at sizing up social situations, and hence often acted inappropriately. A number were preoccupied with their own *systems of ideas and interests*, which were very persistent over time, and often quite original. In addition, many of the children were quite rigid in pursuing their interests, unable to perceive and adapt to the needs of other people and unable also to conform to social demands. *Unusual, metaphorical language* was another feature of these children. One adolescent boy, for example, always held his right arm across his chest and explained this by saying: 'I don't want to feel exposed'. On starting school, he had worn a 'tortoise shell' on his back, which made it hard for him and his mother to get on and off buses on the way to school. When he got home, he always hung the shell on the bathroom towel rail. In retrospect he could not remember whether at the time he thought his protective carapace was real or imaginary. As our later studies made clear, having *an unusual fantasy life* was a further characteristic feature of the condition. Some of the children were outgoing and communicative, some reserved and very quiet.

AN EARLY PSYCHOLOGICAL STUDY OF 'SCHIZOID', AUTISTIC AND NORMAL CHILDREN

From the start, the features these children had in common were recognized as having some similarity to those of children with autism, although the schizoid children were not handicapped in their total functioning as autistic children usually are, and their early development was not abnormal to the same degree. In particular, they did not have the gross early language abnormalities combined with severe difficulties in relating to other people, even their own parents, of autistic children, and their range of intelligence was much higher.

In an attempt to see whether schizoid children could validly be distinguished from autistic children on the one hand and from ordinary school children on the other, small groups of schizoid, autistic and other children were given a series of psychological tasks and tests (Wolff and Barlow, 1978). The groups, of eight children in each, were matched for age (mean age 11 years), sex and non-verbal intelligence (IQ mean of 89, 94 and 92, respectively). The effect of this was that neither the schizoid nor the autistic children were fully representative of the larger groups of clinic attenders from which they had been drawn: the schizoid children in the study were of much lower intelligence than other schizoid children; and the autistic children were the brightest of their group.

The well-functioning autistic children in this study were, like autistic children studied by others (Hermelin, 1978; Hermelin and O'Connor, 1970), repetitive and stereotyped in their responses to the tasks set, had a good rote memory for random series of words, and good visual-spatial perceptions. They were impaired in their perceptiveness of meaning compared with normal children, for example, not improving on their recall for series of words when these words formed a meaningful sentence. These autistic children at the age of 11 were well motivated to succeed at the tasks set for them and, in the tasks which involved describing people (their mother and people in photographs), they used concepts relating to roles and at times to feelings. Schizoid children were, on most tasks and tests, intermediate between the autistic and ordinary school children. They shared the autistic children's stereotypy (in forming patterns with counters), as well as some of their language handicaps and their lack of perception of meaning. On the other hand, the schizoid children were not nearly as repetitive as the autistic children and, somewhat surprisingly, were less well motivated than the autistic group to succeed at tests of memory and intellectual functioning. They actually performed worse on these tests, appearing to be 'distracted from within'. More striking was the fact that the schizoid group were severely (more severely than the autistic children) lacking in the use of 'psychological constructs' when describing people. They rarely attributed emotions either to their mothers or to people depicted in photographs, but talked about them rather in terms of what they wore or did. For example, when asked to describe their mother, the schizoid children would give a list of her daily chores and mention the clothes she wore. They often introduced irrelevancies when talking of their mothers, although not when describing strangers in photographs.

A 12-year-old schizoid boy, asked to describe his mother, responded as follows:

No, I couldn't describe her. I would need to say too much. Curly hair, black kind of blackish, curly hair, wackish [*sic*] brown kind of hair and blue eyes and kind of sharp, pointed nose because she's a nosey and an ordinary woman's lips, stuffed with what do you call it? Lipstick. Just now I think she's wearing a grey coat scarf. Got a blue bag with white things, kind of stripes on them. Two pockets at the side and that's it. That's her broad handbag. She does housework. Got two jobs. At certain times she does the other job and that's when I'm back at school. Until I'm back at school she does this job. Next holiday she'll be doing the other job all the time, even when I'm back from school. What's this job? Typing. She's got and will be getting. And the other job is nursing in an old folk's home and that's all I'm telling you. I'm not telling you any more. I'll describe another person . . .

And he went on to describe his 'girlfriend' (Wolff and Barlow, 1978).

This account focused on the mother's appearance, clothes, household chores and occupation, and contained only a single comment about her feelings or motivations: 'because she's a nosey . . .'.

Anne Barlow's study suggested that there is clearly a resemblance between well-functioning autistic children and less well-functioning schizoid children. Schizoid children, however, are even more impaired in their awareness of the feelings of other people than autistic children are, and they tend not to do themselves justice at intellectual tasks, apparently because of poor motivation and distractibility from within.

2   In search of a diagnostic label

This chapter will examine the usefulness of diagnostic labelling, the changing concepts of schizoid personality disorder, and the diagnoses applied to other series of children who resembled the schizoid children described in this book.

WHY DIAGNOSES ARE HELPFUL

It is often thought that diagnostic labels stigmatize children and obscure their individual uniqueness. Those who argue against such labels hold that what is needed is rather to understand the origins of particular behavioural and emotional difficulties, and to know how the individual child's developmental needs can best be met both within the family and at school. Yet a diagnostic label for a psychological disturbance or for a particular personality configuration does not take away the individuality of a person. On the contrary, it clarifies something the person 'has', not what he or she is, and it often opens doors to a better understanding of the child and to the practical resources, for example, special educational help, that may be needed to promote his or her development.

A diagnostic label for a psychological disorder of childhood is applied when a group of behaviour patterns and expressed emotions tend to cluster together regularly and are much less often associated with other behavioural and emotional features. A diagnostic syndrome is further defined by its age of onset and course over time; by a possible familial incidence; by its response to specific treatment interventions; and by its cause or causes. In general medicine it is this last, causal, feature that best defines diagnostic categories of illnesses, such as pneumonia, a heart attack or meningitis. In psychiatry, knowledge about causation is less advanced, and many diagnostic syndromes are defined more by their symptoms and their course over time.

Many diagnostic labels of child psychiatric conditions, while at first perhaps arousing anxiety, have in fact been very helpful. For example, in recent years it has been recognized that *depressive illness* with its clear implications for treatment, is not at all uncommon, especially in early adolescence (Kolvin *et al.*, 1991; Harrington, 1993), and that it is often associated with other types of disorders, such as antisocial behaviour. It was found that, in order to make the diagnosis, it is essential to ask the young person herself exactly how she feels and what she thinks:

reports from others often underestimate the depth of depressed mood. Moreover, once a diagnosis is made, the treatment options are clear and similar to those for adults with depressive illnesses, about which a great deal is known.

Early childhood autism is another condition whose diagnosis has helped many parents, children and teachers. When the parents of a 3-year-old boy who is not yet speaking, is emotionally unresponsive and preoccupied with lining up his toy cars in immaculately straight lines, screaming if anyone accidentally interrupts the pattern, and also unpredictably screaming when taken out to shop with his mother, are finally told that he has autism, the relief, tinged of course with disappointment and sadness, can be considerable. The mother, perhaps told by others she may be worrying unnecessarily, had seen a television programme about the condition and wondered whether her son was similarly afflicted. It lifts a load from her mind when her fears are taken seriously and she finds her own explanations validated. Now the parents are able to explain to the grandparents, the nursery staff and the neighbours just what the matter is, and are no longer under suspicion of perhaps having caused the disturbance themselves through poor child-rearing. What is more, a new understanding is reached between the parents and their medical and psychology advisers. The nursery or school teacher now has an explanation for the child's unresponsiveness to herself and the other children, knows what teaching methods will best meet his needs and where to turn for advice about how to handle him in the classroom. Most important, a diagnosis of autism is an entrance ticket to a very effective parent organization and, as he or she grows older, special educational resources will be forthcoming for a child with established autism. The diagnosis should mobilize continued professional supervision and support well into adult life, and special work training and residential resources if these are needed.

A diagnosis places a child with a disturbance into a group of other children with the same disturbance. Of course, within such a group children will vary in the severity with which the disorder affects them, and their unique life history, family background and other personal characteristics will always colour their behaviour and how they feel about themselves and the world. Each diagnostic group contains very different individuals, and what they have in common may be less important than what distinguishes between them. But with a condition like a depressive illness or early childhood autism, and with the socially handicapping characteristics of 'loners' that will be described in this book, a diagnosis is vital both for better understanding and for better treatment of the young person and his or her family.

More specifically, a diagnosis can be a pointer to causation and can also promote realistic expectations for the future. This is especially important when the focus, as so often in child psychiatry and psychology, is on the parent–child relationship. Neither parents nor child are helped when a child's inborn, that is, constitutional, difficulties are attributed to family pathology, or when expectations for conformity remain high in the face of inherently limited adaptive capacities. On the contrary, relief and improved conduct frequently follow when a child's difficulties are correctly interpreted as the result of his or her make-up, and allowances are made for this at home and at school. Syndrome definition in child psychiatry is no empty exercise.

It will become clear that the boundaries of the condition with which this book is concerned are not yet well defined and that it is uncertain whether we are dealing with one or a number of syndromes. What is more, the condition (or conditions) has been described by a bewildering variety of terms (Wolff, 1991b). Even more confusing is the fact that the definition and meaning of some of these terms have changed over the years. It is one of the aims of this book to contribute towards a clarification of the syndrome to which we initially applied the label of schizoid personality disorder in childhood (Wolff and Chick, 1980; Wolff, 1984). This label will be used throughout much of this book, although towards the end, and as a result of evaluating the extensive literature on the topic, the term schizoid/Asperger disorder will be recommended.

CHANGING CONCEPTS OF SCHIZOID PERSONALITY DISORDER

We initially applied the label 'schizoid personality' to our children because they resembled descriptions of this personality in adults in the older psychiatric literature.

Schizoid personality in the older psychiatric literature

Although originating in childhood, all personality disorders are described in adult people. Moreover, psychiatrists at the turn of the century were hospital-based and primarily concerned with seriously ill patients. It is perhaps not surprising that before child psychiatry became an established discipline, we had only meagre accounts of the childhood characteristics of adult psychiatric patients. Emil Kraepelin, the father of present-day psychiatry, and especially of the classification of the major psychiatric illnesses, mentioned childhood precursors of some types of schizophrenia, but also made the point that it is possible that 'the peculiarities which meet us in the previous history of our patients could also be found in similar guise in any other group of people taken at random . . .' (Kraepelin, 1919, pp. 236–237). Among these precursors were 'a quiet, shy, retiring disposition', especially in boys, some of whom 'held themselves aloft from all childish naughtiness'. They 'made no friendships, lived only for themselves'. In girls there was irritability, sensitiveness, excitability and self-willedness.

Eugen Bleuler, the Swiss psychiatrist, coined the word 'schizoid' in 1908 to describe people who were shut-in, suspicious, comfortably dull, sensitive and 'pursuers of vague purposes', characteristics he thought were part of the normal range of personality variation (Nannarello, 1953). Yet he also found that the case histories of over half the individuals who later became schizophrenic revealed earlier tendencies towards 'seclusion, withdrawal, together with moderate or severe degrees of irritability. They already stood out as children because they were unable to play with others and followed their own ways instead', and their odd 'intellectual characteristics' made other children regard them as strange, even 'crazy' (E. Bleuler, 1950, p. 251).

Ernst Kretschmer (1925), again investigating the previous personality patterns of psychiatric patients, contrasted the personality traits of schizophrenic patients with those of manic-depressive patients. The former schizoid or, in his terminology, 'schizothyme', people he described as unsociable, oversensitive, but also cold and lacking in 'affective resonance', stubborn and pedantic. Others have included in their descriptions 'a certain unreasonableness' and inaccessibility to argument, with many preconceived notions and superstitions. Affected people may turn to vegetarianism and fanatical outdoor pursuits and become 'persons who have forever shut their ears to reason and who have become entirely absorbed in some idea' (Essen-Moeller, 1946). Kraepelin and other writers noticed some similarity between the features of schizoid personality disorder and the symptoms of schizophrenia, and confirmed the high prevalence of schizoid personality in the past histories of schizophrenic patients as well as in the biological relatives of such patients (M. Bleuler, 1954).

The important point needs to be repeated that, even if schizoid personality traits are particularly often found in the past histories of schizophrenic patients, this tells one nothing at all about the risk of schizophrenia in people with schizoid personalities. This illness is relatively rare in the community; schizoid personality may be quite common and, while a predisposition to schizoid traits probably contributes to the causes of schizophrenia, other and perhaps more important causes are likely to be necessary as well. Only population studies can establish how common schizoid personality traits and disorders are in the general population, and whether such traits are dimensional or categorical, that is, whether they shade gradually into the normal, as Claridge (1985) believes, with some people having the traits in large measure, others very mildly, or whether there is a more definite cut-off point between those with and those without such traits or disorders.

There is a further point to be made at the outset, although it will be discussed more fully later: schizoid personality traits, despite their association in a few people with serious psychiatric illness, may be biologically advantageous for the population in general because of their possible association with originality and giftedness.

Schizoid personality disorder in current diagnostic classifications

In the more recent diagnostic classifications, the meaning of the term 'schizoid personality disorder' has become more restricted, and a new category, 'schizotypal personality disorder', has been devised for personality characteristics previously subsumed under the general term 'schizoid'. In ICD-10 (WHO, 1992), the most recent international classification of diseases, the main features of the newly-defined category of schizoid personality disorder in adult life are: impaired ability to experience pleasure; emotional coldness and detachment; limited capacity to express warmth or anger; indifference to praise or criticism; little interest in sexual experiences with others; a preference for solitary activities; excessive fantasy and introspection; lack of close friends or confiding relationships; and marked insensitivity to social norms and conventions. Curiously, schizoid disorders of childhood are excluded from this definition and appear instead under the childhood category of Asperger's syndrome.

DSM-IV (American Psychiatric Association, 1994), the most recent American classification of psychiatric disorders, defines schizoid personality disorder in terms of four of the following features: neither desiring nor enjoying close relationships; choosing solitary activities; little interest in sexual experiences; getting pleasure from few activities; lacking close friends other than near relatives; indifference to praise or criticism; emotional coldness, detachment or flattened affectivity.

Schizotypal personality disorder in current diagnostic classifications

The American psychiatrist and psychoanalyst, Sandor Rado (1954), first coined the term 'schizotype' for the behavioural and psychodynamic expression of a genetic predisposition to schizophrenia. He saw the 'machinery for psychodynamic integration' in schizotypal people as deficient because of their lack of pleasure, that is their inability to share love and affection, as a motivating and integrating force. He thought that people genetically predisposed to schizophrenia might be stable and well compensated in their adaptation to life, and he labelled such people 'schizoid', in the sense in which Kraepelin and Bleuler used this term. The word 'schizotypal' Rado applied if such predisposed individuals displayed more florid symptoms, and he suggested that schizotypal people too may go through life without ever developing schizophrenia. If these people are intellectually gifted, this helps them towards achievements, and also to compensate for their emotional deficiencies; only if adaptation breaks down altogether will schizophrenia supervene.

Since then, the term schizotypy has been applied to that personality disorder which, although often associated with schizoid and paranoid personality disorders, shows the clearest genetic relationship to schizophrenia (Siever *et al.*, 1990). It is the personality disorder most often found in the closest relatives of schizophrenic patients: in identical more often than in non-identical twins of schizophrenic patients; and in the biological rather than in the adoptive parents of schizophrenics (McGuffin and Thapar, 1992).

Yet the point has been made (Frances, 1985) that it may not be warranted to define the characteristics of this personality disorder on the basis of the features of people (that is, relatives of schizophrenics) who are not themselves patients, since all diagnostic classifications have been designed specifically to apply to patient groups. For our purposes we should merely note that the diagnostic definitions of schizotypal personality at present are in large measure based on non-patient populations. This makes them more rather than less relevant to our own studies of child patients grown-up, because most of these were patients no longer.

In ICD-10, Schizotypal Disorder is now equated with 'latent' or 'borderline' schizophrenia, and classified in the section on schizophrenia. The defining features listed include emotional coldness; odd and eccentric behaviour or appearance; poor rapport and social withdrawal; odd beliefs or magical thinking; suspiciousness or paranoid ideas; obsessive ruminations, but without inner resistance; occasional illusions or depersonalization; vague, circumstantial, metaphorical speech; occasional brief episodes of delusional or hallucinatory experiences. In DSM-IV the term defines a personality disorders with the following features, at least five of which must be present: ideas of reference; magical thinking; unusual perceptual experiences; odd thinking and speech; suspiciousness or paranoid ideas; inappropriate or constricted affect; odd, eccentric behaviour or appearance; lack of close friends other than relatives; excessive social anxiety with paranoid fears.

IN DEFENCE OF A MORE GLOBAL USE OF THE TERM 'SCHIZOID'

The children and young people to be described in this book might be labelled as having schizoid *or* schizotypal disorders and, as we shall see, there was no basis in our study for a clear distinction between people fulfilling the separate diagnostic criteria as set out in ICD-10 or DSM-III and DSM-IV for these two conditions. For this reason the diagnostic term 'schizoid' will be used throughout this book to describe individuals who might fulfil the criteria for either or both the schizoid or schizotypal personality disorders. This use of the term for adults is not idiosyncratic. Tyrer (Tyrer and Ferguson, 1988), who developed an interview for identifying different non-overlapping types of personality disorders, has argued for the use of the term schizoid in a more global way. DSM-III schizoid and schizotypal personality disorder features were both found to excess in the childhood histories of schizophrenic patients (Foerster *et al.*, 1991; McCreadie *et al.*, 1994), and, in a very different sample, of serious offenders, schizoid and schizotypal personality disorders again often occurred together (Coid, 1992).

Moreover, DSM-IV groups schizotypal, paranoid and schizoid personality disorders together as a cluster (Cluster A), and there is recent evidence that all three are biologically related to schizophrenia (Varma and Sharma, 1993; see also Chapter Ten).

So far we have been considering the descriptions of grown-up people with personality difficulties like those of our 'loners'. We now turn to the descriptions of children who resembled the young people in the present study. As we shall see, there is considerable controversy about the best diagnostic terms to be used to describe such children. Some clinicians and researchers believe that there is insufficient similarity between children who present as 'loners' and adults with schizoid or schizotypal personality disorders, and that affected children have more in common with children suffering from early childhood autism, and are therefore best decribed as having a 'pervasive developmental disorder'.

SOME DEFINITIONS OF TERMS

For the sake of clarity, a number of the terms already used are here defined according to current diagnostic classifications.

Personality disorders

According to ICD-10 (WHO, 1992, p. 200), these are deeply ingrained and enduring behaviour patterns manifesting themselves as inflexible responses to a broad range of personal and social situations. They represent either extreme or significant deviations from the way the average individual in a given culture perceives, thinks, feels and particularly relates to others. Frequently, but not always, personality disorders are associated with various degrees of subjective distress and problems in social functioning and performance. These are developmental conditions, which appear in childhood or adolescence and continue into adulthood.

In DSM-IV (APA, 1994) personality disorder is defined as an enduring pattern of inner experience and behaviour deviating markedly from the expectations of the individual's culture. It is judged to be present when personality traits (see below) are inflexible and maladaptive, and cause either significant functional impairment or subjective distress. It is generally recognizable by adolescence or early adulthood.

Personality traits

These are considered to be relatively stable and consistent patterns characteristic of an individual's personality, and not in themselves abnormal (Goldenson, 1984). In DSM-IV they are defined as enduring patterns of perceiving, relating to, and thinking about the environment and oneself, and as exhibited in a wide range of important social and personal contexts.

Pervasive developmental disorders

This group of disorders, beginning in very early childhood, includes autism and a number of related disorders. The inclusive term itself is not explicitly defined in ICD-10, but applies to *distortions* of development in a number of important functions, with severe lifelong difficulties in social and communication skills beyond those accounted for by a general retardation of development, although general developmental delay is often an associated feature.

DSM-IV defines pervasive developmental disorders, which include autism, as qualitative severe and pervasive impairments in the development of reciprocal social interaction; in communication skills; or the presence of stereotyped behaviour, interests and activities. The disorders are usually evident in the first years of life and often associated with some degree of mental retardation.

GROUPS OF CHILDREN RESEMBLING OUR OWN HAVE BEEN GIVEN A NUMBER OF DIFFERENT DIAGNOSTIC LABELS

The first description of 'schizoid' children

I have only recently found what is probably the very first account of schizoid children: a report of six cases from the hospital school of the Moscow psychoneur-ological children's in-patient department, by Dr Ssucharewa, published in 1926. The children were all boys, ranging in age from 2 to 14 years. Since early childhood they had been unlike other children; they were solitary and adapted poorly to the demands of their environment. While themselves excessively sensitive, the child-ren's responses to others were superficial and they showed limited facial expressions of emotion. They had oddities of speech and voice as well as of thinking, with a tendency to abstract, ruminative thought processes; their motor clumsiness was striking and obsessionality a frequent feature. Three of the six children were musical, one was interested in politics and social issues, and two had literary gifts. Five were of above average intelligence, several came from gifted families, and their parents often had similar personality traits. Dr Ssucharewa diagnosed these children as having 'schizoid personality disorder of childhood' ('*Psychopathie*' being the German term for personality disorder). She thought they were like Kretschmer's schizoid types; that they had an inborn predisposition to an unusual personality, which shares some but not all the characteristics of schizo-phrenia, but that their course was quite different from that of patients with schizophrenia, with no deterioration as they grew older.

Later reports of schizoid children

In their study of 500 consecutive child-guidance clinic attenders, Jenkins and Glickman (1946) labelled 75 as 'schizoid'. These children had three or more of a cluster of intercorrelating traits, established by a factor analysis of all recorded symptoms. The schizoid cluster comprised the following items: fantastic thinking; changes in personality; day-dreaming; lack of concentration; carelessness; re-gression towards infantile behaviour. These items were negatively correlated with items defining socialized delinquency. Schizoid children thus statistically defined, like our own schizoid boys, came from socio-economically superior families and, unlike other children, had no adverse background factors to account for their difficulties. In a subsequent analysis of his data, Jenkins (1968) identified 12 per cent of the 500 children as schizoid and presented a somewhat different list of their symptoms: shyness; timidity; apathy; underactivity; sensitivity; lacking close friends. The sex incidence was five boys to each girl, and the commonest age of referral was 9–14 years. It seems probable that the children called 'schizoid' in this second analysis may have included both schizoid and constitutionally-shy children. While superficially similar, Jenkins and Glickman (1946) themselves had pointed out that both neurotically inhibited and constitutionally shy children are very different from schizoid children. The former two groups do not display the eccentricities of schizoid children.

Here it is of interest that four types of childhood solitude have recently been described (Asendorpf, 1993). Some children are constitutionally shy, holding back in strange surroundings and with strange people. This temperamental trait is evident even at 2 years and remains very stable over time. Then there are children who are shy for neurotic reasons, with anxiety and poor self-esteem, fearing, sometimes for good reasons and sometimes irrationally, that they will be ostracized. The third group are children who are in fact ostracized by their peers. And the fourth group, the truly unsociable, avoid human contact because they prefer to be alone. Our schizoid children belong to this last group.

Asperger's 'Autistic Psychopathy of Childhood'

The clearest clinical account we have so far of children who seem to resemble those described in this book is that of the Viennese paediatrician, Hans Asperger (1944), who reported on what he regarded as a new psychiatric disorder in children, which he called 'Autistic Psychopathy of Childhood'. It is a curious coincidence that, unknown to Asperger, Leo Kanner in America had, just a year earlier, written the definitive account of another new child psychiatric syndrome, 'Early Infantile Autism', whose features have, as we shall see, much in common with those of Asperger's children (Kanner, 1943). In addition, Goldstein and his colleagues (Scheerer *et al.*, 1945) just a year later, reported their experimental study of 'idiot savant', an allied phenomenon to be described in Chapter Nine. Both Kanner and Asperger derived the term 'autism' from Eugen Bleuler (1930), who had used it to describe the withdrawal into their own world of schizophrenic patients. So that even then some similarity was noted between schizophrenia on the one hand, and childhood autism and autistic psychopathy on the other. Karl Jaspers (1963), the German phenomenologist and philosopher, defined autism as 'self-incapsulation in an isolated world' and 'being turned in on oneself and one's own fantasies with no regard for outer reality'.

Asperger's paper has recently been beautifully translated by Uta Frith, who also gives us some biographical information, especially about his unique dedication to the remedial treatment of difficult children within a university paediatric setting. Her interpretations, however, of what Asperger *really* meant (especially her belief that his emphasis on the children's giftedness may have been misplaced) and her substitution of the word 'autism' for Asperger's 'autistic psychopathy' may not finally prove to be correct (Asperger, 1944; Frith, 1991).

Asperger (1944) draws on his extensive clinical experience for his account of autistic psychopathy, and illustrates it with four detailed case histories. He points out the similarities to schizophrenia, but the absence of the deterioration or disintegration found in that psychotic illness, and throughout the paper he stresses that affected children may have exceptional achievements. In a mild form, and once one knows what to look for, the personality syndrome is not rare. Despite many individual differences, and the fact that not all children with autistic psychopathy show all its features, the main characteristics of the syndrome he reports are as follows:

1   Its constancy over time is salient. The condition is recognizable from the second year onwards and endures throughout life. The same basic disturbance gives rise to difficulties of social adaptation during pre-school development, makes for disorders of behaviour and learning at school, and leads to occupational

difficulties *and* exceptional achievements, as well as to conflicts in marriage and social relationships in adult life.

2   Asperger describes abnormalities of gaze and poverty of expression and gesture.

3   Speech and voice production are unusual, curiously monotonous in some, excessively soft or shrill in others, and at times with an apparently affected upper-class intonation.

4   The children's language expresses their strange 'autistic intelligence', marked by originality rather than imitation and learning from others. Gifted autistic psychopaths use language in a highly original and creative way, while the less intelligent produce empty phrases. These children become specialists: in the natural sciences, for example, in poisons, mathematics, machinery or art. Asperger makes much of some of the children's originality of thought and of their creative products, but he also describes a few affected children with mental handicap and organic brain impairments. Among these some displayed 'savant' phenomena (although Asperger did not use this term), such as callendrical calculation or the memorization of the tram timetables of Vienna. If of high intelligence, the children develop original and inventive views of the world; if dull, they function like automata. Sometimes they become unproductive eccentrics.

  The children's self-appraisal is surprisingly objective and accurate: they think about themselves. But they are also able to judge others in an astonishingly mature way, being particularly sensitive to the shortcomings of other children. Yet despite their clear-sightedness, their social adaptation is always impaired.

  They often have learning difficulties in reading, spelling and arithmetic and difficulties of concentration, appearing to be 'distracted from within', concentrating on their own inner pursuits rather than attending to the demands of the classroom.

5   The basic disturbance is one of restricted social and emotional relationships with other people. Parents are particularly sensitive to and unhappy about the children's lack of feeling for others, which at times amounts to callousness. Asperger describes some of the children's 'autistic maliciousness' and the hurt they can cause to other children and adults, both physically and emotionally. They are solitary, refuse to join in groups of other children at play, insist on following their own inclinations, meet social demands with negativism and fail to conform at school. They tend to be teased by other children, although the more intelligent gain status through their achievements.

  Motor stereotypies and repetitive behaviour patterns occur. One 7 year old could never finish his meals because of his total preoccupation with watching the fat globules move about on the surface of his soup.

6   Among the emotional disturbances Asperger described are a lack of interest in sex, even in adult life; extreme personal sensitivity with egocentricity, at times associated with callousness towards others and even sadistic communications (for example, cool threats to stab the mother); lack of awareness of interpersonal distance so that some may approach strangers with familiarity; lack of humour, except for puns; and idiosyncratic tastes and attachments to objects, with the

formation of apparently meaningless collections. Asperger makes clear that what is involved is not merely poverty of feeling or emotionality, but a qualitative 'difference of being'. He also stressed the severe homesickness for their own familiar surroundings in the children he admitted to his therapeutic ward.

7   Asperger was clear that the condition is not caused by faulty upbringing, but is likely to be genetic. In each of 200 cases he had then seen in the course of ten years, one or more relatives had had similar personality characteristics, even if these did not amount to the full syndrome. Fathers, if affected, usually pursued intellectual occupations or, if they were artisans, they gave the impression of having missed their vocation. A number of children came from exceptional scientific or artistic families. These observations led Asperger to speculate that autistic personality traits might be socially valuable.

Asperger was very struck by the fact that all his cases were boys. He did see the full picture of autistic personality in the mothers of his male patients, and he found difficulties in social relationships in girls, sometimes following brain disease. But physically unimpaired girls of normal intelligence never showed the complete syndrome as seen in boys. Asperger developed the curious notion that autistic psychopathy might be an 'extreme variant of male intelligence, of the male character', and that in girls the syndrome is either associated with early brain damage or does not fully show itself until adult life.

8   Asperger considered the possibility that affected children were pre-schizophrenic, yet only one of the 200 patients he knew developed this illness. Of course, it is unclear how systematically he followed up his affected children; he certainly lost touch quite quickly with some he described in his first paper. He considered also that, if schizophrenia is determined by multiple genes, then perhaps some find expression as autistic psychopathy. He argues, perhaps not altogether convincingly, that if this were so then there should be an excess of schizophrenic patients among the relatives of autistic psychopaths. His impression was that this is not so. On the other hand, he did see a certain similarity between children with autistic psychopathy and the schizoid personality type Kretschmer described as 'schizothyme' (see above), as well as Jung's 'introverted thinking type'. Neither of these authors had much to say about the childhood characteristics of these adult personalities. In a later publication, Asperger (1961) expressed his belief that the pre-psychotic personality of schizophrenic patients is not the same as autistic psychopathy, yet his description of a 'schizoid' father of a child with early onset schizophrenia reads quite like those of the relatives of his children with autistic psychopathy.

9   As for the prognosis, Asperger found this to be relatively good, except in those children in whom the autistic personality disorder was accompanied by impaired intelligence. At best, these more handicapped people drifted from one menial job to another; at worst, they wandered the streets neglected, muttering to themselves. Yet the more intelligent affected children, and they seemed to form the majority of Asperger's cases, tended to have a good outcome, especially in the sphere of work and hence in their social integration. From among

these he cites a child with extraordinary mathematical gifts, apparent from the age of 3, who became an astronomer. Asperger believed that it is the single-mindedness with which these children pursue their specific interests which leads to their unusual achievements.

The brilliance of Asperger's paper is shown by the many perhaps less obvious aspects of the syndrome which he mentioned even in this very first account: the children's apparent motor clumsiness; their sometimes curiously mature appreciation of good art and good architecture; the fantastic lies some of them tell, for no apparent reasons at all; the fact that, if pressed to comply with social demands against their wishes, outbursts of tears, rage or aggression are common; that they learn appropriate social behaviour best by systematic verbal instructions rather than by modelling themselves on others or sensing intuitively what ought to be done. Asperger has quite a lot to say about treatment, too, but this is a theme we shall take up towards the end of this book.

In later years, when familiar with the work of Kanner and others on childhood autism, Asperger wrote: 'It has become obvious that the conditions described by myself and Leo Kanner concern basically different types, yet in some respects there is complete agreement' (Asperger, 1979, p. 45). He believed that children with early infantile autism and evidence of organic brain damage often came from families in which 'there were unmistakable autistic characteristics, more obvious in the fathers', and he suggested that Kanner's syndrome of early infantile autism was brought on by brain damage in predisposed people.

Asperger suggests that what the two conditions have in common are:

1   an innate disability in forming affective contacts;
2   bizarre behaviour, with stereotypic movements, obsessional attachments to an activity or object;
3   delayed development of the use of personal pronouns;
4   long-lasting homesickness in new surroundings.

He also lists the following differences between the conditions:

Early Infantile Autism	*Autistic Psychopathy of Childhood*
psychotic or near psychotic, but not schizophrenic	typically very intelligent with originality of thought and spontaneity of activity, although not adapted to the environment
avoidance of communication with absence or late development of speech	unusual thinking, with special ability in logic and abstraction; children follow their own path regardless of outside influences; this can lead to the pursuit of useless and abstruse subjects
abnormalities of speech, e.g. monotonous or exaggerated; avoidance of eye contact or 'looking through' the other person	highly grammatical speech begins early, with excellent, spontaneous expressions resembling schizophrenic neologisms
diminished use of gesture	often they don't wish to communicate or make contact with others; they hold forth

	whether or not attended to and speak out of turn
awkward, stereotyped movements, but children can also be very dextrous	they cannot adapt to school but may later pursue their interests with much success, especially in science

Asperger conjectured, 'it seems that for success in science or art a dash of autism is essential' in order to tread an untrodden path with all one's abilities canalized into one specialty. He thought that to presuppose a perceptual defect as the main difficulty was simplistic because, when interested and motivated, the children can understand mime, gesture and facial expression perfectly. He cites Aristotle as defining human beings as creatures who form communities. In contrast, he himself stresses the need for people, including children, to belong to themselves, important especially during phases of creativity.

Asperger describes children with autistic psychopathy as 'highly intelligent ... with interesting peculiarities, yet never the less with behaviour so difficult that they were almost impossible to keep in family or school', and wrote: 'They may achieve the highest university professorships or become artists – yet their quirks and peculiarities will remain with them for life' (Asperger, 1979, p. 45).

Children described by psychoanalysts

For over forty years psychoanalysts have studied the psychopathology of a group of children who seemed to resemble our 'schizoid' children and the children Asperger described. The analysts reported on such children under a variety of different terms: benign psychoses or schizophrenic-like states ((Mahler *et al.*, 1949); severe disturbances of ego development (Weil, 1953); borderline states (meaning conditions in the borderland of psychosis) (Ekstein and Wallerstein, 1956; Geleert, 1958; Singer, 1960).

Analysts highlighted the children's abnormal psychological defence mechanisms against anxiety: denial and projection rather than the more common defences such as sublimation, displacement and reaction-formation (for a discussion of defence mechanisms see Freud, 1946; Wolff, 1989). Psychoanalysts also stressed the adverse effects on such children of interpretative, uncovering psychotherapy, that is actively seeking for the unconscious motivation of the children's feelings and behaviour through exploration of their fantasy life. Instead they recommended a treatment approach of 'ego strengthening', in which the therapist becomes an 'auxiliary ego' and focuses on the actual reality the child must cope with rather than on his or her fantasy life.

Perhaps the best description of such children is given by Annemarie Weil (1953). She points out that, although early developmental abnormalities exist, the condition is more easily recognized during 'latency', that is, during the early and middle school years, because affected children lack the reasonableness and the attempts at self-control and integration so characteristic of this developmental stage. Affected children often have extraordinarily high intelligence or special talents, but at the same time behave in an infantile way. Almost all have a family history either of 'open psychoses' or of 'pre-psychotic narcissistic, bizarre personalities'. The children may be over- or insensitive, hypo- or hyperactive, impulsive or lacking in initiative. Clinically, they come to attention because of three types of difficulties: poor social adaptation, unmanageability, or neurotic-like symptoms. Some are aloof and withdrawn, others are not so but have a need for 'omnipotent control'. Some voice paranoid ideas – 'they don't like me', 'they hate me' – and they interpret what others say in a literal way: 'a boy said he would kill me'. Sometimes there is excessive imitation, for example, of adult styles of talking. Sometimes, as in two of the cases cited in Chapter One, an exclusive relationship with an animal replaces human affection, such as the wish above all 'to be loved by my horse'. Extreme antagonism to other people with temper tantrums and unpredictable acts of aggression can occur, as well as fearfulness, compulsive rituals, obsessional preoccupations and mannerisms, unusually persistent auto-erotic activities and odd attachments to specific objects. The use of symbolic language is another feature.

Weil decribes an affected girl she had treated from the age of 10, whose presenting problem was her severe antagonism towards her sister present since early childhood. This girl had no friends, engaged in fantasy and lies, did badly at school except in the one subject that interested her, religion, and had a special talent for drama. She is quoted as saying: 'I don't love any human. I love something impersonal, the theatre.'

Weil believed such children grow up to resemble their affected relatives and, according to the nomenclature of her day, they might in adult life be labelled as having 'latent schizophrenia' or 'borderline states'. Yet, like Asperger, Weil stressed the hopeful outlook, with improvement and at least 'superficial socialization' in adult life, but with persistence of personality impairments, for example, aloofness or aggressivity. Alvarez (1992) has recently written a more up-to-date account of psychoanalytic approaches to the treatment of both autistic and 'borderline' (or schizoid) children. She stresses the need to appreciate their difficulties in cognitive and emotional terms simultaneously: we must know both how they think and how they feel.

Psychoanalysts have often described children and adults as having a 'borderline' personality, by which they mean a particular intrapsychic organization with an unstable sense of identity, immature defence mechanisms and an impaired but not absent sense of reality.

Much confusion has arisen by changes in the use of the term 'borderline personality disorder' over the years. It does not feature at all in the International Classifications of Diseases, and in the American classifications it has in the past, but no longer, been applied to 'borderline schizophrenic' states. As we saw, schizophrenia-related disorders are now labelled as schizotypal, schizoid or paranoid personality disorders and in DSM-III and DSM-IV the 'borderline label' is applied to describe chronically unstable, vulnerable people with difficult relationships with others, with poor impulse control and an impaired sense of identity or self-image. Depression and unstable mood as well as antisocial and self-destructive acts are common accompaniments (Tarnopolsky and Berelowitz, 1987; Berelowitz and Tarnopolsky, 1993). In childhood, too, borderline disorders have been subdivided into a schizotypal personality disorder group of wide-ranging severity, but rather homogeneous symptomatology, part of the schizophrenia spectrum and related to autism and Asperger's syndrome; and the much more heterogeneous group of 'borderline' conditions with wide-ranging disturbances and many different kinds of associated psychiatric disorders other than schizophrenia (Petti and Ricardo, 1990).

Schizotypal disorder of childhood

In 1986, Nagy and Szatmari reported on 20 children, 18 boys and two girls, seen by paediatricians and psychiatrists and fulfilling DSM-III criteria for schizotypal personality disorder (see above). All had social isolation, social anxiety and magical thinking, with bizarre preoccupations, and the majority were also assessed as having poor rapport and odd speech. They resembled Asperger's children, children described as schizoid by ourselves, and patients identified as having 'Asperger's syndrome' by Wing and her colleagues (see below). The authors stress that schizotypal personality disorder in children may be a mild form of Kanner's infantile autism or a variant of adult schizophrenia, or neither. Their own cases could all be identified as developing abnormally before the age of 5; all were poorly co-ordinated; over half had developmental language abnormalities; more than expected had evidence of some brain abnormality; they were of average intelligence; none met the DSM-III criteria for early infantile autism; most met the criteria for pervasive developmental disorders of childhood (see below); and two developed clear-cut schizophrenic illnesses in adult life. These American authors have also contributed to our knowledge of well-functioning autistic children and of children with Wing's 'Asperger's syndrome', but, curiously, they have rarely referred to their work on 'schizotypal' children in subsequent writings.

Asperger's syndrome

In a seminal paper published in 1981, Lorna Wing described 34 cases (28 male and 6 female), children and adults, of what she called 'Asperger's syndrome'. This paper did much to make Asperger's work accessible to a wider readership. Wing's cases had mainly been referred to psychiatric services, but a few were identified during a population study. Most were impaired in intelligence and none was especially gifted. A number of cases had shown the features of infantile autism in their early years before developing the characteristics Asperger had described. Wing recognized that her patients may have been more seriously impaired than Asperger's, and she found the future outlook in her series less hopeful than Asperger had indicated. Although she wrote: 'There is no question that Asperger's syndrome *can* be regarded as a form of schizoid personality. . .', Wing thought it was more helpful to classify it as a pervasive developmental disorder allied to early childhood autism rather than as a personality disorder. A few of her adult patients showed psychotic symptoms such as delusions and hallucinations, but none was firmly diagnosed as schizophrenic.

On the basis of an earlier epidemiological study of mentally and physically handicapped children, Wing had identified a cluster of symptoms which characterized children with autistic-like conditions:

1 impairment of two-way social interaction;
2 impairment of comprehension and use of language, including non-verbal communication;
3 impairment of imaginative activities with an absence of socially oriented pretend play and a narrow range of repetitive, stereotyped pursuits.

Among children with such impairments, a few had the features of Asperger's syndrome. It is not absolutely clear from this paper how these children would be distinguished from the rest, except that Wing describes them as talking 'grammatically' and as not being 'socially aloof'. Most were motorically clumsy; three-quarters had intense but restricted interests, for example, in astronomy, genealogy, bus timetables, prehistoric monsters; some had specific learning difficulties; and some had antisocial conduct, attributed to their difficulty in making sense of and responding appropriately to social cues.

Wing later (1992) described three types of adult outcome for children with autistic disorders. They could become aloof and indifferent; passive, gentle and easily led; or active but odd. The latter two features are most often found in adults who, among high-functioning autistic children, had been given a diagnosis of Asperger's syndrome. In this later contribution, Wing makes clear that the people she described very rarely married and very rarely succeeded in working life. Thus, they were, as a group, very different indeed from the schizoid children described in this book and, as Wing indicates, quite similar to high-functioning autistic people.

Wing's work gave rise to the idea of an 'autistic spectrum' of disorders, further developed by Gillberg (1989, 1990), who devised six diagnostic criteria for this: severe impairment of reciprocal social interactions; all absorbing, circumscribed interests; stereotyped routines; speech and language problems; problems with non-verbal communication; and clumsiness.

Preliminary mention must also here be made of the work of Tantam (1988a, b; 1991), who used the term 'Asperger's syndrome', as defined by Wing, for a group of quite seriously impaired adult psychiatric patients selected for special study because of 'life long social isolation and conspicuous eccentricity'. While this group of patients certainly resembled the more organically impaired of Asperger's cases, they were as a group probably much more handicapped than his. More than one-third had evidence of brain damage; over half had had the features of childhood autism; in adult life more than a half lived in institutions; only two out of sixty were living independently; only two out of sixty had ever married; less than one-tenth were working; and only one had been in continuous employment since leaving school. These people are indeed similar to a group of well-functioning autistic people followed-up into young adult life (Rumsey *et al.*, 1985), who all had gross social impairments.

The serious difficulties with social adjustment of Tantam's group of patients given Asperger's name is, as we shall see, in marked contrast to the much better adult outcome of our own schizoid group, who also resembled Asperger's children. The explanation is likely to lie in the difference in how the individuals in these groups were identified. Tantum saw adult patients at the seriously handicapped end of the range of the disorder Asperger described, whereas we studied children and young people who included the intellectually more gifted and socially less impaired. It is also likely that the children described in this book are more common in the general population and that the nature of their difficulties is less easily recognized.

Multiplex developmental disorder

Finally, a series of children has been described by Cohen *et al.* (1986) as constituting a subgroup of children with pervasive developmental disorders.

Here we need to be clear that two types of developmental disorders are recognized in childhood: specific developmental disorders, in which the development of one or more particular skills, such as language, reading, spelling, or motor co-ordination, is delayed and develops more slowly than other skills; and pervasive developmental disorders, in which more global aspects of a child's functioning are both distorted and delayed. The abnormalities affect reciprocal social interactions, patterns of communication (verbal and non-verbal), and include the presence of restricted, stereotyped, repetitive interests and activities.

In both the American classifications of psychiatric disorders, DSM-III and DSM-IV (APA, 1980; 1994), and the international classification, ICD-10 (WHO, 1992), autism is classified as a pervasive developmental disorder with an onset in very early life. In ICD-10 the section on pervasive developmental disorders contains a separate category for Asperger's syndrome, which includes schizoid disorder of childhood. DSM-IV now also has a separate category for 'Asperger's Disorder' among the pervasive developmental disorders, but differentiates it from schizoid personality disorder.

Cohen (Cohen *et al.*, 1986) described a subgroup of children with pervasive developmental disorders different from those with early-onset autism, to whom he assigned the diagnosis of multiplex developmental disorder. These children clearly resembled children described as having Asperger's syndrome or schizoid personality, but we cannot be sure how close this resemblance is. A recent Dutch study (van der Gaag, 1993) sought to validate this syndrome and found a group of children who differed from high-functioning autistic children by having a later onset of their disturbance, a higher verbal IQ, more 'psychotic' thinking, more suspiciousness and more aggressive behaviour. On the other hand, they were less impaired than autistic children on measures of empathy and of aloof and rigid behaviour. These children had experienced significantly more environmental stresses than the autistic group, resembling children with disruptive behaviour disorders in this respect. The rather limited follow-up information on this group of children suggests that in later life they functioned very like the patients studied by Tantum. We must be clear, however, that this study concerned very seriously disturbed children, most of whom needed to be admitted to a child psychiatric in-patient unit. The findings cannot readily be applied to less seriously affected people such as the children described in this book.

CONCLUSIONS

It will be clear how much doubt there currently is about how to explain and categorize the conditions exemplified by the children described in this book. We shall return to the debate about the nature of these conditions and what the best name for them might be in Chapter Ten. Meanwhile, we shall use the term 'schizoid' for the children we describe, on the understanding that this term is used broadly, to include schizotypal disorder, and that affected children were like the children Ssucharewa (1926) and Asperger (1944) had discovered, and overlap with the more seriously handicapped groups studied by other workers. These include the children and adults Wing (1981), Tantam (1991), Gillberg (1989) and Szatmari *et al.* (1989a) have reported on under the name 'Asperger's Syndrome', and the children described by Cohen *et al.* (1986) and by van der Gaag (1993) as having multiplex developmental disorders.

The following chapters will deal with studies done in Edinburgh of a group of 'loners', who were systematically followed up from childhood into adult life.

3   A closer look at the childhood picture

Clinical experience alone cannot define a clinical syndrome. While the narrative accounts of his experiences as a paediatrician concerned with unusual children are critical in Asperger's pioneering work, a more systematic look at the features of the sort of children he described, whom we have called 'schizoid', is essential.

Our studies included an analysis of the clinical case records of those 32 schizoid boys whom we were able to follow up in adult life and of their control group of 32 other referred boys, individually matched with the schizoid group as well as possible for age, IQ, socio-economic background and year of referral to the clinic, who had also been followed up (Wolff, 1991). In addition, a similar case-note analysis was done for all the 33 schizoid girls identified over the years and for their individually matched control children (Wolff and McGuire, 1995).

Of course, these case records had not been compiled with research in mind and therefore did not necessarily cover all the items we were interested in. This was especially so for the control group of children, who had been seen by a variety of child psychiatrists whose diagnostic interests and practices are likely to have been different from my own. Moreover, bias may have been introduced in the compilation of the case notes of the schizoid children, all of whom were seen by myself, because of my possible preconceptions about the syndrome. Further bias may have been introduced by the fact that all records were rated by myself and I knew, of course, whether the child whose notes I was rating belonged to the schizoid or to the control group.

It was possible, however, to know how reliably the ratings had been made. A previous study (Wolff and Cull, 1986) had found most of the case-note items rated to be reliable at a satisfactory level when my own ratings were compared with those of an independent psychologist who did not know whether the child rated was in the schizoid or the control group. More recently, reliability ratings by another independent and 'blind' psychologist of all the salient features extracted from the childhood records of the schizoid and control girls were found to be very satisfactory indeed (Wolff and McGuire, 1995).

The present chapter focuses on the childhood features of schizoid boys only. The childhood characteristics as well as the future outcome of schizoid girls, who were much rarer in clinical practice, are dealt with together in Chapter Six, in which possible differences in the clinical manifestation of the syndrome in boys and girls will also be discussed.

THE METHOD OF ENQUIRY

The selection of the 32 matched pairs of boys whose childhood records were rated and who were also followed up, is described in the next chapter (see also Wolff *et al.*, 1991). They had been referred to a child psychiatry department in middle childhood at a mean age of just under 10, ranging from 4 to 14 years. They were of slightly above average intelligence and came from an upwardly skewed social class background.

All symptoms mentioned in the letters of referral and by the parents or child when first seen were abstracted from the case notes, as well as all other symptoms mentioned in the course of the clinic contact. Symptoms included behaviour and revelations of inner discomfort and distress which the parents, the child or his teachers found worrying. On the basis of these symptoms an overall diagnosis of the child's clinical condition was made. Special note was taken of symptoms typical of schizoid personality, that is, being 'a loner' (described as such, or as 'solitary', 'can't make friends, poor mixer', etc.); having unusual fantasies, such as 'romances'; 'can't tell truth from fiction', 'tells fantastic stories'; and special interest patterns or collections. Other typical features of schizoid personality, such as lack of empathy, increased sensitivity, and odd styles of communication, were not regularly recorded in the case notes and could not be rated. In addition, the case notes were searched for evidence of specific developmental delays in language, reading, spelling, writing, motor development and arithmetic, on the basis of psychological assessments made either by local authority educational psychologists or by the clinical psychologists of the child psychiatry department.

A judgement was made as to whether, overall, the child was withdrawn, outgoing or neither, because it is commonly held that schizoid personality is characterized by social withdrawal and uncommunicativeness. My own impression had been that schizoid children can be either withdrawn and uncommunicative or, on the contrary, quite outgoing. The case-note analysis set out to confirm or refute this.

Complications of pregnancy and birth which might indicate possible brain injury were noted, as were any serious physical illnesses or accidents sustained by the child in later life. Possible traumatic life events of an easily identified kind were noted, namely, prolonged separations from family and home, family disruption and severe parental discord. In addition, psychiatric disorders of parents as well as a family history of specific developmental disorders, such as learning difficulties, and of delinquency were recorded. To get some idea of the severity of the disorders of the children, their service uptake was noted in terms of special educational services; community social work services; contact with law-enforcing agencies; and admission to child psychiatric in-patient units.

RESULTS

The presenting complaints

The three most striking findings were how commonly schizoid boys had other behavioural and emotional disorders; the predominance of conduct disorders among their presenting symptoms; and how very common were associated specific developmental delays of learning in this group of children.

Only 10 of the 32 schizoid boys, and of course none of the controls, had been referred primarily because of their personality difficulties with no other independent diagnosable disorder. In brief, the presenting complaints of these 10 boys were as follows:

1 Disorganized work; lives in a fantasy world; eccentric; has a single interest: electronics; solitary and introspective.
2 Had a delusional episode; cannot mix socially; lives in a persecutory dream world; does not want to go to school; restless; odd movements.
3 Elective mutism; stammer; enuresis; socially withdrawn; picks at himself; fights at school; associates with a wild boy.
4 Elective mutism; poor mixer.
5 Obstinate; obsessional questioning; insensitive to the feelings of others; noisy and objectionable; always interrupting at home; friendless and too quiet at school; cannot get off to sleep at night; lacks initiative; will not get up to dress for school.
6 Callous about his adoptive father's disability; falsely told his speech therapist (who was treating his stammer) that his parents were dead and he lived with grandparents; excessively unguarded; good at creative writing; gave talk on astronomy at school; joined railway society; refuses to play team games or to join Scouts; has temper tantrums at school; threatens to throw things; withdrawn and a poor mixer (has only one friend); obsessional habits; makes little eye contact when talking to others.
7 Elective mutism; a loner; shy; avoids school sports; afraid to sleep alone; hyperkinetic; explosive if crossed; aggressive and threatening under stress; once threatened mother with a poker.
8 Solitary; others gang up on him; mimics other boys; sullen, quarrelsome and aggressive; loses control and screams; restless; attention-seeking; very objective about himself; has enjoyed music since the age of 3.
9 Repetitive, even perseverative; obstinate; sometimes sits alone in the dark; talks nonsense to himself; is too unguarded; under stress he threatens to burn the school down; wets himself daily; keen on music in an adult way; knows about 'the olden days'; does not want to be a Scottish boy.
10 Restless; flares up for no reason; concentrates only when interested, very difficult to shift from his own goals; has had very fixed ideas since infancy; likes solitary play with lego; cannot hold a rational conversation: only talks about *his* concerns; destroys the belongings of other children; has difficulty expressing his thoughts; gets frustrated and often cries; cannot cope in the

school playground: hits and pushes, but without malice; he is extroverted and too unguarded; but affectionate and popular with other children; does not pick up social cues, but is neither withdrawn nor solitary; in the classroom puts his hands over his ears; seems to lack normal anxiety.

Pure conduct disorders, that is, antisocial behaviour, occurred in 5 boys in both the schizoid and the control groups. However, whereas among the control children there were 9 with mixed conduct and emotional problems and 10 with a pure emotional disorder, among the schizoids only 6 had a mixed disorder and only a single schizoid boy presented with a pure emotional disorder.

A further difference in the presenting complaints was that 6 of the schizoid boys, but none of the control children, were referred only because of school failure. This is closely linked to the excess of specific developmental disorders in this group.

Other symptoms

Serious or multiple delays, in comparison with what could be expected for the child's age and IQ, in language acquisition, in learning to read, spell or do arithmetic, or persisting clumsiness were recorded for 15 schizoid boys, but only for 4 of the control children.

Three other features specifically looked for as likely characteristics of schizoid personality in childhood also differentiated significantly between the two groups. These were being a loner, recorded for 24 of the 32 schizoid boys, and 4 of their 32 controls; having multiple or striking unusual fantasies, present in 11 of the schizoid but none of the control children; and having definite special interest patterns, found in 17 schizoid and no control children.

Unfortunately, social withdrawal or its opposite were often not remarked upon in the case notes of the control children. Ten schizoid boys were rated as withdrawn, 18 as outgoing and 4 as neither. Of the controls, 3 were withdrawn, 7 outgoing, 3 neither and in 19 cases there was not enough information. All that can be said is that schizoid boys are by no means generally withdrawn or uncommunicative. Three of the schizoid boys had presented with elective mutism, and 3 had had some features of early childhood autism at some time in their lives but never the full syndrome.

The special form of conduct disorder, that is, whether manifesting as aggressive behaviour or stealing, showed no statistical difference between the two groups, although there was a non-significant excess of aggressive behaviour among the schizoid boys.

Neurological damage and other adversities in the lives of the children

It was thought possible that schizoid children might have sustained more early neurological damage of a minor kind because of the known clinical association of schizoid traits with developmental receptive-language abnormalities (Bishop,

1989), which usually have a genetic basis, but are sometimes associated with evidence of neurological impairment; and because in both autism and schizophrenia early brain damage is thought to play a part.

In fact, the pointers to such damage, while more common in the case notes of schizoid children, failed to distinguish between the groups statistically. Obstetric complications of any kind had been recorded in 15 schizoid children and 10 controls; possible evidence of cerebral dysfunction, such as a history of epilepsy, an abnormal EEG, abnormal neurological signs on examination, pervasive hyper-activity with poor attention span, or a marked discrepancy between verbal and performance items on intelligence testing had been recorded for 10 schizoid and 5 control children.

On the other hand, it was anticipated that life events and circumstances of a traumatic kind might be found less often in the records of the schizoid children, because their difficulties were thought to have been mainly caused by constitutional factors rather than by adversity, as among the controls. In fact, while global ratings of adversities differentiated very well between the groups, only some specific adversities were found more often in the control group, but not usually to a statistically significant degree. Ten control but only 4 schizoid children came from disrupted families, and family size was greater among the controls (their average sibship being 2.3 compared with 1.8 for the schizoid group). In addition, a history of delinquency in other family members was doubtfully present in only one schizoid boy but definitely present in 5 controls, and this difference was significant. On the other hand, psychiatric illnesses in mothers and fathers, a well-recognized source of stress for children, were equally common in both groups, and severe family discord and prolonged separation from parents and home had been experienced slightly more often by schizoid children.

Yet overall ratings of childhood privations and of childhood stresses, ratings subsequently found to be adequately reliable, judged the control children to have been exposed to very significantly more adversity of both kinds. Ten control children were judged to have experienced marked and 10 mild privations, compared with none and 6 in the schizoid group. Eighteen control children were thought to have experienced marked and 10 moderate stresses, compared with 7 and 9 in the schizoid group.

Other characteristics of the families

In view of the marked association we had found between schizoid personality and specific developmental delays, it was not surprising that a family history of such delays, usually in one or other parent or in a brother or sister, had been recorded significantly more often in the schizoid group: in 6 schizoid but no control children.

More doubt must attach to my personality assessment of the children's parents, because these ratings were not open to reliability testing. Only I had seen the parents of the schizoid children, and ratings were of course influenced by actual interview impressions at the time. Moreover, the parents of control children were seen by different staff members and more of them might have been given a personality-disorder diagnosis, had I seen them all myself. In the event, on the basis of the case-note information, I judged 6 mothers of the 32 schizoid boys to be mildly or doubtfully schizoid themselves and 12 definitely so, compared with one mother mildly or doubtfully and one definitely schizoid among the controls. Of the fathers of schizoid boys, I judged 11 to be mildly or doubtfully schizoid and 7 definitely so, compared with 3 and none in the control group. What is unquestionable is that one mother of a schizoid boy had a chronic, relapsing paranoid schizophrenic illness, but that no parent of a control child was affected.

Special services provided for the children

Two children in each group had spent time in a children's home, and the families of 4 schizoid and 6 control boys had had local authority social work help.

One boy in each group had been in a list D school, the equivalent of the former 'approved' school, and altogether 6 schizoid and 5 control boys had been before a Children's Hearing, the Scottish equivalent of a Juvenile Court.

The uptake of local authority special educational services, too, did not differentiate statistically between the groups. The services given to the schizoid and to the control children, respectively, were as follows: psychological assessment and advice only – 10 and 11; special day school – 5 and 3; special residential school for children with emotional and behavioural difficulties – 6 and 3.

On the other hand, a non-significant excess of schizoid boys had spent some time in a child psychiatric in-patient unit – 9 compared with 4 among the controls – and this suggests that the schizoid boys may have been thought to be psychiatrically somewhat more disturbed than their controls.

WHAT CAN WE CONCLUDE FROM THESE FINDINGS?

The presence or absence of some of the postulated core features of schizoid personality in childhood, such as impaired empathy, increased sensitivity and odd styles of communication, had not been systematically recorded in the case notes and could not, therefore, be rated. On the other hand, being a loner and having specific interest patterns did, as predicted, distinguish schizoid from other children. In addition, a feature Wing (1992) singled out as typical of autistic disorders and of Asperger's syndrome – abnormalities of imaginative activities – also characterized our schizoid boys. However, instead of impaired imagination, our children were characterized by having unusual fantasies.

The striking association with specific developmental delays, especially of language-related skills (Wolff, 1991a), is important because it strengthens the idea that schizoid personality has a constitutional, probably genetic, basis. It suggests also that schizoid personality may, like autistic disorders, be related to a group of other developmental language disorders: the congenital dysphasias, where the difficulty is essentially one of not being able to use language for communication (Bishop, 1989; Cantwell *et al.*, 1989; Brook and Bowler, 1993).

The precise relationship between these clinical syndromes and developmental language disorders has not yet been established. Nor can we be sure whether the social difficulties associated with delays of language and reading, found to excess among the siblings of autistic children (Bolton and Rutter, 1990; Bolton *et al.*, 1994) resemble the features of our schizoid boys. It is of great interest that a follow-up study into adult life of 20 boys with severe receptive developmental language disorders (Rutter and Mawhood, 1991) found these to have high rates of serious social and emotional difficulties. These took the form of impaired capacities to form friendships and loving relationships, excessive anxiety and an apparent lack of feeling for other people. While the authors say that these social impairments did not fit any accepted diagnostic pattern, it does seem that the similarities with schizoid personality, as we described it, may have been considerable. This view is strengthened by the fact that 2 of the 20 boys and one of 5 similarly language-impaired children, who also had autistic features, developed schizophrenic illnesses, as did similar proportions of our own children (see Chapter Seven). Moreover, Baltaxe and Simmons (1992) found developmental language delays or disturbances to characterize the early development of normally intelligent children who were later (between 7 and 14 years) diagnosed as having either schizophrenia or schizotypal personality disorder. These authors point out the overlap of symptoms found in autism, schizophrenia and schizotypal personality.

Co-morbidity, that is having other psychological disorders in addition to their schizoid personality difficulties, was very common in our group, only 10 children being without such additional disturbances. This is in line with the findings of Szatmari *et al.* (1989a) for children they labelled as having Asperger's syndrome. The high incidence of co-morbidity is of great practical importance. Unless a careful assessment is made, many children with schizoid personality will be missed and their treatment will not be accurately tailored to their needs. As a result, their doctors, psychologists, teachers and parents may continue to have unrealistic expectations for the affected child's capacity for change. Missing the diagnosis is the more likely, especially in children of good intelligence and without obvious handicaps, because of the often mistakenly held belief that schizoid children are withdrawn, shy and uncommunicative. The case-note analysis here described clearly shows that this is not so.

4   The personality of loners in later life

Here we are concerned with how enduring the specific personality features of children diagnosed schizoid in early life turned out to be. The social adjustment in adult life of affected people will be dealt with in the next chapter.

FROM THE WRITINGS OF A GIFTED SCIENTIST

Blackest void prevailed, silent, terrifying beyond imagination, and unknown, for there was none to know it. All infinity, boundlessly yawning with cold velvet vacuum, lay like a sphere, with no surface, whose centre was ungainable since the faster it was approached, the further it receded; but time was not, and nothing was.

In the empty finsterness, a strange threshold softly resolved, imperceptibly slowly but inexorably increasing in strength, warping the very essence of nothingness, and insidiously thickening the void. At last a critical level seemed to be attained, and suddenly there was created and anti-created from the very space a fearsome morass of energies, whose sum properties remained naught; but whose divided powers held tension between themselves, sinisterly forming configurations discrete and extant.

The eternal problem had been cast; to dispute it, the two antiposed entities, whose summed reality was not; but whose division thus contrived struck diametric opposition and absolute enmity. Although such existed only by virtue of its adversary, yet they sought to destroy one another, for the peace of the former state was not, as was the division, unstable.

So began a typed manuscript sent to me by ANTHONY G following a research interview which took place when he was 28 years old. A second batch of 'stories' started as follows:

The professor adjusted his spectacles nervously and peered in the vague direction of his breakfast. Ferguson shut the door behind him, and there was silence in the professor's study.

A tottering pile of books overbalanced at that moment, and fell in cascades all over the professor's desk, dispersing his breakfast. They were very old books, and most of them fell to pieces. He climbed out from under the debris, and sighed with a peculiar accent.

His gaze fell on a page at random. He did not recall it; but it held his attention. He extracted the remains of the crumbling volume whence it had come, and looked carefully.

This book, written in ancient *Mnton*, was full of interesting patterns, weird diagrams, and highly involved technical paragraphs. One such paragraph read:

'Take two aahbones, and place them on pinnacles. Rheum a bon mine, purple a souple of meserobes, and stand in a trickle of vaboves. Put a sibl flame threshold round yourself, and draw the following diagram on the ground with an archidraicht circle. You will gain a clue about the Bars of Time.'

The professor dropped the book to the floor with a deafening crash. The Bars of Time!

He knew a little about the Bars of Fate, and the Bars of Destiny. But the Bars of Time were a much sought-after affair throughout the Universe. That *he*, Professor Beaking, should gain a *clue*! After aeons of time, the Bars of Time may again be found!

At the time of the research interview, Anthony's mother dated the onset of his difficulties to when he was 13. In that year he had enrolled as a boarder at the school he had previously attended as a day boy, because the father had changed his job and the family had to move to another city. Anthony became unhappy, increasingly withdrawn, and his work, which had previously been good, deteriorated. He found it very difficult to fit in with other children, his teachers failed to understand him, and his reports were terrible. But he remained interested in and good at science, especially physics and electronics. He enjoyed art, but loathed sport. Following the psychiatric referral, when he was 14, and advice to the school, less pressure to conform was put on Anthony; he was encouraged to start an electronics club and this increased his status among his peers. Nevertheless, he was glad to leave school at 17 with three 'A' levels and a number of 'O' levels. He now entered a moderately prestigious University to read Electronics and began to shine in his own academic field. He went on to take an MSc in Astronomy at one of the then new British Universities, and a PhD in Astrophysics at Oxbridge. Between the MSc and PhD courses, Anthony held a University post as a lecturer.

His parents were, however, still uncertain about his academic giftedness and could say little about his progress since leaving school because he told them nothing and would not allow them to visit him at university. He compartmentalized his life, tolerating no overlap, and his mother was especially distressed because the parents were forbidden to go to any of his three graduation ceremonies. Although hurt, they acquiesced with his wishes.

The mother said Anthony was very private and very withdrawn. One never knew what he was thinking and she felt he would never change. Both parents accepted that they could not expect to be able to communicate with him. When at home, he stayed in his room except for meals. He would not allow anyone to see his face, which he covered with his long, dark hair. The mother described this as falling like a curtain at the table, making for great difficulties in eating. The parents thought they got on quite well with Anthony on his own terms, they could laugh together at times, and they were grateful that he still came home. He writes to them, but in a curious childlike script with mixed capital and small letters, ignoring the normal rules of spelling, grammar and punctuation. The information content of his letters is negligible, and sometimes even they cannot crack his private code. The mother reported his interests as writing imaginative fiction and drawing psychedelic posters, which she found brilliant but disturbing. She knew his appearance alarmed other people because he was always dressed in black, including leather boots, and a long black mane hid his face. He was, she thought, quite unaware of the feelings of anyone else.

During the research follow-up interview, Anthony himself reported that he had no close friends and never has had. He said he had once gone out with some girls, but: 'I very quickly ran off furiously in the other direction. Not wanting to be tied down was part of it. I'm always at a loss what to say.' Later he commented: 'I'm too harmful, I'm dangerous to know because I don't understand people and their relationships. . . . I have decided I must stay right out of that sort of thing.' He had not been to a party for five years, since his undergraduate days. At that time he 'made great efforts to be sociable and learn social skills', and he could be quite extrovert at parties, and 'jump up and down as long as I didn't have to speak to anybody'. Now he only attends social gatherings where he knows and has to speak to no one. He used to like acting in undergraduate reviews, standing up in front of an audience and 'let them have it', being really vicious and angry and then rushing from the theatre, thinking 'I really let them have it that time . . . you'll think I'm a terrible person, a real misanthrope'.

Anthony, too, reported that he compartmentalized his life. 'I hate having to do more than one thing at a time. I've decided that I am going to work and do nothing else for the next few years. I work 17 hours a day and sleep for 7 hours and do nothing else at all. It makes me pretty crotchety. . . . One day I may decide to concentrate on making friends and I will do nothing else, no music, no theatre, no work, just concentrate on making friends.' He often feels extremely lonely. He rushes home from work and deliberately avoids the other people living in his flat. 'I have managed to successfully avoid them for a whole year. I've never met any of them in that time.' He goes to his room, locks the door, locks the windows and reads. Sometimes he lies awake thinking 'Who am I? What am I doing in this metropolis alone with no friends and no one to talk to? If the distress of being alone became too strong, then maybe I would go out and make friends, but at the moment the price in terms of discomfort is too much.'

When discussing his writings, Anthony said his ideal would be to live in a castle in the wilds of Scotland, surrounded by lions, skeletons and skulls. He would live entirely alone, see no one and do just what interested him. He had been writing stories since childhood, a page or two at a time, always carefully filed away but never completed. The same theme recurs: 'It is rather baroque, about a man who is 260 years old and lives in a castle and never sees anybody'.

During his psychiatric assessment at the age of 14, he reported:

I find it very difficult to get my work done properly. I do very badly in most things except the things I'm interested in . . . e.g. higher maths and all types of science . . . and electronics. . . . I'm extraordinary [to other people] and I apply my imagination. I've got a type of dreamed up island and draw endless cartoon strips. Specially at prep school it occupied my time . . . [on the island there are] very forward people scientifically and a lot of trade in electronic equipment and fairly good justice and very democratic [government] . . . the professor lives there . . . [and] a bit of a funny point: it's *Mnton* but also in the north-west of Scotland.

Of his difficulties in getting on with other youngsters, he said: 'people are just nasty because I'm an abnormal person with different tastes'.

At that time the mother reported that her father had been 'brilliant, but difficult to live with', a solitary and socially awkward engineer, and that finally her mother had left him.

We shall see later that, ten years on, Anthony's life had turned out rather happier than perhaps even he had expected. Here the point needs to be made that his dreamed-up island of *Mnton*, which had been in his mind since he was 4 years old, was not in itself characteristic of the personality of loners. He was the only one of 32 schizoid boys studied in detail who had invented a fantasy place for himself with a definite location, a language, and a legal and political system. Such fantasies, sometimes shared by friends or siblings, are rare but are created by many different kinds of children. The phenomenon has been called the 'paracosm' (Silvey and MacKeith, 1988). What was unusual in Anthony's case was the persistence of his fantasy well into adult life and the language in which it was expressed. Anyone coming to his writings with no knowledge of their author might think they exemplified the sort of language disorder typical of schizophrenic patients: odd associations, neologisms, much use of metaphor, diffuse and unfocused thinking – features, the reader will have observed, that were absent from Anthony's ordinary conversation.

THE FIRST FOLLOW-UP OF YOUNG MEN

The first follow-up study we undertook was a predictive validation study. That is, it aimed to show whether or not the condition of schizoid personality, broadly defined and identified in childhood, could be successfully diagnosed in a group of patients grown-up, by a psychiatrist who had no knowledge of their earlier clinical picture. For this purpose a control group of other children, referred to the same child psychiatry department, but given other diagnoses were also interviewed 'blind' for comparison. These other children were individually matched with the children thought to be schizoid for age, sex, measured intelligence, social class of origin (as indicated by the father's occupation), and the year of referral to the clinic.

A further aim of the study was to find out whether or not the postulated core features of schizoid personality – solitariness; impaired empathy; excessive sensitivity; rigidity of mental set including circumscribed, pervasive interest patterns;

and unusual, odd styles of communicating – could also be identified in later life by an independent interviewer and would differentiate schizoid children from their matched controls.

The research was undertaken by Jonathan Chick (Chick, 1979; Chick *et al.*, 1979; Wolff and Chick, 1980; Cull *et al.*, 1984), who interviewed all the young people, and by Anne Cull who saw their mothers.

The child patients followed up

Because the condition appeared to be so much commoner in boys than girls, only boys were selected for this first study in order to make the sample more uniform. This was further ensured by choosing only schizoid boys with typical features of the condition. Control children were chosen by a staff member not otherwise involved in the study to match each schizoid child as indicated above.

Of the 30 schizoid young men we attempted to enrol in the study, 3 could not be contacted and 5 refused to participate. Of 36 controls we tried to contact, one had died, 5 could not be contacted and 8 refused.

Twenty-two schizoid and 22 control people took part in the study, including 19 matched pairs. Their mean age at childhood referral was 10 years (range 5–14) and at follow-up 22 years (range 16–28). The mean full-scale IQ at initial referral was 108 for the schizoid children and 106 for their matched controls.

The research interview

A semi-structured interview was devised to assess the young people's current life adjustment as well as the postulated core features of schizoid personality. A detailed glossary with definitions of terms for the interviewer was prepared to ensure uniform ratings of the young people's responses and of the interviewer's own global ratings made at the end of the interview.

To test the reliability of the ratings, a second observer was present during nine interviews and made independent ratings. There was complete agreement between the raters on the overall diagnosis of schizoid personality, and good agreement on responses to questions designed to capture the core features of the syndrome and to questions about the individual's life adjustment.

The follow-up interview also included the same test of psychological construing we had previously used in our comparative study of schizoid, autistic and normal children (Wolff and Barlow, 1979), a test for intro- and extraversion (Eysenck's Personality Inventory), as well as two brief intelligence tests.

The findings

The main result of this study was that after an average period of twelve years, an independent psychiatrist correctly diagnosed 18 of the 22 former schizoid child patients as 'definitely schizoid', but only one of the former controls. On looking back at the childhood case notes it became clear that this control boy, one of the youngest of the group, had had typical schizoid features. Two former schizoid children and one control were diagnosed as 'doubtfully schizoid', and 2 former schizoid patients and 20 controls were thought not to be schizoid at all.

There had thus been *two misdiagnosed cases*: one boy, correctly thought to be schizoid at follow-up who, when first referred at only 5 years of age, was thought to have an obsessional state; and another boy, who had been correctly diagnosed as schizoid in childhood and whose diagnosis was missed at follow-up when he was 17. At that stage the boy was found to be very reticent at interview, monosyllabic, fixed in his views, using metaphorical expressions. He declared a long-standing and passionate interest in ice cream. The error at follow-up was largely due to the young man reporting himself as a good mixer and as having 'friends all over', being especially 'close' to an ice-cream vendor.

All the *five postulated core features* of schizoid personality distinguished very highly between the groups, except that among the questions designed to capture 'rigidity of mental set', only special-interest patterns were characteristic of the schizoid boys grown-up. An additional, sixth, feature which characterized the schizoid group very highly was that of having an unusual fantasy life.

Both groups of young people had normal scores on intro- and extraversion (Chick *et al.*, 1979) indicating, as we had suspected, that schizoidness is not to be equated with introversion, that is, with the more common form of social inhibition and shyness. Our test for psychological construing once more showed that, when describing other people, schizoid subjects tend not to use perceived emotions or motives. Furthermore, the scores on this test were highly associated with the interviewer's and the young people's self-ratings of lack of empathy (Chick *et al.*, 1979).

The interviews with mothers, which followed the same lines of enquiry as the interviews with the young people themselves, were used to help construct a comprehensive life history for each of the 43 people involved (one mother refused to be seen). At the end of the study discrepancies in child and follow-up diagnoses were resolved by discussion, and this led to 23 people being diagnosed as schizoid and 20 as not schizoid. The life histories were then presented to two independent psychiatrists to rate for the presence or absence of schizoid personality. Both agreed at a statistically significant level with the consensus diagnosis; one rater very highly (weighted kappa 0.85), the other less highly so (weighted kappa 0.65) (Cull *et al.*, 1984). (Weighted kappa is a statistical method to test for agreement between series of measurements or ratings of the same phenomena made by different raters or at different times. 1.0 signifies complete agreement; 0.0 no agreement at all.) It needs to be stressed that this part of the study was done before the more recent American psychiatric diagnostic classifications, DSM-III, DSM-III-R and DSM-IV (APA, 1980, 1987, 1994), were in common use, and that the term schizoid was, as throughout this book, applied by the two psychiatrists rating the life histories in a more global way to include what are now called schizoid, schizotypal and paranoid personality disorders.

Even at that early age (a mean of 22 years) it was found that, while the work adjustment of the schizoid group was as good as that of their matched controls, fewer had had heterosexual relationships and they had had more psychiatric symptoms, especially suicidal behaviour (in 5 of 19 schizoid people; but in none of 19 controls). Two schizoid young men had developed schizophrenic illnesses and this concerned us. But there were only 23 schizoid people in this first study and we shall see later that, when bigger groups were examined, the proportion of schizoid children who became schizophrenic in adult life was much lower.

The social and psychiatric adjustment of schizoid children grown-up will be discussed more fully in the next chapter. Here a further illustration will follow of the revelations the young people themselves and their parents made to us at the time of this first follow-up.

ON THE BORDERLANDS OF AUTISM?

THOMAS J was originally referred for a psychiatric assessment when he was 10 years old because of educational failure, solitariness, poor concentration and elective mutism: he spoke only to his family at home, never to anyone at school, except, occasionally, in a whisper. His speech even at home was inhibited, slow, high-pitched and monotonous. He was very reserved at school, a poor mixer, and he had gaze avoidance, failing to look others into the eyes. His concentration was limited. Intelligence testing showed his abilities to be low average on performance tests and below average on verbal tests. His school attainments were commensurate with his age and ability levels, but he was exceptionally good at drawing, and here his favourite subject was trains. His special interests were sewage systems and trains. He wanted to become a railway porter when he grew up. At play, mainly with older boys, he tended to imitate what they did rather than play imaginatively. Apart from his artwork, he lacked drive and anyone who met him was struck by his general immobility and fixed, blank expression.

Thomas's birth and early development had been normal, except that he was 'slow in wanting to speak, although not in beginning to speak'. Unlike autistic children, he had never engaged in verbal repetitions or 'echolalia'. He always preferred solitary, unimaginative play. He came from a professional family which the mother, for reasons that never became clear, had left when he was 5 years old. His conscientious and hard-working father had brought up all the children on his own since then.

Thomas was 20 at the first follow-up. He reported that he had been very happy and had done well at the small Rudolph Steiner school to which he had been transferred following his psychiatric assessment: 'The teacher interested me in things'. He left at 16 to attend a training centre and was then offered two jobs (this at a time of full employment). He disliked the first and left after three weeks, but had remained in the second, at a garden centre, ever since. He particularly enjoys sweeping leaves and weeding: 'Hoeing is my favourite.' He dislikes loading lorries because this involves contact with other employees: 'I'm not happy working with other people, I feel rushed, I like doing jobs on my own.' He eats lunch with some other workers and recently gave up his chair to a girl who joined this group, so that he now sits on a box at lunch time: 'It's not very comfortable'. If his boss is at all critical of him he broods on this at night. He dislikes it when other employees are lazy and fool about.

He still lives at home with his father and sister. He mentioned two 'friends', neighbouring boys who greet him in the street but with whom he has no other contact. He has had no girlfriend and when asked where he learnt about 'the facts of life', he said: 'It's a subject I avoid. I never mention anything about it.'

He maintains his long-standing interest in his model railway, has been to art classes and, at 19, developed a special interest in 'houses', especially old houses with character and design in the Adam style: 'I've developed a fascination for things like buildings . . . and aircraft have captured me.' He reads books about architecture and draws houses and aeroplanes a great deal. One of his lesser worries is that he lives in 'a 1940s bungalow . . . living in a shoe-box house'. He loves order and hates to see houses which are untidy. Thomas's desire for order showed in other ways too: 'If I was Prime Minister, I would have everything working fine and orderly, in style, just ordinary people going about their daily routines. . . . I like to see tidy people . . . it may be the way I've been brought up. . . . In the bus I want to tell people to be quiet.' He feels very strongly about alcohol: 'I don't agree with it . . . my main drink is chocolate.' When asked about religion, he described himself as 'an ordinary Christian', and went on to declare his opposition to the Mormon faith a relative had recently joined: 'I feel it's man-made, not the real Christianity.'

The remarkable aspect of this boy's activities and inner life was that, despite his limited ability level, he had a number of intellectual interests and pursuits and that, despite his persisting slowness of speech and monotony of intonation, he expressed himself with unexpected vividness and clarity.

To anticipate the outcome of our second follow-up study, at 29 years of age Thomas was still in the same job, now living harmoniously with an older sister in her house. He had joined a rambling club and was going to art classes. He had two elderly men friends, whom he visited. He had never had a sexual relationship and considered marriage not to be for him. He produced somewhat conventional oil paintings copied from photographs, but also more original and very detailed crayoned, pen and ink drawings, largely from memory, of old houses, city scenes, landscapes and aeroplanes, the latter copied from magazines, with verbal captions poorly spelled (see Chapter Nine). He was more outgoing now, his speech was clear, and there was now only a hint of gaze avoidance. But he still had a rather fixed smile, a limited range of facial expressions and restricted body movements.

At this interview the sister revealed that their mother had been a perfectionist, erratic, tending to 'pontificate' and to theorize about God and the planets. She was an outgoing woman, but with little understanding of other people, being insensitive, for example, to the needs of her children. Her second marriage, too, had ended in divorce.

ARE SCHIZOID CHILDREN GROWN-UP SCHIZOTYPAL?

A second follow-up study aimed to clarify further the diagnosis of this group of children. They certainly resembled Asperger's cases of autistic psychopathy. The question was, would they in adult life also have the features of schizophrenic spectrum disorders, that is, schizotypal, paranoid and schizoid personality disorder, as in DSM-III, DSM III-R and DSM-IV (APA, 1980, 1987, 1994)?

This second follow-up (Wolff *et al.*, 1991) also shed more light on the young people's later social and psychiatric adjustment, which will be described in the following chapter.

We had planned this time to see both men and women, but had much more difficulty in tracing and gaining access to the girls, who were fewer in number. The systematic, controlled, 'blind' follow-up interviews were therefore once more confined to schizoid boys and to a control group of other clinic attenders matched to our schizoid children as in the first study.

The children followed up

Of the total cohort of 115 schizoid boys seen in clinical practice, attempts were made to follow-up the oldest of them, including those who took part in the first study. We aimed to see about 30 matched pairs of former child patients this time.

In the event, we attempted to trace 55 schizoid boys grown-up, found 43, and were able to enlist co-operation in the study from 32. Among the controls, again selected from the clinic records by an independent worker to match the schizoids as well as possible, we attempted to trace 69, found 49 and gained co-operation from 32. Matching of the two groups turned out to have been good. The mean age of both groups at the time of the child psychiatric referral was just under 10 years (range 4–14 years). The mean verbal IQ at referral of the schizoid boys had been 107 and of the controls 108, and their performance IQs had been 105 and 103 respectively. Schizoid boys had come from a somewhat higher socio-economic background, 19 of the 32, compared with 14 of 32 controls, having had fathers in non-manual occupations. At the time of follow-up, the mean age of both groups was 27 years (range 18–37 and 18–38 respectively). On the Mill Hill Vocabulary Scale they scored means of 106 (range 88–130) and 107 (range 89–130), and on Raven's Matrices 101 (range 75–130) and 110 (range 78–130), respectively. The two groups of young men themselves were now very similar in occupational status, only 10 in each group having non-manual jobs. Nine schizoid and 6 control participants were unemployed at the time.

The research method

All interviews were done by a social worker who was again 'blind' to the childhood diagnosis and to the early histories of the people she saw.

The research interview consisted of three dovetailed parts:

A semi-structured interview previously used (Chick, 1978; Wolff and Chick, 1980), with systematic and largely pre-coded questions about the subject's work, social, marital and sexual adjustment; about physical and mental health, alcohol consumption, and antisocial conduct; and a series of questions about personality functioning designed to reveal the core features of schizoid personality as we had defined them. These were solitariness; impaired empathy and emotional detachment; rigidity of mental set, especially the single-minded pursuit of special interests; increased sensitivity, with paranoid ideation at times; and unusual or odd styles of communication, including under- and over-communicativeness; and an unusual fantasy life.

Scoring, done during the interview, was according to written definitions. In addition, at the end of each interview, global ratings of personality features, personality disorder, and psychiatric illness were made using a glossary of definitions. Contacts with law-enforcing agencies after the age of 16 were verified from data obtained from the Scottish Criminal Records Office, and contacts with psychiatric hospitals from a hospital records' search, both previously described (Wolff, 1992).

The Baron Schedule for Schizotypal Personality Disorder (Baron *et al.*, 1981, 1983) was used. This leads to ratings on scales assessing the ten features of schizotypy which define this personality in DSM-III: illusions, depersonalization, ideas of reference, suspiciousness, magical thinking, impaired rapport, odd communications, social isolation, social anxiety and *transient* delusions and hallucinations. The reader will notice that this list includes items very similar to those we had identified as the 'core features' of schizoid personality in our young people: solitariness, lack of empathy, increased sensitivity (including suspiciousness), and odd communications, but contains in addition items relating to odd sensory experiences and none defining our fifth core feature: rigidity of mental set, special interest patterns in particular.

The third part of the interview was the *Diagnostic Interview for Borderlines* (DIB; Gunderson *et al.*, 1981). We included the DIB because some workers had found the features of schizotypal and borderline personality to coexist in many cases and we wanted to help to clarify this issue.

The social worker's interviews were audio-recorded when this was permitted and an independent social worker and a clinical psychologist rated twelve interviews to assess the inter-rater reliabilities of the codings made. These were very good for items concerned with work adjustment, marriage and sexual adjustment, physical and mental health, and antisocial conduct; they were less good for the personality ratings, lower than in our first follow-up study, when the second rater had been present during the encounter. It is possible that these personality ratings were in part dependent on the interviewer's actual observations during the interview, and not only on what was said and hence recorded on the audio-tape.

I myself saw each participant after the main interviews with the social worker had been completed, in order to re-establish contact with the young people, make my own assessment of their life adjustment, measure their current intellectual level and give them some additional pencil and paper tests (referred to in Chapter Ten).

The personality characteristics of the two groups of people at follow-up

Once again the 'blind' research social worker was able to distinguish clearly between the groups, although she was less certain in her diagnostic assessments than the research psychiatrist had been in our earlier study. She identified 16 of the 32 schizoid people as 'definitely' and 11 as 'doubtfully or mildly' schizoid, misdiagnosing 5 as 'definitely not schizoid'. She diagnosed 23 of the 32 controls as 'definitely not schizoid', 6 as 'doubtfully or mildly schizoid' and 3 as 'definitely schizoid'.

Once again, the ratings of items capturing our five core features of the syndrome (solitariness, impaired empathy, the single-minded pursuit of special interests, increased sensitivity, and odd styles of communication) also differentiated very highly between the two groups of young people.

Special gifts

An impressionistic assessment of special giftedness in childhood or adult life, the pursuit of which scored on the scale of 'special interests', identified 10 of the 32 schizoid young men and 3 controls. Among the schizoids, 4 as children had had exceptional drawing skills, which had persisted in 2; 3 had had exceptional or idiosyncratic literary skills, which had persisted in 2; 2 had been gifted at electronics and/or maths, gifts which determined their later career choice; and one, exceptionally musical as a child, became a musician. Among the controls identified as 'gifted', 2 became outstanding athletes in adolescence, and one developed a late talent for art and worked as an art teacher.

Schizotypal and borderline personality features

The Schedule for Schizotypal Personality (SSP) showed highly significant differences between the two groups. The score which defined schizotypal personality disorder according to the DSM-III definition identified 24 of the 32 schizoid people as schizotypal, but only 6 of the 32 controls. The schizoid group did not have excessively high scores on all of the 10 SSP scales. Only ideas of reference, magical thinking, social isolation and, especially, impaired rapport and odd communications differentiated significantly between the groups.

The DIB scores were higher among the schizoid than the control people, but not at a statistically significant level. Only 4 people overall had abnormal scores on the DIB, all within the schizoid group. One of the five subscales of the DIB showed a significant difference between the groups: the scale for psychotic experiences, on which the schizoid subjects scored more highly.

HOW SHOULD WE INTERPRET THESE FINDINGS?

As in the first follow-up, the findings indicate considerable stability over time of the syndrome of schizoid personality as we had defined it, and of its component core features. Affected children, as indicated in Chapter One, were quite similar to those described by Asperger (1943) as having autistic psychopathy of childhood. Now we found that three-quarters of these children when grown-up also fulfilled the criteria for schizotypal personality, a personality type known to be associated with but not predictive of schizophrenia.

The social and psychiatric adjustment of both groups of young people will be described in the following chapter. Here we present the life circumstances and self-appraisal of the gifted scientist, described above, when seen again at the time of the second follow-up.

THE GIFTED SCIENTIST AT 37

ANTHONY G had taken much trouble over coming to see us from a distance and was eager to help with the project. He was charming, as he had been in childhood, friendly, clearly highly intelligent and very insightful about himself in a somewhat detached way. He looked young for his age, was still dressed in black leather, but his face was no longer hidden from view. He was working successfully in his own field and had been promised a tenured university post: 'My work gives me satisfaction . . . if I'd had different ideals I'd have got satisfaction from other things.' He indicated that in the world he grew up in, an academic and 'scintillating' career were the accepted aspirations: 'If I were 14 now, I'd not follow the same course.' He thought he might have done an apprenticeship in some useful trade and been a 'primary producer', but 'I'm very glad I was around when it was all right to be an astrophysicist and glad I wasn't born 20 years later'. Now 'the future looks blacker . . . in our era space travel has become a reality and one doesn't know what will come next. Improving our understanding of ourselves, what being conscious and being alive means. . . . One has a way of seeing the world which may not be the only way.'

Anthony was now happily married and had two children. He told us that he had no social contacts other than those arranged by his wife. Of himself he said: 'I'm still much the same. Basically I'm a private person. There are private areas my wife and I don't share, but we get on very well.' His marriage formed a bridge between himself and his mother. She found him bewildering: 'She and I find our hearts are in the right place but we don't communicate very well.' He also mentioned that he knew, although she had never said this to him, that his mother had often wished he had been different. About one of his small daughters he said: 'I feel she and I are rather similar. She has the same sort of sinister bent. She likes dark and strange things', but she is very sociable.

Looking back to his childhood hospital referral at 14, Anthony said: 'Yes, I did suffer then. [I thought] if I were more convivial, different aspects of the world were more open to experience and I wondered what I was missing. Now, having been around more, I feel lots of people feel much the same. I feel I've had a charmed life and I feel pretty content. . . . I've never really had any bad experience.' He mentioned his job, his family and his ability to support them 'and that wouldn't have happened if I hadn't been launched on a flying start, on a crest of a wave', and he described a 'euphoric feeling' he always has. When I commented on his splendid mind, he said it had been a matter of luck.

When asked about his stories, Anthony said: 'They've gone on ice. But I'd really rather like to live in a castle in the wilds. That's the real me.' He had written no stories for ten years, but he writes notes about his dreams and intends to write stories when there is less pressure on him. He would want to be read. When reminded of how he invented new words and used totally original language, he said: 'I try to invent less words because it puts people off. It's too easy and English is full of weird words. There's no real excuse for inventing words.' He had enjoyed it, although he thinks it was 'a pointless exercise'.

He thought that his maternal grandfather had probably been a bit like himself: 'If we'd been contemporaries we'd have got on rather well.' He worries about a brother, less gifted than himself but with whom he feels he has things in common, who was unhappy and drifting, interested in psychology and music.

Anthony G, although clearly still showing the features of schizoid personality, was functioning well and his personality could not now be described as abnormal. But at 14, and again at 28 years of age, he had suffered and his social adaptation had been seriously impaired.

5   The later life adjustment of schizoid boys

This chapter focuses on the social and psychological adjustment of the groups of schizoid boys and their matched controls who were personally interviewed in our two follow-up studies. We shall examine their work achievements, their social circumstances, their personal relationships, as well as their mental health, including alcohol problems and delinquency. (The methods used in the study have been fully described elsewhere: Wolff and Chick, 1980; Wolff et al., 1991.)

At a mean age of 22 years, 19 boys diagnosed 'schizoid' on referral to a child psychiatric clinic and their 19 matched controls given other diagnoses (Chick, 1978; Wolff and Chick, 1980) were seen. In addition, at a mean age of 27 years, 32 schizoid boys and their matched controls (Wolff et al., 1991) were interviewed.

It must be stressed that all these young people had been referred as children to a child psychiatry department, and that they were therefore not representative of the general population. The degree of social impairment in every area of functioning of the people who formed the control group is bound to have been considerably greater than for people in the general population. It is also very likely that loners, that is people we would diagnose schizoid, who have never been psychiatrically referred as children will have an even better social adjustment in adult life than the individuals who took part in our studies.

SOCIAL ADJUSTMENT

Work

At the time of the first follow-up (Wolff and Chick, 1980), the measures of work adjustment used (present occupational status; job(s) lost because of poor relationships; longest time in any one job; overall work adjustment) showed no differences between the group of boys diagnosed schizoid in childhood and the group of their matched controls with other childhood diagnoses. The occupational status of both groups was wide, ranging from successful engineers and academics to unskilled manual workers and the unemployed.

At the second follow-up, there was again no statistical difference between the groups in their present occupational status; in work stability and appropriateness of their work status, taking into account the individuals' levels of ability and education; or in work relationships. But, on this occasion, schizoid young men had a worse overall work adjustment (on the basis of all measures taken together) than their matched controls. Yet it was remarkable that, at a time of high national unemployment, as many as 14 out of 32 schizoid people had been in full-time and continuous work (including further education) since leaving school, compared with 16 of the 32 controls.

Domestic circumstances

At the second follow-up there was no statistical difference between the two groups of young men in their life circumstances, that is, whether they were living with their parents at home, with other relatives, in lodgings, with friends, alone in their own home, or with a wife or partner. Similar proportions of schizoid young men (20 out of 32) as of controls (19 out of 32) had left home; and the ages at which they had done so (20 and 19 years respectively) were almost identical.

Marriage and sexual relationships

At the time of the first follow-up, 5 control but no schizoid young men were married, and 8 control but only 5 schizoid men had a definite current girlfriend. The difference between the groups was statistically significant.

At the second follow-up, too, differences were found in the marital status of the two groups, but these were now no longer statistically significant. Eight schizoid young men had been married compared with 13 controls; 3 in each group were engaged to be married or were cohabiting with heterosexual partners; one schizoid young man was cohabiting with a homosexual partner; and 20 schizoid compared with 16 control people were single. The mean age at marriage was 25 and a half and 23 years for schizoid and control people respectively.

A scale devised to measure overall sexual adjustment at the second follow-up showed marked differences between the two groups, especially when the items of this scale were combined to measure 'any significant sexual relationship ever' (found in 18 schizoid subjects and 30 controls) and 'none, or fleeting sexual relationships only' (found in 14 schizoid subjects and 2 controls). Only 2 schizoid young men had had homosexual relationships and one of these had a stable partner. All other relationships in both groups were heterosexual.

Other social relationships

Questions were used in both follow-up studies to assess the individuals' current social interactions with other people and their recent participation in group activities and entertainments. On both occasions small but significant differences were found between the groups; schizoid young men being less sociable than their matched controls.

Conclusion

It is clear that the overall social adjustment in adult life of boys given a diagnosis of schizoid personality was relatively good. In childhood these young men had been quite similar to the children Asperger had described in 1944. Our findings, while in agreement with Asperger's own impressions of improved social adaptation in later life, are in marked contrast to those of Tantam (1986, 1988a, 1988b) for what he and others (e.g. Wing, 1981; Frith, 1989) have called 'Asperger's syndrome'.

Tantam (1991) recruited 60 adults who had been identified by other psychiatrists as 'eccentric' and 'socially isolated'. Of these 46 had either met Wing's criteria for 'Asperger's syndrome' in childhood – the triad of severe impairment of two-way social interactions, difficulty with communicative language and impaired imaginative functions – or had in adult life shown poor verbal and gestural expression, unusual special interests, unconventional social behaviour, communicative language disorder, poor peer relationships and clumsiness. Only 4 per cent of Tantam's series had had higher education, compared with 47 per cent of our 32 young men. Only 9 per cent of his subjects were currently employed, compared with over 44 per cent of ours. Fifty-three per cent of his group were in residential care, compared with none of our 32 boys personally followed up. Only 3 per cent of his series, compared with 53 per cent of our 32 young men, were living independently. Only 2 per cent of his series had married, compared with 25 per cent of ours; and only 1 per cent of his series had ever had a heterosexual relationship, compared with 50 per cent of ours (see also Chapter Six for comparisons between Tantam's series and our cohorts of both boys and girls).

The conclusion must be that the people Wing, Tantam and others described as having Asperger's syndrome, all of whom had been in psychiatric care as adults, are far more handicapped in later life than the children we have called schizoid. The condition Asperger first reported is clearly wide ranging in severity and it is very likely that most affected young people cope much better in later life than the recent studies of Asperger's syndrome, as defined by Wing and others, have suggested. This should give hope to parents, teachers and the young people themselves.

MENTAL HEALTH

Minor psychiatric symptoms

At the time of the first follow-up, the schizoid young men had had significantly more psychiatric symptoms as well as medical care for psychiatric or emotional problems since leaving school than their matched controls. These difficulties usually took the form of 'minor' psychiatric conditions such as depression and suicidal thoughts or actions. At the second follow-up too, the schizoid group had had more psychiatric treatment than the controls. Seven schizoid young men had been admitted to a psychiatric hospital compared with 5 controls; and 8 schizoid people had attended such a hospital as out-patients only compared with 2 of the controls. But there was now no longer a difference between the groups in their suicidal thoughts or behaviour.

Major psychiatric illness

Of the 22 schizoid young men and the 22 controls from whom the 19 matched pairs for the first follow-up were derived, 2 had developed schizophrenic illnesses, both in the schizoid group. Yet, five to nine years later, at the time of the second follow-up, the same 2 schizoid people and no others were found to have schizophrenia, now out of 32 matched pairs of subjects. We shall see in a later chapter that when the total cohort of 119 schizoid boys and 32 schizoid girls who had reached the age of 16 years were examined for psychiatric illness, the incidence of schizophrenia among the schizoid people, both men and women, was even lower. These findings highlight the danger of drawing conclusions from small numbers of cases.

JONATHAN W was 10 years old when he was referred to the child psychiatry department. The presenting complaints were poor school work, reluctance to mix with other children and constant rocking movements.

Jonathan's birth and early development had, on the whole, been normal, but he had surprised his mother by his insistence on feeding from only one breast. He had also rocked in his crib since infancy. He walked at 18 months, was 'late' in becoming toilet trained, but spoke well by the age of 2. He had been 'shy' with other children since the pre-school years; he had food fads; and he had always been obstinate, concentrating only on what interested him: of late, ancient ruins and castles.

The father, a business man, had for some time been handicapped by extreme social sensitivity. He was totally preoccupied with how other people regarded him. A brother of Jonathan's had had a transient delay in language development. The mother was warm and empathic, supportive of all members of her family.

Jonathan himself, when first seen, was long-winded and confused in his verbal expression. He had, and knew he had, word-finding difficulties: 'I get all muddled up with my words'. He was a handsome boy, but rocked constantly in his chair. He looked warm and friendly, but revealed himself to be remote and detached, and his ability to make emotional contact with others was severely impaired. He was of above average intelligence on non-verbal tasks; just average verbally. While his reading comprehension was good, reading accuracy was poor and he was retarded by three years in spelling.

At 17, just before the first follow-up, Jonathan was admitted to hospital with a sudden onset of a schizophrenic illness: he believed he had been hypnotized at school by some Chinese boys whose voices he heard in his head and who, he thought, were influencing him and willing him to jump off a high building.

At that time, his mother said, he had always been an insensitive child, oblivious to the needs of others and also of their responses to him. As he grew up he lost interest in most things, spending much of his time in the year preceding his illness listening to records, rocking, withdrawn from the family and, indeed, unable to tolerate their presence in the same room. He had also become obsessional, for example, going to great lengths to obtain every single book on the reference list for his history classes at school, and insisting that books which got worn had to be replaced.

Jonathan was 26 at the time of the second follow-up. He was still living at home, doing a little work in his father's business. He attended a psychiatric hospital regularly and was on medication for his psychotic illness. He had no friends. He remained very handsome, but he still had constant shaking of the knees. While highly sensitive himself, he lacked empathic understanding for others. He was overtalkative and almost totally preoccupied with his schizophrenic illness and what he called his 'paranoia'. He blamed himself for his illness and for not always being kind to other people. He said he did not have 'a real, anchored personality', and he felt guilty about his sexual thoughts involving a girl in the neighbourhood. He worried in case he might be accused of rape. He mentioned as his main interests: Roman history, the Bible and his coin collection.

Alcohol problems and drug-taking

At both the first and the second follow-up there were no differences between the groups in their self-reports of drinking behaviour. At the time of the second follow-up, six people in each group had a possible drinking problem. Questions about drug-taking were systematically asked only at this time. The incidence of drug-related problems was low and no differences were found between the groups.

Nevertheless, one of the control subjects had a very serious drug problem and had been in prison on that account; and one schizoid man had been drinking so excessively, taking methyl alcohol when unable to get ordinary drink, that he had induced a severe visual defect and was almost blind.

Although of good intelligence and from a middle-class background, this young young man had left school with no qualifications and begun drinking in his teens. He had left home because his aggressive and assaultive behaviour when drunk had caused much upset. He had done a number of odd, menial jobs, been a punk model, been sent to prison for shop-lifting and assault, and had often slept rough. At the time of the second follow-up interview he was 30 and had been totally off drink for two years. He was smiling, gentle, detached and vague. He said that he found himself talking about himself 'as if I'm talking about a stranger', and later: 'They tell me I'm anxious, I'm not sure why.' He had few regrets except for 'good times that have passed', and of his essential solitariness and fleeting human relationships he said: 'Things aren't right. I never know why.'

Delinquency

At the time of the first follow-up the two groups were quite similar in their responses to questions about having been in trouble with the police since leaving school. At the second follow-up, too, the scale assessing antisocial behaviour since leaving school in terms of contact with a variety of law-enforcing agencies, ranging from none to having been in prison, showed no differences between the two groups. Nine of the schizoid young men and 12 of the controls had had such contact. We must be clear that many young men in the general population have court convictions (20.5 per cent of men aged 16–26 years in England and Wales in 1984: Home Office, 1989). Furthermore, many children come to child psychiatrists because of antisocial childhood behaviour, and such children are at even greater risk than children in the general population of becoming delinquent in later life.

INDIVIDUAL VARIATIONS IN OUTCOME

In the last chapter we saw that the specific personality features of our schizoid group of former child patients which we had attempted to define and identify had remained very stable over time. Yet, just as among the control group of people, there were also great individual variations in personality functioning in both childhood and adult life. These individual differences were in part determined by the young people's ability levels and their educational achievements, but probably also by their social and family background and their life experiences. Our studies did not aim to identify the origins of such individual variations in either group, and the research design did not enable us to relate possible early adversities systematically to later life adjustment.

Nevertheless, our interviews with the young people who helped us with our study shed much light on their individual life paths. In the remainder of this chapter we will describe some of the members of our control groups, as well as some of the schizoid individuals, to illustrate the very wide range of their later life adjustment in relation to their earlier experiences.

An example of a happy outcome from the control group

JOHN A was followed up when he was 33. He was working successfully in the probation service, although he would have preferred a career in engineering. He was happily married to a nurse and had three young children. He described himself as someone who had changed a lot over the years, especially in self-confidence. At times he thought he was quite cynical, pessimistic and detached, seeing people as themselves responsible for the mess they get into. At the same time, he came across to the interviewer as a warm and caring person, much involved with his family and many friends, and more sensitive than perhaps he cared to admit. He had a number of interests, but none took priority over his family life.

When seen in the clinic at the age of 10, John's mother had had many complaints to make about him. She found him oppositional, dirty, untidy, restless, discontented, prone to temper tantrums and a poor mixer. He was jealous of her relationships with anyone other than himself. Although intelligence testing showed him to be of superior ability, his school work was poor, and his teachers described him as too quiet and bullied by other children.

John's father worked away from home most of the time and when at home could never relax. The mother was an unhappy and angry woman, who had been much attached to her own father and remained in conflict with her mother throughout her life. She was tired and depressed, preoccupied with possible bodily ailments and obsessional about cleanliness.

John had cried a lot as a baby, and suffered from nightmares after an admission to hospital following an accident at 18 months old. His mother slept with him because of the nightmares and, whenever the father came home, John resented his presence. His anxieties had been reinforced by a further hospital admission for surgery at the age of 9.

At his follow-up interview, John thought his mother had expected too much from him as a child and had attributed her own unhappiness to him. He could see now that the problem had been hers rather than his own, and he had come to terms with this. He thought his mother had been 'neurotic', and his father 'down to earth' but unable to avoid constant friction when he was at home.

In summary, this young man had made a very good adult life adjustment despite his childhood emotional difficulties and social inhibition and despite the fact that these had prevented him from making the educational progress his high intelligence should have guaranteed. His childhood troubles were thought to have been brought about by his mother's personality difficulties, the marital strains between his parents, and the traumatic accident and hospitalizations of his early years.

A less happy outcome from the control group

MICHAEL W was followed-up when he was 24. He was then living with his 19-year-old girlfriend and working as the caretaker for a number of bed-sitters in a tenement. This, his first 'serious' attachment, had lasted for a year. They have occasional rows when she walks out, but have never come to blows. He hopes they will marry and said he wanted 'to commit myself to something'.

Michael described himself as self-employed: he and a friend have a van and pick up and sell scrap metal. He had been claiming unemployment benefit, too, but a 'snooper' caught him.

He had been a 'Hell's Angel' and had had 'lots of good times and ugly times'. He had been in and out of young offenders' institutions, mainly for car and cycle thefts, but also for assaults during fights in which others had got badly injured. His longest prison sentence was two and a half years. That had made him change: 'You leave it, but it never leaves you . . . others are still in it ... that's why I've got short hair and changed my address ....' He thinks that, over the years, he has slowed down. He kept off drugs because he was afraid. He said: 'I'm happy the way I am, the way I look. I dress to fit in with my friends not society.'

He was a most charming young man to meet, but terribly dirty and greasy, dressed hippy style. He made excellent emotional contact, talking freely about his childhood family, his lifelong trouble with people in authority, and his lasting resentment at the way he had been treated as a child in a series of approved schools.

Michael had been referred to the child psychiatry department when he was 5 and a half years old, together with an older brother. Both boys were oppositional at home and at school, destructive and stealing other children's property. Michael also had nightmares. The family was materially very deprived, and an eviction for rent arrears had been very traumatic for both children. The parents had never married because the mother wanted to remain in control of her life, having had a previous, mutually violent marriage. During the boys' early years their mother had left them in doubt as to whether their father, whose name they did not share, was their real father, and he took little part in his children's upbringing. The mother was both indulgent and punitive, her child-rearing being characterized by lack of supervision and inconsistency which even the boys declared to be wrong. At his follow-up interview, Michael still described her as 'unpredictable, temper-wise'.

Over the years, the parents, although harmonious with each other, had been unable to change their way of bringing up the boys, and the children began to truant and to get into more and more serious trouble. At 24, Michael said he was 'not bothered' by the fact that his parents had never married, but that he himself *would* marry 'for the children's sake'.

When he was 8, Michael was savaged by an Alsatian and was in hospital for some time. The boys had been offering chocolate to two dogs who were in a fenced-off enclosure when one of the animals broke loose. Michael then developed anxiety symptoms and nightmares about dogs, and became socially withdrawn but his delinquent behaviour continued.

Michael had spent some time in a residential school for emotionally and behaviourally disturbed children, but ran away repeatedly and his educational progress was very poor, despite his average abilities. His truanting, stealing and later joy-riding got him into more and more trouble, and he spent his adolescent years in a series of approved schools.

It was only at the time of follow-up that we discovered, through a hospital records' search, that Michael's mother had in fact been chronically addicted to alcohol since the boys were children, had made a number of suicide attempts and had drink-related court convictions.

In summary, this normally endowed and emotionally responsive boy, always loyal to his family and friends, had been reared in poverty by affectionate parents who were unable to instil inner standards of control in their children. The mother was a poor role model for self-disciplined behaviour, inconsistent in her child-rearing methods. The fact that alcohol was wrecking her maternal skills became clear only much later. The father played a peripheral part in the family.

The eviction and the accident with the dogs were major traumata. The close ties between the two delinquent brothers led to an escalation of antisocial behaviour in both boys. Michael's educational retardation had prevented him from enjoying school and getting further training of any kind. His adolescent and young adult years were marred by the consequences of his repeated criminality. While he is hopeful about the future, this hope is tinged with uncertainty.

A well-adjusted man from the schizoid group

MATTHEW had been referred at the age of 10 because he had run away from his boarding school together with two other boys, and had had to be brought back by the police. His parents described him as a non-conformist, insensitive to the needs of others, oppositional, impulsive and obstructive. He had been a poor mixer at school; impertinent to older boys, bullying towards others. He had grandiose ideas, a vivid imagination and was fearless. Once, in a temper, he had lain down in the middle of the road waiting to be run over. At night he had trouble getting off to sleep. He was of very superior intelligence, rather better at verbal than at visuo-motor tasks, and his arithmetical skills were retarded for his age and ability level. He had been enuretic until the age of 3.

Matthew's father was a professional man of high intelligence, who thought Matthew was very like himself in personality. The mother had a chronic disabling physical illness and this was why the two children of the family had been sent to boarding school. Tragically, both parents were killed in a car crash when Matthew was 13 and his sister 15. He was then no longer in contact with the clinic and neither he nor his teachers took up the offer of further psychiatric support at that time.

The follow-up interview took place when Matthew was 34. He had had a university education and was now in a secure job he enjoyed as a Health and Safety Inspector. Part of his work was to interview victims of factory accidents. He was happily married to a former nurse and had a very gregarious son aged 3.

When discussing his mother's chronic illness, Matthew said it had had no impact on him at all. Similarly, while his sister had burst into tears on hearing about the parents' accident and death, he said: 'It didn't really hit me at all. I was independent or had a hard shell. It sank in slowly. . . . I used to go to the telephone and then I'd remember they were no more.' He had looked up the details of the accident in a library newspaper. An aunt and uncle had offered to make a home for the two children and Matthew accepted this, settled down, and still remains in close touch with these relatives as a member of their family. In fact, his school work and general adjustment had improved after this transition. His older sister, in contrast, could not accept a new family, failed her school exams, went into lodgings and took a job requiring no initial qualifications. She spent only holidays with the aunt and uncle. But she, too, undertook a professional training and, after an unsuccessful first marriage, is now once again and more happily married.

At the end of his interview, Matthew asked what I had thought of him as a boy, and I described his childhood personality and introduced the word 'loner'. This, he said, 'fitted' and a lot of things 'fell into place'. He had never been popular at school ('the boys cheered when they were told I was leaving'); at university he had had a very small circle of friends and spent his spare time going for long, solitary walks. He said: 'I'm trying to be more considerate now. I'm not a very considerate person. I'm quite self-centred; I can filter things out.' In his very first job he left after 'a personality clash with the chief engineer'. In fact, he believes he has changed jobs more than was good for his financial advancement; but he always lands on his feet.

Matthew's special interests are the stage (including acting) and photography. He had taken 2,000 photographs of a drama group he used to belong to and later used the slides for fund-raising. He had also been the photographer at a recent family wedding. He said: 'I have a theory that the shyer the photographer, the longer the telephoto lens and the further the photographer from his subject . . . [but] I'm getting better. The lens is shorter!' He also said: 'I'm still a cynic.'

Although at follow-up both Matthew and the 'blind' research interviewer rated his empathy as 'definitely impaired' (a feature of his personality which he was trying hard to improve, especially in relation to his wife), he was overall judged to have no psychiatric symptoms and a normal personality. And he just failed to score within the schizotypal range on the Baron scale.

In summary, unlike his normally responsive sister, this boy appears to have been protected from the impact of the traumatic circumstances and events of his childhood by his personality make-up, especially by his emotional detachment and lack of empathy, and perhaps also by his absorption in his own ideas. Later, his difficulties with relationships somewhat impaired his work adjustment, but overall he had been able to remedy this. At the age of 34 Matthew came across as an attractive, friendly and outwardly warm person, despite the emotional detachment he described as a feature of his personality.

A delinquent outcome in a schizoid boy with a 'Minimal Brain Damage' syndrome and Elective Mutism in childhood

GARY had been referred to the clinic when he was 7 because he refused to speak at school. His mother reported him as shy, slow to warm up, but also as obstinate and aggressive, explosive under stress. He had once threatened his large mother with a poker. She described him as a 'loner' with just a single friend. He was afraid to sleep alone at night and he was easily excited, for example, by television. He was overactive, fidgety and with a poor attention span. He had serious spelling problems and, despite normal intelligence, he could not yet spell or write his name. The mother had seen a programme about autism and wondered whether Gary was autistic.

Gary was the survivor of non-identical twins born prematurely, but weighing seven pounds at birth. He was born with a bleeding tendency and required transfusion after birth for severe blood loss. Although he had never had a fit, an electroencephalogram when he was 7 had shown an abnormality suggestive of epilepsy.

The family was united: the father, a labourer, 'shy, like Gary'; the mother subject to depressive illnesses and responding with great emotionality to the stresses induced by her son's difficulties.

Gary's hyperkinesis was well controlled with stimulant medication. Because of his learning difficulties and his aggressive behaviour in a big classroom, he was taught in a small special class for much of his school life, and there he coped quite well. But whenever attempts were made to reintegrate him into a bigger ordinary class, his behaviour would once more break down.

Gary was 21 at the time of the follow-up. He had left school at 16 and completed a motor-mechanics course at a further education college, but he as he put it: 'I got bored with cars'. He had had some short-term labouring jobs, but had been mainly unemployed.

Gary had married at 17, having met his wife at college, and they had a young daughter. He was clearly very fond of his wife and said he would like to have more children. At interview, he was still large and obese, as he had been in childhood, but he was now quite communicative and disarmingly frank about his personality difficulties and his delinquency.

He said: 'Ive been drinking a bit. Every day when I get money I drink, 3–4 pints and sometimes spirits.' When drunk he becomes violent, but is pleased that he has never hit his wife or baby. During rows she hits him. He has once torn the living room door off its hinges, and he has injured people in pub fights. He has briefly been in prison for non-payment of a fine for a motoring offence and he is now awaiting a court appearance for house-breaking together 'with another three guys' while drunk. The others had gone in and he had been the look out. There was also a charge of the theft of a motor cycle. The court had asked for psychiatric reports.

Gary said: 'I feel paranoid about folk all the time' and added that he's got it in for the police and the court. For the past two years, whenever he walks down the street, he thinks people are staring at him, but he doesn't know if they really are. He thinks that other people think 'that I'm an arsehole or an idiot. I go in bad moods and, if it gets bad, I'll hit them'.

About his childhood mutism Gary said: 'I was just shy. It did bother me. I'd get a red face if I talked to someone.' He was clear that his difficulties were not due to any shortcomings in the way his parents had brought him up.

The 'blind' research social worker assessed Gary as 'definitely schizoid', with both an antisocial and schizotypal personality disorder, using DSM-III criteria. She found him smiling inappropriately, with poor eye contact, odd rapport, some incoherence of speech and with definitely impaired empathy and oversensitivity with paranoid ideas. His score on the Baron scale for schizotypal disorder was also abnormal.

In summary

This young man's schizoid personality traits in combination with his constitutional impulsiveness, the result of birth injury, severely impaired his ability to cope with relationships with other people in the outside world, although he did have the capacity for affection within his family circle. The fact that he was, in addition, of only just average intellectual ability and had made poor progress at school contributed to his poor work adjustment, and the boredom of his unemployment in turn may have contributed to his alcohol problem. This then both increased his paranoid ideas and precipitated his violent and antisocial behaviour.

The psychiatrist who assessed him for the court, while recognizing Gary's constitutional handicaps, was more impressed by the fact that he did not have a treatable psychiatric illness, and he did not consider that the nature of Gary's personality disorder merited any special consideration by the court. The future outlook for this young man must remain very uncertain.

So far we have been considering the clinical picture of schizoid personality in childhood and adult life as it manifests itself in boys. The next chapter deals with the childhood features and with what is known about the later outcome of schizoid girls.

6   Schizoid girls in childhood and later life

We shall now describe the clinical features of schizoid girls as they emerged from an analysis of their childhood case records and from a series of follow-up interviews with some of them in early adult life.

THE CHILDHOOD PICTURE IN GIRLS IS RARER AND MORE PUZZLING

Asperger himself (1944) (see also Frith, 1991b) had been intrigued to find that the condition he discovered and labelled 'autistic psychopathy of childhood' occurred almost exclusively in boys. He had come across similar difficulties in girls, but never the full syndrome, unless the girls had suffered from brain damage due to encephalitis, an illness quite common at that time. Asperger noted that not only fathers but also many of the mothers of his affected patients had features of autistic psychopathy, and he wondered whether perhaps in girls these features become apparent only after puberty. He also speculated that the condition might be 'an extreme variant of male intelligence' because, as he thought, boys are more abstract and logical in their thinking than girls.

The reported sex incidence of Asperger's syndrome and related conditions in children has varied from 10:1 to 2.3:1 (Ehlers and Gillberg, 1993; Gillberg, 1989; Mouridsen et al., 1993; Nagy and Szatmari, 1986; Szatmari et al., 1989a; Tantam, 1991; Wing, 1981). Our own group of schizoid children consisted of 115 boys and 34 girls, reduced to 33 in the studies now to be described because of the uncertainty of the diagnosis in one case. This is a ratio of 3.5 boys to 1 girl. The aggregated sex ratios of children and adults reported as having schizoid/schizotypal/Asperger disorders is 4.6:1 (Wolff and McGuire, 1995).

Wing (1981) thought that Asperger's syndrome might have different manifestations in girls and boys, and that affected girls are more outgoing. That had been my impression, too. I thought they might also, as a group, turn out to be more sociable and more communicative. These impressions, as we shall see, were not correct.

There is some evidence that autistic disorders manifest themselves differently in males and females. Rutter and Schopler (1989) reported that, for autism in general, girls are more seriously affected. But among higher-functioning autistic people girls are said to be less seriously handicapped (McLennan *et al.*, 1993) and, as we discussed in Chapter Two, a case has been made for considering that severely affected children with Asperger's syndrome are indistinguishable from high-functioning autistic children.

If, as in high-functioning autism, girls with schizoid personality (mild Asperger's syndrome) in the general population are less seriously affected than boys, one would expect them to be referred less often to a child psychiatric clinic. This is clearly the case. One might then also expect that, when such girls *are* referred, they will have more co-morbidity, that is, more associated psychiatric or educational difficulties, and will have suffered from more adversities in their lives than schizoid boys. We shall see that to some extent this was found to be so. It had in fact sometimes been quite difficult to diagnose schizoid personality in the girls because, unlike schizoid boys, they often resembled other referred girls, not only in their symptoms but also in their experiences of family adversities.

AN INITIALLY PUZZLING CASE

SANDRA had been treated since early childhood for constipation and soiling. At the age of 9 she caused much concern during a stay in a children's ward because she kept wandering about the hospital and told stories to the staff and children which turned out to be pure fantasy, for example, that her mother had just had a new baby. Sandra had also been running away from school and home, often taking the neighbours' dog, and once their little boy, with her.

At school Sandra had friends and made good progress, but she often acted strangely. She had stuffed her nostrils with paper; had once sellotaped over her mouth; had chased other children with dog's dirt; and had put her blazer down a toilet.

Sandra had been adopted in infancy and details about her birth were not known. Her development had been normal apart from bed-wetting and soiling. She was of normal intelligence, but with a markedly lower verbal than performance intelligence score.

When seen at the child psychiatry clinic, she was outgoing but superficial in her communications; she had odd grimaces and motor mannerisms; she seemed to lack feeling and talked quite callously about sticking pins into her budgie. It was unclear whether this was fact or fantasy. She was a gifted drawer.

Sandra was admitted to a psychiatric in-patient unit, but often ran away, sometimes taking other children or neighbouring pets with her. Once she cut the heads off all the flowers in a nearby garden, and another time she was brought back by the police having shop-lifted an odd assortment of goods, including two left shoes. She had given a false name and address to the police.

She was never able to explain what prompted her actions and her emotional life remained mysterious. She did not seem unhappy nor particularly worried. No light was shed on her almost total lack of conformity to accepted standards of behaviour during the many hours spent with her by a sensitive psychotherapist. She did not seem to dwell on her adoptive status and her origins, and appeared to be fond of her affectionate but bewildered parents, especially her father. Despite being encouraged to do so, Sandra did not express anger or resentment and she was always pleasant to be with.

Because of her unpredictable wanderings and her parents' inability to cope with her behaviour, Sandra was discharged to a Rudolf Steiner boarding school. Sometimes during the holidays she embarrassed her parents by shouting from her bedroom window that her mother was ill-treating her. But, despite frequent escapades, her school placement lasted until she was 17. Sandra was very well liked and the parents, too, were pleased with her progress. Yet her wanderings continued. She often entered the houses of wealthy people; she abducted riding horses, 'always equipped and dressed in appropriate gear'; and she told fantastic stories. The head of the school wrote: 'Her intuitiveness and presence of mind seem to have been bordering on the miraculous'. Once pebbles had to be surgically removed from her ears. Shortly before leaving school she disappeared, and a major search for her was launched. She heard of this on the radio while staying with 'friends' in a distant town.

Sandra was last seen at the child psychiatry department at the age of 17, looking ungainly and with a strange hair cut. She was cheerful and outgoing, but seemed basically shy, lacking in empathy and seriousness. She had a number of friends, but no plans for her future. A social worker was helping to arrange work training for her.

During her follow-up interview when she was 32, she remembered her in-patient stay with some pleasure, smiling ruefully as she recalled some of her outrageous behaviour, and she spoke of her psychotherapist with much affection.

THE GIRLS IN CHILDHOOD

For the childhood case note analysis, the samples consisted of 33 girls diagnosed as having a schizoid personality and 33 other referred girls, chosen from the departmental case register by an independent psychologist to match each of the schizoid girls as closely as possible for age, year of referral, tested IQ and occupational class of the father. The method for the case-note analysis was exactly the same as that described in Chapter Three for the boys (Wolff and McGuire, 1994).

Because all case notes were abstracted and rated by myself, and I was of course not 'blind' to the children's diagnosis, an independent psychologist read and rated the records of 8 schizoid girls and 8 controls without knowing which was which. *Inter-rater reliabilities* for 26 variables on two-, three- or four-point scales were on the whole satisfactory, ranging from weighted kappa 0.0 for special interest patterns (which may have been due to their rarity in the girls or to inadequate definition of the behaviour) to 1.0, with a mean of 0.73 (Wolff and McGuire, 1995).

The findings

The childhood ratings were analysed in two ways. First, ratings for the 33 schizoid girls as a group, were compared with ratings previously made of the case records of the group of 32 schizoid boys. Next, the differences between ratings of schizoid and control girls were compared with the differences previously found between schizoid and control boys.

Group differences between schizoid boys and girls

There were only two significant differences in the childhood features of the groups of schizoid girls and boys: girls had had fewer organic illnesses which might have caused organic brain impairments, and they less often had the specific interest patterns which had been so characteristic of schizoid boys.

Differences between matched pairs of schizoid and control girls

Features of schizoid personality

As with the boys, the case records did not permit rating of three of the features we had thought to be characteristic of schizoid personality in childhood: impaired empathy and emotional detachment; excessive sensitivity, at times with paranoid ideation; and odd styles of communication – because these features were not systematically recorded, especially in the case notes of the control children. For two of the other three core features, schizoid girls and boys both differed significantly from their matched controls. The characteristic of being a 'loner' discriminated as highly between schizoid and control girls as it had done between the pairs of boys; unusual fantasies, distinguished almost as highly between the pairs of girls as it had done between the boys. Schizoid boys had been no more withdrawn than their matched controls, but schizoid girls, contrary to expectation, were marginally more often withdrawn than their controls.

The one clinical characteristic which very significantly differentiated schizoid from control boys, but did not distinguish between the pairs of girls, was that of having special interest patterns or collections (and this had also been found significantly more often in schizoid boys than girls). One might speculate that this could be due to the lower intelligence we had also found in the girls and perhaps to their lower levels of intellectual pursuits in general. Yet special interest patterns had been a feature of a number of schizoid boys who had only modest intellectual abilities. At follow-up, too, proportionally fewer women than men were found to have such special interests, but at that time the difference between women and men was no longer statistically significant.

Associated developmental disorders

As with the boys, significantly more schizoid than control girls had *specific developmental delays*. Severe learning difficulties had already been mentioned by Asperger as frequently associated with the disorder he described (Asperger, 1944, 1991). They should probably be thought of as an integral part of the disorder, although in our series of boys and girls, like other key features of the syndrome, they were by no means always present.

Specific developmental disorders differentiated between schizoid girls and their controls even more highly than between the groups of boys (15 schizoid and 4 control boys had had serious or multiple specific developmental language, educational or motor delays, compared with 13 schizoid girls and only one control). In the general population, specific developmental disorders, as well as educational difficulties, are always much commoner in boys than girls (Rutter *et al.*, 1971) and it is thought that this is due to the increased vulnerability of boys to many biological and social adversities.

In our schizoid groups, one girl and one boy had had *severe early language delays*, which cleared up entirely in both. The point was made in Chapter Three that some children with severe developmental language disorders have similar interpersonal and cognitive difficulties to those of autistic children or children with more severe Asperger's syndrome (Bishop, 1989; Cantwell *et al.*, 1989; Rutter and Mawhood, 1991; Brook and Bowler, 1993). Severe early language delay also overlapped with our schizoid/Asperger children in both boys and girls. Among our schizoid boys, three had displayed *symptoms of autism* in early childhood: gaze avoidance and echolalia. In contrast, none of the schizoid girls had done so.

Elective mutism, previously reported in children of low average intelligence with Asperger's syndrome (Fine *et al.*, 1991) and in the biological relatives of children with Asperger's syndrome (Gillberg, 1989), occurred in 3 boys and 3 girls of the total of 65 schizoid children whose case notes were analysed, a rate far higher than that found in the general population (Kolvin and Fundudis, 1981) and probably also than that in children referred to a child psychiatric clinic. This suggests that in all children with elective mutism a diagnosis of schizoid/Asperger disorder needs to be considered. Elective mutism, like schizoid/Asperger disorder, is associated with developmental language delays (Kolvin and Fundudis, 1981), and it has also been reported as an unusual precursor of schizophrenia (Eldar *et al.*, 1985).

Co-morbidity

It has been pointed out (Szatmari *et al.*, 1989a) that, in contrast to autism, other associated psychiatric disorders are common in Asperger's syndrome. This can obscure the underlying diagnosis, and our study suggests that this may be especially so in affected girls. In half the boys and two-thirds of the girls the presenting symptoms were of other psychiatric disorders, mainly conduct or mixed disorders. As in the case of the boys, fewer schizoid than control girls had been referred only with complaints of emotional disorders, and more with educational failure.

The incidence of conduct disorders of any kind before or during the clinic contact had not distinguished between schizoid and control boys, but the group of schizoid girls were strikingly different from their controls in this respect. Twelve of the 33 schizoid girls, compared with only 3 of the 33 girls in the control group, had been seriously conduct disordered, that is, they had been charged with an offence, or had engaged in multiple or serious thefts, or very aggressive behaviour leading to school exclusion or injury to another person, or had been responsible for serious fire-raising. The figures for boys were 9 and 8 respectively. Stealing and aggressive behaviour alone did not distinguish schizoid from control girls (nor between schizoid and control boys).

Background factors

Schizoid boys, as we have seen, had predominantly come from a middle- and upper-class socio-economic background. This was not so for the girls, but the difference between the boys and girls was not statistically significant. In line with this, the measured IQ of schizoid girls in childhood was also non-significantly lower, especially on verbal tests (their mean IQ on the verbal scale of the Wechsler Intelligence Scale for Children [WISC] was 99.0, compared with 107.6 for the boys). We shall see that, at follow-up, the girls were again of lower socio-economic background and of lower IQ than the boys, and that the differences now *were* statistically significant.

As in the case of the boys, schizoid girls did not differ from their controls in the numbers who had been affected by obstetric complications or who had evidence of mild brain dysfunction.

Coming from a broken home did not distinguish schizoid from control girls, just as in the case of the boys, and prolonged separations from parents and home, equally common in both groups of boys, was more common among control than among schizoid girls.

However, overall ratings of family delinquency, socio-cultural deprivation, childhood stresses and childhood privations of any kind had been made significantly more often in control than in schizoid boys, suggesting that the behavioural and emotional difficulties of boys in the control group were more related to environmental adversity than were those of the schizoid boys. Among the girls, in contrast, although separation experiences had been more common among the controls, childhood privations of any kind were only non-significantly more common in the controls, and family delinquency, socio-cultural deprivation and childhood stresses were rated as equally common in both groups. This suggests that the difficulties of schizoid girls, in contrast to those of schizoid boys, may to some extent have been brought about by adverse circumstances.

It has been argued above that if schizoid personality manifests itself less obviously in girls than in boys in the general population, the onset of social malfunctioning may be later in women, as Asperger himself (1944) had thought, and schizoid girls disturbed enough to be psychiatrically referred would have more co-morbidity, more associated developmental disorders, and would also have been exposed to more adversities in their lives.

In fact, the schizoid girls in this study had not on average been referred earlier to the clinic than the boys, and did not have more developmental disorders than the boys, but they did have more co-morbidity. In addition, and in contrast to schizoid boys, schizoid girls had been exposed to almost as much environmental adversity as the girls in the control group, they were somewhat less well endowed intellectually than the boys, and came from a less privileged social background. This is what we would expect if the expression of the underlying tendency towards schizoid disorder were milder in girls than in boys.

Services received

In line with their relatively higher rates of specific developmental disorders, significantly more schizoid than control girls had received special educational services, ranging from assessment and advice only, to placement in a special residential school. For the boys, there had been only a trend in that direction.

Contact with law-enforcing agencies (from appearing at a Children's Hearing to admission to a List D school) did not differentiate between the groups of either girls or boys. Social work services (ranging from supervision, to admission to a children's home, to permanent alternative family placement) were received only slightly more often by schizoid compared with control girls. There had been no difference for the boys. But admission to a child psychiatric in-patient unit, which had been only marginally more common in schizoid boys, had occurred significantly more often in schizoid than in control girls. These differences were due to the lower rates of both social work contacts and psychiatric admissions in control girls as compared with control boys.

In summary, in a child psychiatric clinic, schizoid personality is seen less often in girls than in boys. The condition is harder to diagnose in girls because they more often have associated difficulties. The manifestations of schizoid personality in girls are the same as in boys, except that girls less often have special interest patterns. Referred schizoid girls also tend to come from a less privileged social background than the boys, and are less often of very high intellectual ability.

THE GIRLS IN LATER LIFE

It had been planned to follow up the girls in the same way and at the same time as the boys, to follow up the matched group of control girls also, and to have an independent interviewer, who did not know of the childhood diagnoses, carry out the main assessments, just as in the study of the boys. In the event this was not possible, because it proved much harder and took much longer to trace the girls. In part this was due to the difficulty of tracing former child patients who had changed their name by marriage, in part due to the fact that the schizoid girls were found to be geographically extremely mobile.

In our follow-up of the boys we had always planned to interview only a proportion of them. In the event, 32 matched pairs of schizoid and control boys were seen in adult life. But, because there were far fewer girls than boys in our total group of children identified as schizoid, we attempted to trace and interview all 33 of them. Because the research interviewer was no longer available by the time the tracing had been completed, I myself carried out most of the interviews, and the attempt to see the control girls as well was abandoned. Instead, the follow-up information on schizoid girls was compared as far as possible with that obtained previously for schizoid boys.

Tracing and co-operation of the girls

Of the total group of 33 schizoid girls, 2 had died by suicide before the survey was completed (one of these had initially agreed but later refused to be interviewed). (One other girl, sadly, committed suicide after taking part in the study.) Three of the girls had emigrated before the start of the study. Four proved to be untraceable, one of them extremely mobile. Of the remaining 24 girls, one, also very mobile, agreed to take part in the study over the telephone, but was never in at the times we arranged to meet. Six of the 24 girls traced refused to take part in the study, an effective refusal rate of 29 per cent, compared with 25.6 per cent for the boys.

Did the 17 girls who took part in the follow-up study differ from the 16 who did not?

All the information extracted from the childhood case records for the 17 schizoid girls who were seen for follow-up was compared with that for the 16 girls who were not interviewed. Significant differences between these groups were found for only three items: the girls interviewed had been in contact with the clinic for a significantly longer time; they had been rated as less emotionally and socially withdrawn; and fewer of them had had other, associated child psychiatric disorders (8 of the 17 girls followed-up had presented with educational failure or features of schizoid personality only, and 9 with other child psychiatric syndromes; among the girls not followed-up, the figures were 1 and 15 respectively). For all other ratings of age, IQ, symptoms, family and social background, and services received, there were no significant differences between the groups. The girls who took part in the follow-up study thus knew the author better than those who did not, were less withdrawn (and presumably less secretive), and were likely to have been somewhat less disturbed, but in all other respects they were representative of the group as a whole.

The follow-up method

The research interview has already been described in the previous two chapters. We were particularly interested in the girls' scores on the 'Diagnostic Interview for Borderlines' (DIB, see Gunderson *et al.*, 1981). This had not differentiated schizoid from control men at follow-up, but we thought that schizoid women might have more borderline features than schizoid men, because among psychiatric patients more women than men are known to have this type of personality disorder. We shall see that this supposition, too, as with our guess that schizoid girls are more 'outgoing' than schizoid men, turned out to be wrong.

As with the men, the women's intelligence was tested.

One girl, then in residential care, suffering from the residual effects of a schizophrenic illness (see below and Chapter Seven), was so withdrawn that she was able to respond only to parts of the interview.

How reliable were the interview ratings?

We saw earlier that reliability testing of the main interview had been satisfactory. The only indication that I had not been biased in favour of finding schizoid features in the young women interviewed comes from a comparison of the overall ratings of schizoid personality made of the 6 girls who had been seen for follow-up by the 'blind' research interviewer with those made by myself for the remaining 11. The research interviewer diagnosed 5 out of 6 girls as 'definitely schizoid' and one as 'not schizoid'; I diagnosed 5 out of 11 as 'definitely schizoid', 5 as 'mildly or doubtfully schizoid', and one as 'not schizoid'. The statistical analysis of the results has been described elsewhere (Wolff and McGuire, 1995).

Results

The comparisons presented here are between the 17 schizoid girls and the 32 schizoid boys, all of whom had been interviewed again in adult life.

The schizoid girls had the same mean age at referral (just under 10 years old) and at follow-up (27 years old) as the schizoid boys. The girls had been referred on average three years later than the boys and were followed up correspondingly later also. The mean duration of childhood clinic contact had been the same for both groups.

Occupational status as well as verbal IQ were significantly lower at follow-up for the schizoid women than for the men, and their educational qualifications were also significantly lower. It is unlikely that this is entirely due to differences in the educational levels between men and women in the general population, because it applied in our groups to school qualifications, too. Only one-third of the schizoid men had left school with no qualifications at all, compared with over half the schizoid girls. Fifteen of the 32 schizoid boys had had a college or university education of some kind, with three completing a university degree, compared with only one of the 17 girls, who was attending college at the time of the study.

Features of schizoid personality in girls and boys at follow-up

The scores of the girls were no different from those of the boys on many personality features which had previously distinguished between boys in the schizoid and control groups, suggesting that the schizoid women shared the personality characteristics of the schizoid men. These were: past solitariness; current social integration; being a poor 'mixer'; feeling the 'odd man out'; lacking in empathy; oversensitivity; an unusual fantasy life; unusual thought processes; marked guardedness or lack of guardedness; and the single-minded pursuit of special interests (although this was 'definite or striking' in only 4/17 women, but in 13/32 men). In addition, the interviewer's ratings of unusual eye contact, smiling and motor behaviour were also quite similar for the girls and boys at follow-up.

The girls were rated as using less 'metaphorical' language than schizoid young men, and as being less often over- or undercommunicative. Schizoid girls were found to be less sociable than the boys, but it may be that in the general population, too, young women of this age participate in fewer social outings and lead a more restricted social life than men. A preference for solitariness was expressed as often by schizoid girls as by the boys, and so was a self-assessment of being 'emotionally detached'.

DSM-III schizotypal and borderline personality disorders

The Baron scores for schizotypal personality disorder were no different for schizoid women and men, and very much higher than they had been in the group of male controls. Fourteen out of 16 women who completed the Baron schedule scored within the schizotypal personality disorder range (87.5 per cent) compared with 24 of the 32 (75 per cent) schizoid men.

On the Baron subscales, too, the women scored similarly to the men, with abnormal scores on the scales for ideas of reference, magical thinking, impaired rapport, odd communications and social isolation.

The schizoid women had higher mean DIB scores for borderline personality disorder than the schizoid men, who themselves had had higher mean scores than the control men, but none of these differences were statistically significant. Of the DIB subscales, only that for psychosis had significantly differentiated schizoid from control men. This scale was scored very similarly for schizoid women and men. However, the schizoid women also scored significantly worse on the scale for social adaptation ($P < 0.05$), in line with their self-reports of an even less active social life than the schizoid men.

At the end of the interview, more of the women than the men were given an overall clinical DSM-III diagnosis of schizotypal personality disorder: 9 out of 17, compared with 7 out of 32; but proportionally fewer were diagnosed as having a DSM-III schizoid personality disorder: 3 out of 17 compared with 9 out of 32.

Psychosocial adjustment

Here comparisons between schizoid male and female subjects are much more problematical in the absence of a control group of girls. Girls in the community marry earlier, have children earlier and their working lives are different from those of boys. Nevertheless, the data available for the girls is presented here for clinical interest, because they were a consecutive group with schizoid/Asperger syndromes presenting to a child psychiatric clinic.

Ratings of work adjustment and work relationships, which had not distinguished schizoid from control men, were also similar for the schizoid women. But overall work adjustment, significantly worse for schizoid than control men, was even worse in schizoid women, although not significantly so.

One schizoid girl, with evidence of mild cerebral damage, who later developed a schizophrenic illness with decline of IQ, was living in a Rudolf Steiner community. This was the only one among our 65 schizoid and control boys and girls known to be in institutional care in adult life.

Proportionally more schizoid girls at follow-up were living with a partner, and the girls had left home earlier than the boys, but these differences were not significant. The same proportion of schizoid girls as boys had married (5/17 compared with 7/32), non-significantly lower than the proportion of control boys (12/32). While schizoid boys had had significantly fewer lasting heterosexual relationships than control boys, there was a trend for schizoid girls to be more often involved in significant heterosexual relationships than schizoid boys (14/17 compared with 17/32).

Exactly the same proportions of schizoid women and men had had treatment for psychiatric disorders, rates significantly higher than those for control men. Schizophrenic illnesses occurred in later life in 2/17 schizoid women and 2/32 schizoid men, but in none of the 32 control men. Suicidal behaviour was significantly more common for schizoid women than for schizoid men (any suicidal action, 10/17 and 6/32 respectively), and this is in line with the higher rates of attempted suicide in young women than young men in the general population. But, as will be reported in the next chapter, although the numbers were very small and therefore only suggestive, even deaths from suicide in later life were found to be commoner in our total group of schizoid girls (3/33) than in the boys (3/115), and this is not what one would expect from population norms. There were no known deaths by suicide in the control groups of either sex.

Antisocial conduct, in terms of any convictions after the age of 16, was equally common in schizoid women and men (5/17 and 8/32 respectively), when, as we shall see in Chapter Eight, in the general population women are always much less delinquent than men. Excessive drinking, too, was mentioned exactly as often by schizoid women as men (6/17 and 10/32 respectively), when in the general population men are much more often affected. In addition, a few of the schizoid girls at follow-up were found to have had serious difficulties in bringing up their children: 3 of the 17 women interviewed had children in permanent care or placed in other families.

It is of interest to compare the psychosocial adjustment of our total groups of 32 schizoid men and 17 schizoid women with that of Tantam's cases of Asperger's syndrome (1991). Among our 49 subjects followed up, only one was in residential care out of our total cohort of 149 boys and girls), two-thirds were living independently, over half were working reasonably well, and over a quarter had married by the age of 27. Among Tantam's (1991) cases, over half were in residential care, only 3 per cent were living independently, less than one-tenth were working and only 2 per cent had been married.

In conclusion, the 17 schizoid girls followed-up resembled the 32 schizoid boys seen again in adult life in being more solitary, lacking in empathy, having increased sensitivity, special interest patterns and unusual thought processes. Like schizoid boys, most of the women in later life fulfilled the criteria for schizotypal personality disorder, and 2 of the 17 had developed schizophrenic illnesses, from which one had recovered but the other had not (see Chapter Seven). While the overall psychosocial outcome for the girls was reasonably good, as it had been for the boys, their lower ability levels precluded them from the occupational achievements shown by some of the men. This, as we argued earlier, may have been due to a referral bias in childhood, and may not apply to more mildly affected women in the general population.

IS THERE A FAMILY HISTORY OF SCHIZOID PERSONALITY TRAITS?

We did not have the resources for a systematic study of psychiatric illness and personality disorder among the biological relatives of our schizoid boys and girls. My clinical impression had been the same as Asperger's (1944) and Wing's (1981). I, too, thought that many of the parents had schizoid personality traits.

An attempt was made to put this impression to the test in two ways:

1 descriptions of the children's parents found in the case records were rated for possible schizoid traits (for those children who had biological parents and where the case notes were detailed enough for such ratings);
2 at follow-up, each individual was asked for global descriptions of his or her biological parents' personalities, and these descriptions too were rated as indicating possible or definite schizoid traits.

It must be made clear that these ratings were quite impressionistic.

In childhood, 18 of 31 schizoid boys had fathers rated as doubtfully or definitely schizoid, compared with 3 of 24 control boys. The figures for girls were 10 out of 30 and none out of 21. For mothers the comparable figures for the boys were 18 out of 31 and 2 out of 26, and for the girls 6 out of 29 and 3 out of 21.

At follow-up, 11 of the 30 fathers of schizoid boys were rated as doubtfully or definitely schizoid, compared with 10 of the 28 fathers of controls and 8 of 15 fathers of schizoid girls. Only 3 of 30 mothers of schizoid boys were rated as having schizoid traits, exactly the same number as for the 29 control boys. Nine of the mothers of 15 schizoid girls were rated as themselves possibly schizoid.

Thus, in childhood, when the parents had actually been seen in the clinic themselves, significantly more mothers and fathers of schizoid than of control boys had been thought to have schizoid personality traits, and this was so also for the fathers of schizoid girls. Schizoid girls also had more schizoid mothers than did control girls, but this difference was not statistically significant.

Clearly, no reliance can be put on the ratings of parents' personalities at the time of the follow-up when these were based only on descriptions provided by their children.

MAKING THE DIAGNOSIS MAY BE DIFFICULT AND ERRORS CAN OCCUR

As we saw in Chapter Four, at the end of our first follow-up of 22 matched pairs of schizoid and control boys (Wolff and Chick, 1980), the interviewer and the author together reviewed all the diagnoses made in childhood and adult life. We found that one boy in the control group had been correctly diagnosed as 'definitely schizoid' by the research interviewer at follow-up, and one boy diagnosed as schizoid in childhood had clearly been misdiagnosed by the interviewer as 'not schizoid' at follow-up.

Making the diagnosis can be especially difficult in girls. I once saw an extremely uncommunicative girl with school refusal and diagnosed her as having a phobic anxiety state with severe social inhibition. She puzzled me because I could make no real contact with her. Years later her mother told me that in her twenties this girl had twice, and inexplicably, stolen babies. Retrospectively I diagnosed her as schizoid. Later still I heard that, while serving a prison sentence, she had developed schizophrenia.

Among the girls who were followed up, two who had been diagnosed as schizoid in childhood were later found to have perfectly normal personalities. One had at that time been interviewed by the research interviewer, the other by myself. One girl in the control group, who had not been seen by myself in childhood, was later diagnosed as 'definitely schizoid' on the basis of her adult psychiatric hospital case notes, and in retrospect also on the basis of her childhood records. Despite these findings, the childhood groupings of the girls were not altered, so that both the analyses of the clinical features in childhood and in adult life were, if anything, biased against finding differences between schizoid and other referred girls.

TWO GIRLS IN THE SCHIZOID GROUP WHO HAD NORMAL PERSONALITIES IN LATER LIFE

The following two young women had been diagnosed as mildly schizoid in childhood and were found to have no features of this personality when interviewed in later life. The childhood diagnosis had probably been mistaken. An alternative explanation is that only very mild schizoid features had been present, but were no longer evident in later life.

MARY was only 5 and a half years old when she was first seen in the clinic because of her unhappiness and inability to make friends. She was in frequent fights at school. She excelled at gym, composed poems and produced strange drawings. The mother complained of her bed-wetting and soiling, but also of temper tantrums, restlessness and negativism. She felt rejected by her daughter, whom she described as fearless, stubborn and unpredictable. Twice Mary had drunk poisonous substances. Sometimes she saw 'monsters'. At interview she was 'distant', lacked appropriate shyness, was overtalkative and laughed incongruously.

Mary's birth and developmental history had been normal, but she was poorly co-ordinated and had transient reading and maths problems in her early school years. She was of average ability.

Her bed-wetting and soiling improved with treatment, but she was referred again two years later because she was said to have attacked a neighbour's baby. At that stage Mary said she thought other girls talked about her behind her back.

The mother had had recurrent depressive illnesses since Mary's birth, and the father attributed the child's difficulties to the mother's excessive strictness with her.

At follow-up by the research interviewer, this former patient was found to be happily married and with two young children. She had a steady, part-time job. She now had no features of schizoid personality and her Baron and DIB scores were normal. She had no psychiatric or personality disorder; but she described herself as somewhat lacking in confidence and concentration, and said she had always found number work difficult and this had prevented her from further training . She felt she had ability which was 'blocked'.

Mary was very glad to participate in the study because she always felt she had been misunderstood as a child, and she described her difficulties then as a reaction to her mother's punitiveness, which she could now understand as a result of the mother's depressive illness and associated irritability. She also thought that her school difficulties had contributed to her lack of confidence. Her one remaining concern was that she could not be as emotionally responsive to her husband as she would like to be.

Mary was thought to have lacked empathy in childhood, to have been excessively sensitive and to have had an unusual fantasy life. But she was only 5 years old at the time and the diagnosis of schizoid personality was probably incorrect. She certainly suffered from her mother's inability, because of her own illness, to be affectionately responsive to her.

JOYCE was 9 years old when she was referred to the clinic because she was rebellious, difficult and physically aggressive at home, especially to her mother, and persistently jealous of her younger brother, accusing the mother repeatedly of favouritism. Over the previous year she had become increasingly withdrawn and complained of feeling 'strange'. She got on well at school. At interview she was outspoken and judged to lack sensitivity for the feelings of others. She said: 'Why don't you leave it to us? Why try to help us? Leave us alone. . . . I'm not going to co-operate. You haven't a clue what I'm talking about.' Also: 'I'll go on a diet if she [her mother] gives up smoking.'

Joyce had been born by Caesarean section, two weeks premature. Her development was normal except for some reading and spelling problems when younger. The mother described her own mother as insensitive to the feelings of others and never listening to their point of view. There were no other family problems.

Follow-up by the author twelve years later, revealed a mature, warm and confident girl, who made excellent contact, had no features of schizoid personality, scored within normal limits on the Baron and DIB scales, and had no psychiatric or personality disorder.

She was cohabiting steadily with her boyfriend, whom she hoped to marry; both were students. She enjoyed her work and had realistic career plans. She led an active social life and her relationships with her parents were good.

Joyce said she still had a slight spelling problem, and she remembered herself as a shy child, apprehensive of new things and people. She had had an imaginary companion for some years, and she recalled also an ongoing childhood fantasy (a 'paracosm' – see Chapter Four), set in a fantasy world and shared with a friend, about a girl called 'Zuluanne Chippolata'.

Looking back, Joyce thought that at the time of the referral she had been merely 'unsettled, growing up' (she had been an early maturer), and that coming to the clinic had helped. Between the ages of 10 and 13 she gradually became a vegetarian ('I realized that what I was about to eat was the animals in the field' – the family lived in the country), and her mother, who co-operated fully with the diet, thinks thereafter Joyce became much calmer.

ONE GIRL AMONG THE CONTROLS WHOSE CASE RECORDS REVEALED A SCHIZOID PERSONALITY DISORDER BEGINNING IN CHILDHOOD

This young woman in the control group had not been seen by myself in childhood. It was only during a records' search for possible psychiatric hospital attendances that the true diagnosis became clear.

JANE was referred to the clinic at 15 years old because she had cut her wrist. She was unhappy, solitary and friendless, disliked school and felt inferior. But her behaviour at school was 'exemplary'. In the playground she would stand and read. She was suspicious of everyone and told her headmistress she thought the world was against her.

At home Jane was said to be withdrawn, but also quarrelsome and aggressive. She often wandered off, telling no one where she was going. She went to bed late and insisted on playing her radio well into the night. She would 'drop her eyes' when looking at strangers. She had some obsessional habits as well as an eye-blinking tic. She was learning German and had a German pen pal, the father thought to spite him, since he had been a much traumatized POW in Germany during the war. Jane had two passionate interests: Germany and horses, visiting a milkman's horse regularly. In fact, the suicidal gesture occurred when her parents on one occasion refused to allow her to visit the stables.

She had been three weeks postmature, but well at birth. She had started talking only at 2 years old, and was still poor at verbal expression. She had had no friends since the age of 5. Recently, she had been preoccupied with religious themes, wanting to enter a nunnery and to make a nun's habit in her sewing class at school.

There was considerable family stress, because the father, previously cheerful and healthy, had come back from the war chronically anxious, uncommunicative and with many psychiatric difficulties. The mother was protective of him and the children.

Jane was of average ability. At her first interview she expressed the wish to live on top of a high building, so that no one could come up without her knowing. She was hostile to her father because of his ingrained hatred of the Germans.

A diagnosis of early onset psychosis was considered, but her difficulties were later ascribed to the family tensions.

She was referred to an adult psychiatric out-patient department in her late twenties after some years of marriage, because she was depressed, with suicidal ideas, and regretted getting married. She could not relate to people, was happiest with horses and read widely. She had a steady job she disliked, but had also worked in stables in her spare time since she was 8. She had owned two horses, and the death of one had precipitated her present illness.

Jane thought no one could help her and at one point wrote to her doctor: 'I still get very depressed . . . [and] try to block that by closing my mind to reality and entering my own private world . . .' . In the course of the next sixteen years there were a number of re-referrals. She separated from her husband, continued to visit the milk horses every Saturday (never omitting to go because 'they'd miss me'), worked steadily and effectively at a skilled job, but remained depressed and anxious, feeling that she was making nothing of her life. Yet she was afraid that if she entered psychiatric treatment she might 'lose a part of myself'. Cognitive therapy was attempted, but she dropped out and wrote to the therapist: 'Thank you for putting up with me. . . . I feel I'm too stuck in my ways . . .' .

Her notes record her as 'odd', speaking in an almost inaudible voice and making little eye contact, but she clearly evoked much positive concern from the people who tried to help her. Her recurrent complaints included a feeling that life was empty, that she had no future and that she had no feeling for anyone. Occasionally, there were transient physical symptoms: lameness, numbness, visual difficulties, inability to use her hands. During her interviews she sometimes sat near the door, indicating: 'I prefer to sit by the escape route'. She said: 'A bit of me wants to change and a bit of me doesn't.' She thought that 'I will eventually kill myself.'

The diagnoses recorded in the adult case notes were of depressive illness, abnormal personality and schizoid personality disorder. The only DSM-III-R diagnostic category for which the case notes provided sufficient criteria was schizotypal personality disorder.

THE LATER OUTCOME IN SCHIZOID GIRLS WAS AS VARIED AS IN THE BOYS

The point was made in Chapter Five that the later life adjustment of schizoid boys was very varied despite the personality features they shared. This was so for the girls also. While some, like Jane described above, clearly suffered greatly from their inability to have close relationships with other people and felt that life was empty, others appeared to be quite cheerful despite their sometimes chaotic lives.

It was my impression that this depended largely on whether they were introverted and introspective, attributing their difficulties to their own personality make-up, or whether they were extraverted, outgoing, tending then to blame other people when things went wrong.

Schizoidness is not related to introversion. Our first group of schizoid young men had normal intro-/extraversion scores (see Chick *et al.*, 1979 and Chapter Four). Some schizoid people are withdrawn and inward, others outgoing.

SANDRA, whose childhood picture was described earlier in this chapter and whose psychiatric illness features in the next chapter, illustrates the later life adjustment of an outgoing schizoid girl.

It had been very hard to trace Sandra for *follow-up*, because her two marriages and many moves of home. She was finally interviewed when she was 32. She was in her second marriage and her husband cared well for her. Neither partner worked and he seemed to look after all practical aspects of life. They had a small child. The dark and ill-cared for house was full of many kinds of animals, and only now did the extent of her passion for animals become clear. She said she had read widely about animals. Her only contacts with the outside world were through the kennel club where she had once won a dog championship. Sandra had never held a job for more than a few months. She had nothing in common with her neighbours who, she felt, disapproved of her way of life: she did no house work or washing. She kept in touch with her one friend, an animal breeder, mainly by telephone. Her husband, like a previous partner, who had also looked after her devotedly, had been seriously delinquent. Older children by previous associations were cared for in other families. She had been fined for shop-lifting, had assaulted 'friends' when younger, used to be an excessive drinker, and had been admitted to hospital many times with drug overdoses. She also reported, more vaguely, having at one time been forced into prostitution.

Sandra was very friendly, cheerful and outgoing, but she made poor emotional contact. She now attributed her childhood troubles to her mother's cruelty, and also reported that a teacher at her boarding school had treated the children cruelly and had been in trouble for this. She thought social workers were 'vindictive liars'. She was generally mistrustful of people, and sometimes she thought that people in the street looked oddly at her and talked about her. The psychiatric diagnosis made at follow-up was of a schizotypal and antisocial personality disorder. She had abnormal scores on seven of the ten Baron schizotypal scales, but did not reach a borderline personality disorder score on the DIB.

In childhood, this girl had lacked empathy and feeling for other people, and had had a vivid fantasy life with pathological lying. Her pervasive special interest in animals and her basic solitariness, as well as her sensitivity and paranoid ideation, became clear only in later years. She had had no specific developmental disorders and the only evidence for communication difficulty at follow-up was that she often gave tangential replies, wandering off the point.

We shall see in the next chapter that Sandra's mention of a psychiatric hospital admission for 'post-natal depression' led to the discovery of a well-documented schizophrenic illness from which she had recovered.

CONCLUSIONS

The similarities we found in the clinical picture in childhood and at follow-up between the girls and boys go some way to support the diagnosis of schizoid personality in girls. The differences we found between the sexes could in part be due to referral artefacts, that is, to the selective referral of schizoid girls with more severe behavioural disorders.

There was no difference between the age of referral of boys and girls: usually the middle-school years. But our findings do suggest that the referred schizoid girls came from a less privileged social background and may have had more environmental adversities in comparison with their controls than the boys. In addition, they were of marginally lower tested intelligence, significantly so at follow-up. But there was no evidence for an excess of organic cerebral impairment in either girls or boys.

Our schizoid girls certainly had more associated psychiatric disorders, especially conduct disorders, and their rate of developmental disorders, while similar to those of the boys, was very high in comparison with that of other referred girls. However, contrary to expectations, schizoid girls, both in childhood and in later life, were no more sociable and outgoing than schizoid boys.

7 What is the risk of later psychiatric disorder?

In our first controlled follow-up study of 19 matched pairs of schizoid and other referred boys at a mean age of 22 years (Chick, 1978), we found that schizoid young men had had significantly more contacts with psychiatric services than the controls. In addition, five of the schizoid group had made a suicide attempt and five others had had suicidal thoughts, compared with only a single control boy who reported having had suicidal ideas. Five schizoid young men had symptoms of minor psychiatric illnesses: marked depression in two, dramatic mood swings in one, panic attacks in one and obsessional ruminations in another, compared with one young man in the control group with panic attacks and another with a phobic-anxiety state. One person in each group had an alcohol problem.

These symptoms often seemed to be a reaction to the constraints imposed on the young people's social and working lives by their personality difficulties. This study also suggested that more schizoid children might in later life develop schizophrenic illnesses than was to be expected for a general population: 2 out of 22 schizoid people had developed this illness by the time of the follow-up. But it was the same 2 patients who were again identified as having schizophrenia in our second follow-up of 32 young men at a later stage.

The present chapter reports on what is known about the psychiatric difficulties in adult life of the whole group of schizoid children seen over the years, 115 boys and 34 girls, from whom those who were personally interviewed had been drawn. All were aged over 16 at the time. The focus will be on comparisons of the use of psychiatric hospital services by the schizoid and control children in later life, and of the frequencies of recorded suicide attempts and of deaths attributable to suicide in these groups. The incidence of schizophrenia was of particular interest because of the possible genetic links between schizoid and schizotypal personality disorders and this illness (see Chapter Two), but also because we wanted to know whether or not the future outlook for children with schizoid personality is clouded by a substantial risk of developing a serious mental illness.

TWO BOYS WITH CHILDHOOD DELUSIONAL EXPERIENCES WHICH DID NOT RECUR

There were in fact two boys among the group as a whole who had caused concern in childhood because of a possible diagnosis of schizophrenia when they were first seen. Their most worrying symptoms at that time had been hallucinations and delusions. As it turned out, these were transitory in both cases and neither boy developed any more serious psychiatric illness by the time of the follow-up, when they were 34 and 35 years old respectively. These two were the only children in the whole group who had had such symptoms on their initial referral.

DAVID, already mentioned in Chapter One, had had no recurrence of the paranoid symptoms that had first brought him to the clinic when he was 11. He did, however, have two depressive illnesses associated with marked anxiety, which had seriously interfered with his school and university studies at the time. During the first illness he had made a suicide attempt. On both occasions he was admitted to hospital and treated with medication and psychotherapy, and on both occasions he made an excellent recovery. When seen again at the age of 34, he remained as vulnerable and sensitive as he had been in childhood, inclined to belittle his own achievements and settling for a more humdrum job than his considerable gifts had led even him to expect. On the other hand, he was happily married to a supportive wife and had a small daughter. While very helpful to us with our study, he was quite anxious about the possible effects on his peace of mind of recalling his past difficulties and unusual childhood experiences.

Indeed, several schizoid children refused to take part in the follow-up for fear that reminiscing about their earlier difficulties might lead to a recurrence of distress. Whereas David participated fully in the study, one boy offered to be seen informally but declined the research interview, and one girl wrote to say she would be too upset to take part. Another boy, Malcolm, mentioned during a long and friendly telephone conversation that he was still extremely sensitive and had to avoid all encounters that might make him anxious: 'I'm still a sensitive person and I try to avoid emotional experiences for that reason, and I deliberately live a quiet life. . . . The only part of life in which I am subjected to stress is work. . . . Stress is widespread and I'm vulnerable to it myself.' He declined to be interviewed, but he undertook the pencil and paper tests that formed part of the follow-up study and allowed me to see his parents. They completed a full interview on his behalf, although this could not of course be used for the follow-up study, which relied on personal interviews. This boy, too, had had delusions and hallucinations in childhood.

MALCOLM had been referred at 14 years old by the school psychologist because he was extremely withdrawn, with no social contacts, looked dreamy and emotionless and appeared 'surrounded by a world of his own creation'. He could not communicate with other boys, had no interest in work and his concentration was poor. His drawings were regarded as 'weird'. He stood out at school (this was in the late 1960s) because of his mincing gait and effeminate gestures. His parents thought his speech was odd: 'too proper'. He could not stand gym and he spent breaktimes in the toilets. Before being referred, he had taken to wearing gloves in the classroom and he had asked to be allowed to sit on a cushion. He himself had requested the psychiatric referral.

When seen at the clinic he said he felt different from other people because he likes to be alone and he spends hours in his bedroom. He has no friends. He collects antiques and records of classical music and is also interested in the Church. He writes stories and draws a lot. At present he feels he needs help because he is afraid he'll 'go funny'. He gets worked up when he shouldn't and for three months he has had strange experiences. He saw furniture, plants and animals moving; he felt his skin itch all over and this compelled him to laugh against his will, which embarrassed him; he believed the teachers on the sports field intended to hit him and to push a wall on top of him. He also thought the teachers were planning to murder him and dig holes for him to fall into on the football pitch. He felt all this had been precipitated by his hearing other boys engage in sex talk and swearing at his secondary school; he can't stand this. He said: 'Sex is too awful to be true', and he had developed a magical theory of procreation whereby God impregnated all women. About sex education he said: 'I don't know why people are poisoning my mind.' He liked old things and would have preferred to live several hundred years ago, or in England. He revealed a fantasy that he would be unkind to his future wife, chaining her up by an iron collar. He also had a religious vision: 'Christ came. I had the vision of an angel and I will be made a saint on 5 October.' During his clinic interviews he was very communicative and eager for help, and his delusions and hallucinations disappeared on small doses of a major tranquillizer never to return, although vague paranoid feelings about teachers and other boys persisted.

Malcolm remained excessively sensitive, feeling 'funny all over' if people looked directly into his eyes. He also engaged in much fantasy, suggesting to me that his close relatives were thieves and drinkers, and that he might murder me and then dress up as 'the other Dr Wolff'.

His birth, by breech delivery, had been difficult, but his early development quite normal. He tested at a just average level of intelligence and was mildly retarded educationally. School progress was poor except in the subject that interested him: he had won an arts prize at primary school. The family was united. The mother said: 'I was similar to Malcolm, very quiet, but I had friends and he doesn't. . . . I'd like to see him with a different personality, a more everyday person.' The paternal grandfather had been gifted and gone to art college, but, because of circumstances, had worked below his capacity and training all his life.

At follow-up the parents reported that Malcolm had been working steadily as a clerk with the same firm for seventeen years. He still lives with his parents and is solitary except for taking part in family social events. He is a regular concert-goer, but, apart from this, spends his evenings in his room reading, writing or listening to records. His passion for classical music, quite foreign to the interests of his parents, his sisters and their social circle, has been longstanding. He has a large record and tape collection, and is knowledgeable about classical music and the lives of composers. He also visits stately homes, reads about architecture and has an abiding interest in beautiful things. His parents know little about his work or opinions. Retesting on a verbal intelligence scale now showed him to function within the superior range.

This young man has clearly learnt to live within the confines of his personality characteristics of which the most noticeable is his extreme sensitivity. His stable life adjustment is a tribute to his understanding of himself, but also to the support and tolerance of his parents.

AN INVESTIGATION OF PSYCHIATRIC HOSPITAL RECORDS

Method

For the total of 149 schizoid children, 115 boys and 34 girls, who had all reached the age of 16 at the time, 149 other referred children had been selected by an independent psychologist to match each schizoid child for sex, age, year of referral, IQ and occupation of father as closely as possible. A psychiatric records search was then undertaken for all these former patients who, at the time of the survey, were known to be alive and had not emigrated. This left 109 schizoid boys and 32 schizoid girls, and 110 control boys and 32 control girls.

The Information and Statistics Section of the Scottish Home and Health Department undertook a computer search of all recorded psychiatric hospital admissions in Scotland for these groups of former child patients. In addition, the records departments of local psychiatric hospitals helped to trace all hospital admissions and out-patient visits in adult life recorded for these groups.

Of course, the records search will not have been complete because some former patients may have had admissions to psychiatric hospitals in England; a number will have attended psychiatric hospitals as out-patients outside their former locality; and, in the case of the girls, a change of name on marriage would have lost them to the records search. One married woman, for example, was traced and interviewed, and only then was it found that she had had a hospital admission with a clear-cut schizophrenic illness under an earlier married name, as well as a number of admissions following suicide attempts. The omissions from the records are, however, likely to have been similar for both the schizoid and the control groups (except that fewer control than schizoid women were personally interviewed, so that it is just possible, but unlikely, that more psychiatric illness was recorded for schizoid than for control women), and comparisons between them are still valid.

All case notes traced were read and abstracted. One disadvantage was that I could not be 'blind' to whether the notes I was reading were those of a former schizoid or control child. But I was primarily interested in a rather crude set of questions: Had there been a hospital attendance? Had there been an admission? Had there been a suicide attempt? Was there evidence for a DSM-III diagnosis of schizophrenia? The answers to these questions are not likely to have been compromised by any clinical bias I may have had.

Results: How well had the groups been matched?

At the time of the records search, the mean ages of schizoid boys and girls and of their matched controls were quite similar, ranging from 26.4 to 26.8 years. The maximum childhood IQ was very similar for the schizoid and control boys, with means of 102.2 and 104.3 respectively. However, over half the control girls had never been tested and there was a non-significant difference between the schizoid girls (mean IQ 101.7) and their controls (mean IQ 93.1). There was also a statistically significant difference between the occupational status of the fathers of the schizoid boys and that of their controls. Half the schizoid boys came from occupational classes I and II (that is, professional and higher managerial), compared with less than one-third of their controls. There was no occupational class difference between the two groups of girls. In particular, there was no upwardly-skewed occupational background among schizoid girls as there was among schizoid boys.

Results: Are schizoid children more prone to psychiatric disorders in later life?

We need to remind ourselves once more that both schizoid and control children came from a clinic population, that is, they had been disturbed enough in childhood to be referred to a child psychiatry department. It is well known that such children are at greater risk than children in the general population of developing psychiatric disorders in later life, especially if the form of their childhood disturbance was a conduct (or antisocial) disorder (Robins, 1966, 1991; Zeitlin, 1989). It may well be that schizoid people who had not been referred to a psychiatrist in childhood are less at risk of later psychiatric problems than were our groups of children. This needs to be remembered when we attempt to draw conclusions from our findings to schizoid people in the general population.

The records survey, like the smaller interview studies, showed that significantly more schizoid people had made use of psychiatric services in later life. This survey has been published (Wolff, 1992). The slightly different results here reported are due to the discovery, after the survey was finished, of one additional schizoid girl who had made many suicide attempts and had developed a schizophrenic illness, and the news given to me by the mother of another schizoid girl that her daughter had recently died after falling from the upstairs window of her flat.

Twelve out of 109 schizoid men and 10 out of 32 schizoid women had had at least one psychiatric hospital admission, compared with 4 out of 110 control men and none of the 32 control women. There was no difference between the groups in their records of out-patient psychiatric attendances only. In the schizoid group, 9 men and 4 women were thus recorded; among the controls, 6 and 6 respectively. It is clear that proportionately more women than men in both groups had had psychiatric care of some kind after the age of 16, and this corresponds to the greater use of psychiatric services made by women in the general population.

The nature of the psychiatric disorders: suicidal actions

By no means all hospital admissions resulting from self-injury were picked up in this survey because most would have been to a general and not a psychiatric hospital. Information about suicidal actions came from those young people who had been personally interviewed, from psychiatric hospital records which mentioned previous suicidal behaviour, and from hospital or Health Board records of deaths from suicide. The incidence of non-fatal, self-injurious behaviour here described will therefore have underestimated its true incidence, but this underestimate is likely to be the same for both the schizoid and control groups. It is unlikely that any deaths have been missed.

In the schizoid group, by the time of the survey, two young men and two young women had died by suicide; none among the controls. One further suicidal death in a young woman occurred some five years after the records survey. Of these deaths, one took place in prison, one in the course of a manic-depressive illness, a third in the setting of a schizophrenic illness and alcohol addiction, and a fourth in the course of heavy drinking. In addition, one boy, a glue-sniffer, had died by suicide before the age of 16 while on holiday from an approved school. The overall rate in the total cohort of 110 schizoid boys and 32 girls by the age of just over 26 and a half years was 4.0 per cent, which compares with an estimated population incidence by the age of 27 of .0026 per cent. Although for statistical comparisons our cohorts of former patients were much too small, there does appear to be an increased risk of death by suicide among schizoid people, greater perhaps when there is also, and this was very rare, a psychotic illness. Yet this risk, although probably increased, was still low.

The differences in the incidence of non-fatal self-injurious actions were smaller. Five schizoid young men and 6 young women had had one or more hospital admissions after a suicidal act, compared with 4 men and no women in the control group, and one individual in each group, both men, were known to have made mild attempts without subsequent hospital admissions.

The nature of psychiatric disorders: schizophrenia

Four schizoid boys and three schizoid girls had developed schizophrenic illnesses, compared with one of the controls, a young man with no evidence of previous schizoid personality traits. Overall, therefore, 5.0 per cent (7 out of 141) of schizoid people and 0.7 per cent of controls had developed schizophrenia by a mean age of 26.5 years. This compares with a lifetime prevalence rate in the general population of 0.8–1.0 per cent, and an estimated prevalence rate by the age of 27 years of 0.31–0.49 per cent, say 0.4 per cent, calculated for a British cohort (Done *et al.*, 1991).

Despite the sizeable numbers of schizoid and control children available, these numbers were still too small for statistical analysis. The results suggest, however, that the later risk for schizoid children of developing schizophrenia is low, but about twelve times as high as that for the general population. Our schizoid group of people may thus be similar to groups of people with schizotypal personality and other schizophrenia spectrum disorders known to be genetically related to schizophrenia.

Among the 8 schizophrenic patients we found in our schizoid and control groups, this illness was associated with definite organic brain dysfunction in 2 schizoid young men and in one schizoid girl, and with possible organic brain dysfunction in another schizoid man. Furthermore, the mean maximum tested IQ in childhood of the 7 schizoid people who later developed schizophrenia was lower (84) than that of the 134 who did not (103). These findings are in line with those of others (Castle and Murray, 1991) that neurological abnormalities and premorbid deficits in IQ are characteristic of schizophrenic patients, especially men, and that the intelligence and school performance of men, although not of women, who later develop schizophrenia is less than those of their siblings and age group (Offord, 1974). Lowered IQ has also been found to precede schizophrenia beginning in childhood (Werry, 1992b). These findings suggest that low intelligence may increase the vulnerability of people predisposed to schizophrenia, so that in schizoid children of high intelligence the risk of later schizophrenia may be even lower that for the group of schizoid children as a whole. Offord (1974) suggested some twenty years ago that IQ and a predisposition to schizophrenia may be inherited separately, and that high IQ or the more favourable circumstances of families of high intelligence, associated as these are with higher socio-economic circumstances, will protect predisposed children from later schizophrenia.

THE LINKS BETWEEN SCHIZOID AND SCHIZOTYPAL PERSONALITY, ASPERGER'S SYNDROME AND SCHIZOPHRENIA

The evidence here is still incomplete. There is one report of the later development of schizophrenic illnesses in two children, one of very low intellectual ability, who had been diagnosed as having Asperger's syndrome (Clarke *et al.*, 1989). Tantam (1991) gives the incidence of schizophrenia in his group of adults with Asperger's syndrome as 3.5 per cent. Nagy and Szatmari (1986) found that 2 of their 20 children with schizotypal disorders developed schizophrenia in later life; and van der Gaag (1993), in his follow-up of children with 'multiplex developmental disorders', all of whom were so disturbed that they needed hospital admissions in childhood, found that 2 out of 12 had developed schizophrenia in late adolescence and a further 6 now fulfilled the diagnostic criteria for either schizoid (4) or schizotypal (2) personality disorder.

Most investigators have looked backward, at the previous personality features of patients with schizophrenia. A study done some years ago of that very rare group of patients who developed schizophrenia in childhood found that such children had often 'pursued philosophical questions unusual for . . . their age' long before the onset of their illness, and that over half had had difficulty making contact with other people (Eggers, 1978). This finding was confirmed by a more recent study (Werry, 1992a), which found schizotypal personality and/or neurodevelopmental abnormality in over 50 per cent of children and adolescents with schizophrenic illnesses. It seems that the earlier the onset of schizophrenia in childhood, the more likely it is that there have been prior schizoid or schizotypal personality traits (Werry, 1992b).

But, as we saw earlier, adult schizophrenic patients, too, have retrospectively been found to have had an excess of schizotypal and schizoid personality disorders prior to their illness (Foerster *et al.*, 1991; McCreadie *et al.*, 1994). Moreover, 'incongruous behaviour' of a type quite similar to that of our schizoid children and of Asperger's patients, in combination with specific developmental delays, again as in our and Asperger's groups, were found to characterize a small group of psychiatrically referred children who developed schizophrenia in adult life (Zeitlin, 1991).

There has also been one long-term follow-up study of adult schizotypal patients admitted for treatment to a psychiatric hospital. Fenton and McGlashan (1989) found that such patients were especially prone to develop schizophrenic illnesses later, 12 out of 30 schizotypal patients being affected, compared with only 6 out of 75 patients hospitalized with a diagnosis of borderline personality disorder. We must remember, however, that these schizotypal people were so disturbed in adult life that they required hospital treatment and are not, therefore, representative of schizotypal people in the general population. For these people the risk of later schizophrenia is likely to be very much smaller.

'High-risk' studies of the offspring of schizophrenic mothers compared with children of healthy parents should also provide evidence about the link between schizotypal personality and later schizophrenia. Sadly, in most of these studies, the children's personality and development were not assessed clinically, so that we cannot be sure how many such children had schizoid or schizotypal personality features and/or specific developmental disorders in early life as compared with their control groups, nor how many, if so affected, later developed schizophrenia (Fish *et al.*, 1992; McCrimmon *et al.*, 1980). Moreover, in one of the most meticulous high-risk studies, carried out in Denmark (Cannon and Mednick, 1993), it now appears that children were specifically excluded from follow-up if they were found to be seriously mentally disordered when first interviewed at a mean age of 15 years (Munk-Jorgensen *et al.*, 1993).

We are on surer ground when we look at studies of the biological relatives of people with schizophrenic illnesses. These are known to include an excess with schizotypal and schizoid personality disorders (Varma and Sharma, 1993). Comparisons of the biological and adoptive relatives of schizophrenic patients who had been adopted had shown an excess with schizotypal and paranoid personality disorders among their biological relatives (Kendler and Gruenberg, 1984). And in a Finnish study it was found that the adopted away children of schizophrenic mothers have higher rates both of schizophrenia and of schizophrenia spectrum disorders than adopted people who had healthy parents (Tienari *et al.*, 1991). In this study the mental health of the adoptive families also contributed to the outcome in that, when a child from a schizophrenic mother was reared in a well-adjusted adoptive family, the risk of later schizophrenia or of a spectrum disorder was much reduced. Curiously, in these studies the sex ratios of relatives identified as schizoid or schizotypal is never referred to.

It has been found that monozygotic (identical) twins are more alike when both schizophrenia and schizotypal personality disorder are assessed than when only schizophrenia is taken note of. Recent studies have also now shown increased rates of schizophrenia and schizophrenia-related conditions in relatives of schizotypal personality disordered patients (Siever *et al.*, 1990), and of schizophrenia among the biological relatives of psychiatric patients with schizotypal personality disorder, compared with relatives of control groups of non-schizotypal psychiatric and non-psychiatric patients (Battagglia *et al.*, 1991).

SEVEN SCHIZOID CHILDREN WHO DEVELOPED SCHIZOPHRENIA

Case 1

JONATHAN, who at 16 developed what was to be a chronic schizophrenic illness with acute exacerbations in response to minor stresses, has already been descibed in Chapter Five. The main symptoms of his illness were paranoid hallucinations and delusions, and abnormal thoughts telling him what to do. He felt his head had been divided into two, and that something was trying to get into his head to control other people's thoughts and to make him blush. Latterly, he had also had musical hallucinations. Several relapses were ushered in by suicide attempts: wrist-cutting, pill-swallowing, jumping off a bridge. His insight into his illness enabled him to co-operate fully in his treatment with long-term anti-psychotic medication. He felt better living in a hostel than at home, but was able to work only sporadically in his father's business.

Jonathan fulfilled DSM-III criteria for a diagnosis of schizophrenia, undifferentiated type, chronic with acute exacerbations.

Case 2

KEVIN was first referred at the age of 10 because of impulsive and violent behaviour at a series of ordinary and special schools. His mother suffered from chronic paranoid schizophrenia. He himself had had severe measles with acute hallucinatory experiences when he was 6, and his impulsivity, restlessness and aggression began thereafter. He was of low average intelligence, with specific learning delays, and he disrupted all school activities by his restless wanderings around the classrooms and his aggressive attacks on other children. He was a loner, talking to himself about fantasized wild animals, peaceful only when travelling on city buses whose numbers and routes he knew by heart. He caused much trouble at home and in the neighbourhood by staying awake noisily until late into the night and then 'lying in' by day. He made obscene phone calls, was rude and physically aggressive to neighbours, and was perceived the more threatening because at puberty he grew into a very large, obese boy. A number of special-school placements failed, and at 16, during a psychiatric hospital admission for further assessment, he created such physical chaos and fear among other patients by his unprovoked violence that he was transferred to the Scottish Special (secure) Hospital.

Kevin's first follow-up interview took place in that setting. He was open but vague about his earlier troubles, ascribing them to lack of discipline: 'If the school had been more firm with me it wouldn't have happened. The headmaster was too soft. . . . The trouble was my parents weren't firm enough with me. If they gave me an inch I'd take a yard.' About one of his obscene phone calls, he said he did not think the woman was upset: 'She needn't have answered the phone or listened to me.'

In the Special Hospital Kevin isolated himself from other patients, was noted to be clumsy, poorly coordinated and to lack initiative. He liked cooking and in the kitchen he was no trouble. After his discharge at 21, he began to complain that he was mentally ill, that his mind was not his own and that he heard threatening voices. He also believed people were talking and laughing about him. He was seen in the street talking and gesticulating to himself.

Until then, adult psychiatrists had tended to make a diagnosis of 'sociopathic personality disorder', although some had diagnosed schizophrenia at the time of his admission to the Special Hospital. Now when his auditory hallucinations became unmistakable (he heard voices in his head telling him that he should hurt other people and commit suicide; he tasted poison in his food, which looked to him abnormal; he was fearful, yet observed to laugh to himself incongruously), a diagnosis of paranoid schizophrenia was made (confirmed when, at 24, he reported that pigeons stared at him as if they could read his thoughts and that radar was in the atmosphere). He has had excellent and sustained care from hospital psychiatrists and his family doctor, has generally taken his anti-psychotic medication, and has remained more stable living in a hostel rather than at home with his family. He has a girlfriend, but is unable to hold down a job.

Kevin fulfilled DSM-III criteria for schizophrenia, undifferentiated type, chronic, as well as for schizotypal personality disorder. In childhood he was thought to have suffered minor brain damage at the time of his measles infection.

Case 3

ALAN was first referred at 8 years of age, for advice about schooling. He had a learning disability (IQ 60), was a poor mixer, made little eye contact and his social responses were inappropriate. He had abiding mechanical interests and aptitudes, and was good at using screws, nuts and bolts. He also had an excellent sense of direction. He conversed in a rather adult way and, even then, was preoccupied with possible medical abnormalities in himself, being especially concerned about the shape of his nose. Physical examination found him to have a coarse tremor of both hands with abnormal (choreoid) movements and to be ambidextrous. Special investigations showed enlarged lateral ventricles of his brain, especially on the left, compatible with cerebral atrophy. His EEG, too, was abnormal, but without epileptic activity.

Alan had been born after a very long labour, was a placid, unaffectionate baby, walked at 14 months, but still spoke little and unclearly at 3. At this time he had a severe attack of measles and also a nose injury due to a fall.

By the age of 18, he was in better touch emotionally, but his conversation was repetitive, concerned mainly with his health and his worries about his nose, which was indeed very crooked. He had made little educational progress and was still being cared for and educated in a Rudolf Steiner settlement.

At 21, Alan was referred to the adult psychiatric services because of his increased social withdrawal, inappropriate laughing to himself, and constant talk about his bowels, his circulation, his skin colour and sexual functions, all of which he felt were abnormal. He also thought a girl at the settlement could read his thoughts, and he was suspicious that things like sour milk might be put in his food and that this would affect his bowels and his mind. A diagnosis of a psychotic, schizophreniform illness, superimposed on an organic intellectual impairment, was made. Alan responded well to anti-psychotic medication, but failed to take it regularly and had recurrences of schizophrenic symptoms. He went to the police complaining that 'people are affecting my body . . . people's minds are thinking about me and affecting my body and my food . . . people try to change me.'

By the age of 24, having taken his medication more regularly and now living in sheltered housing, Alan had lost his hypochondriacal preoccupations and psychotic symptoms. Sadly, these returned when his dose of medication was reduced. He wore a large wooden crucifix, was seen to cross his face in a bizarre way, said: 'parts of my brain are not working', and mentioned 'private' sexual preoccupations.

He, too, fulfilled DSM-III criteria for undifferentiated, chronic schizophrenia, as well as for schizotypal personality disorder, for pervasive developmental disorder of childhood and for mild mental retardation. Brain damage in childhood was well documented.

Case 4

ROY was referred at the age of 13 because of his excessive anxiety and weeping about his poor school progress. He was of low average ability, had always been a loner and had been a slow developer, especially in language. A paternal uncle was described as emotionally withdrawn. His mother had had depressive illnesses. Roy had been treated for thyrotoxicosis at the age of 8.

Roy's adult psychiatric referral occurred at the age of 20, following a further thyroid operation complicated by hypoparathyroidism. He complained of being 'nuts' and embarrassing other people in the street, who then turn round and talk about him. He said he heard voices and that his hospital visits were mentioned on the radio and in the newspapers. Occasionally, he thought his food was poisoned. Since his surgery he had been apathetic, with occasional outbursts of anger against his parents. Sometimes he felt they were against him. He destroyed furnishings during some outbursts. He now rarely went out, but still worked as a storeman.

During his hospital admission, Roy was found to be a loner, spent all his time on his own and had many persecutory ideas. After discharge, he took his medication only sporadically; relations with his parents remained poor and explosive; he had only a single friend and no girlfriends. But he did work most of the time, was interested in CB radio, and remained under the care of a community nurse.

Roy fulfilled DSM-III criteria for schizophrenia, undifferentiated type and for schizotypal personality disorder.

Case 5

FAY was first referred at 11 years because of her school refusal, starting after a change of school. She was extremely anxious about leaving her mother, depressed, weepy and with a nervous tic. She was withdrawn, socially isolated, and labelled as 'shy' at school. She was also irrationally possessive of her mother. She was of borderline intelligence, with specific spelling difficulties in addition, her twin brother being more able. She had been the first born, weighing 5 pounds at birth. Her mother, too, had always been 'shy' with periodic depressions. The father thought the two were similar in personality.

Anti-depressant medication improved Fay's mood state and a special school placement helped her to complete her schooling. But she remained friendless, inarticulate and 'impenetrable', working in hotels sporadically but often unemployed. She spent her time listening to records in her room.

By the age of 17 she had developed odd ideas about dead men and that her mother might not be her real mother. She now took repeated overdoses, usually when drunk. She also appeared at court, having stabbed a passer-by outside a pub. She eagerly accepted psychiatric out-patient help, and talked about her depressions and her very troublesome and frightening fantasies.

Over the next twelve years a pattern was established of repeated brief psychiatric hospital admissions, usually after very serious suicide attempts by wrist-cutting and pill-taking. Fay was often deeply depressed and now also clearly addicted to alcohol. Sometimes she was found drunk in the street. She believed she was a lesbian; she had never had a boyfriend and had wanted to go out with a girl, but had never done so. She was preoccupied with childhood 'visions' of her grandmother for whose death she blamed herself and whom she wanted to join in death. In her late twenties her thoughts became even more bizarre: 'I can kill people sometimes. I look into the back of their eyes and blood runs. Then they die.' She now heard voices whispering about her, saying; 'You don't live here. We'll get you out.' She commented: 'It looks like they've succeeded, because I'm moving.' Her mood was noted to be flat and inappropriate and both auditory and visual hallucinations were recorded.

Fay's suicidal actions became more and more dangerous: she threatened to jump off high buildings; she swallowed Domestos; and she complained that her voices were telling her to kill herself. Yet at 29, just before her death of a final overdose, Fay was living in her own flat with a woman friend. She was still addicted to alcohol and, despite medication, still hallucinating.

The psychiatric diagnoses recorded in this tragic case include alcohol addiction; mental subnormality; pre-psychotic personality; borderline personality; acute psychosis; alcoholic psychosis; and sociopathic personality disorder. The DSM-III-R diagnoses assigned on the basis of the psychiatric case note information are: alcohol dependence; schizophrenia, undifferentiated type; schizotypal personality disorder; and mental retardation.

The case notes also reveal letters, apologizing for 'the trouble' she was causing and pathetic in their appeal, which this girl wrote to some of the psychiatrists who had been most sensitive in attempting to help her. Yet she often discharged herself from hospital, and it seemed never to have been possible to engage her in a long-enduring treatment relationship with any one person. What had not been attempted, difficult perhaps within the current framework of mental-health legislation, yet not impossible in view of her repeated seriously self-destructive behaviour, was to keep her in an active therapeutic ward for a long period of time, as an involuntary patient if need be. She was often keen to be helped, but was so driven by her inner experiences that she could never see any treatment through. Fay's disorder was clearly very chronic, and no brief intervention could possibly have influenced the outcome.

Case 6

SOPHIE, was first referred when 10 years old because of her inability to read, despite average intelligence. She also had word-finding difficulties. She was solitary and detached with an unexpressive face. She made abnormal eye contact, tending to stare at other people. She talked in a monotonous, manneristic voice and lacked appropriate shyness with strangers. She was still enuretic. She had a family of imaginary companions with whom she would have realistic conversations using different voices. Although gentle in her behaviour, she expressed quite violent ideas in words. She wished the staff of the child psychiatric in-patient unit were 'footballs' and that she could 'drop blocks of ice on them'.

Sophie's development had been normal, including the onset of speech, except that she had always been clumsy, slow to learn to dress herself and to use eating utensils. She had been a sleepy baby, slow to feed and, in later childhood, neurological examination revealed incoordination of her left arm and hand. Her EEG was abnormal in a non-specific way. A number of eccentric but academically brilliant relatives were described on the father's side of the family.

Sophie remained rather solitary, but was well cared for both by her parents and at school where her specific learning difficulties were understood and catered for. She enjoyed school and then worked on her parents' farm.

At 16 and a half she first began to hear voices, which frightened her. About a year later she was admitted to a psychiatric hospital because she had become acutely distressed and was found wandering towards a river: 'The voices have had an argument with my imagination and have not yet made it up.' She spoke to her voices in a special religious type of chant and felt this gave her some control over them. Much of her talk now concerned religious themes, e.g. : 'The devil wants me out of the parish'. Her mood was depressed, she felt life was not worth living, and in the psychiatric records both thought disorder and compulsive touching of furnishings were noted. Her EEG was again abnormal. She was treated with both anti-psychotic and anti-depressive medication, improved and was discharged home after three months.

At 18 years old Sophie was again assessed psychiatrically because there had been a steady deterioration in her condition. Her speech was now chaotic, one metaphor leading to another and, while her occasional hallucinations were no longer troublesome, she had become sluggish, unresponsive and altogether lacking in initiative. A schizophrenic defect state was diagnosed.

Sophie took part in a follow-up interview when she was 25, now living in a Rudolf Steiner Community. She was passive, barely able to respond to the interview. Her face lacked expression, as it had always done, but now she had distinct gaze avoidance, too, and her verbal utterances were monosyllabic. She indicated she did not like company. Intelligence testing showed marked deterioration, with a score within the mildly handicapped range on the Raven's Matrices test.

Sophie's caregivers in the Community reported that she is still at times hallucinated but no longer 'tortured' by her voices. She does simple needlework and can help with cooking and baking in the kitchen. But, unless encouraged to get up, she would just lie in bed or even stay in her bath. Occasionally she acts unpredictably: pouring bleach over herself; hitting her sister; dropping a rabbit she had been cuddling. She has an obsessional habit of shredding the leaves of plants. She chooses to be called by her nickname at home but by her proper name in the Community. She had been a lively, engaging and imaginative child. Now she functioned as a dull, sluggish and totally remote person.

We had not predicted this outcome. Indeed, one of the boys who had clinically been very similar to Sophie in childhood, with clear evidence of early brain damage, severe specific developmental difficulties and an exceptionally vivid fantasy life, was when seen again at the age of 26 years, found to be working steadily, content with his rather restricted life style, and still in the parental home. He had no symptoms of psychiatric illness and, despite limited intellectual abilities, he had become an avid reader of books about mathematical theories and science fiction.

Case 7

SANDRA, already described in Chapter Six, was admitted to psychiatric hospital four months after the birth of a daughter and following an acute onset of hallucinatory experiences, during which she had threatened her boyfriend with a knife. Over the previous four years she had been drinking heavily and had made more than thirty suicide attempts by taking overdoses.

Sandra now heard whispering through her ears, 'hollow voices', as if in a tunnel, saying things like: 'Why don't you put rat poison in the dinner?' ; 'Why don't you stick a knife in him [her cohabitee]?' ; 'That girl's a slag'; 'That guy's an alcoholic'; (and later, while in hospital) 'Put your head through the window; harm yourself with scissors'. She argued with the voices, especially with a female one, and she felt that her 'brain ran riot' and she could not think straight. She complained of thought-blocking and was noted to have a flat mood. A diagnosis of paranoid schizophrenia and personality disorder was made, and she was successfully treated with anti-psychotic medication.

Two further brief admissions occurred: one following a relapse of hallucinations and suicidal ideas; the other, on a compulsory hospital order, some two years later while drunk and threatening to stab a male friend. Since then, although not on regular medication, Sandra has had no recurrences of schizophrenia, merely transient episodes of paranoid feelings and ideas from time to time. As the account in Chapter Six makes clear, there has been no deterioration in her mental state or social functioning.

ONE CASE OF SCHIZOPHRENIA AMONG THE CONTROLS

Case 8

TIMOTHY had been referred to the child psychiatry department when he was almost 8 years old, because he had become depressed and had developed nightmares after a neighbour commented that his club-foot deformity made him walk like 'a pigeon'. He had then asked his mother: 'Why did you buy me with feet like that?'

His mother suffered from recurrent depressive illnesses with suicidal ideas. The father was hard working, but the family was large and poor. Timothy himself had suffered from epilepsy in addition to his congenital deformity and had been in and out of hospital throughout his life. He loved sports, however, was fond of animals, and very kind to a spastic cousin. He did not enjoy school.

When seen in childhood, he was a sturdy, healthy, but frightened and rather suspicious boy, frowning and angry, who hardly talked except to complain of his nightmares.

Timothy was first referred to an adult psychiatrist at the age of 23, at the start of a long prison sentence. The records revealed that a year earlier, after visiting his mother in hospital where she had had a major operation, he met a man who had once attacked him as a teenager. He had felt that 'It was him or me' and had stabbed this person, injuring him severely. Some of his brothers were also in trouble with the law at the time, but for more minor offences. Timothy had had a previous custodial sentence for a similar offence. His worries now were that he might keep repeating such assaults. He was depressed, unable to sleep, and treatment for a reactive depression was started. Some months later he began to feel the prison authorities were being unfair to him and he was found to be tense and aggressive. By this time he had become a strict vegetarian.

Five years after that Timothy was re-referred because of repeatedly aggressive behaviour to other people in the prison. He was now actively hallucinating and paranoid, shouting at imaginary persecutors. He remained fearful that he might injure someone. He complained that people were tuned into his brain; that voices told him to 'screw their eyes out'. He now revealed that he had heard voices for years, but could never bring himself to mention this. A diagnosis of paranoid schizophrenia was now made, probably present for very many years, and he was started on anti-psychotic medication to good effect.

It was noted that Timothy did not come from a typically delinquent background, that his family was a close one and that he, like his father, to whom he was very attached, had always been a hard worker. Sadly, it was difficult to persuade him to take his medication regularly and further episodes of psychotic experiences and aggressive behaviour occurred.

THE ANTECEDENTS OF ADULT PSYCHIATRIC DISORDER IN THE SCHIZOID AND CONTROL GROUPS

Because we had childhood data systematically and reliably recorded for 32 schizoid boys and 33 schizoid girls, as well as for equal numbers of matched control children, it was possible to relate this to later psychiatric morbidity using one rather crude index: any psychiatric hospital attendance or admission (see the Appendix, p. 171). It needs to be said that these groups of children were not representative either of the schizoid group as a whole (only about a quarter of the boys could be included), or of other clinic attenders (the control children were of slightly higher socio-economic background and IQ than other clinic attenders, because they had been chosen to match the schizoid children).

Among the controls, psychiatric hospital contact in adult life was associated with childhood evidence of cerebral dysfunction, with childhood conduct disorder, particularly with childhood aggression, and with the duration of contact with the clinic. There was also an almost significant relationship with lower childhood verbal IQ. Among the schizoid children, only two factors were related to later psychiatric hospital contact: a record of fantasies of violence (present in only seven schizoid children, six of whom later became psychiatric out- or in-patients), and an overall rating of childhood privations.

In summary, schizoid children are more likely than other referred children to suffer from a variety of psychiatric symptoms in later life, most of them not grave. While serious and life-threatening suicidal behaviour is commoner among schizoid children grown-up than among other childhood clinic referrals, only very small numbers are affected. The same applies to the later development of schizophrenic illnesses. It will also be clear that, while it is possible to predict the psychiatric outcome for groups of schizoid children referred to a psychiatric clinic, prediction for individual children is not possible. Two subjects who had aroused considerable concern in childhood had in fact remained well. Yet others, unpredictably, developed transient or chronic schizophrenic illnesses in later life. It had not been possible to examine the family histories of the children systematically for close relatives who might have had schizophrenia or other psychotic illnesses, and it may be that those few children who later became seriously ill had other genetic disadvantages which we did not pick up and which contributed to their subsequent psychotic illness. The only predictive feature that emerged from this study was that high IQ appears to protect schizoid children against the development of later schizophrenia.

In the next chapter we shall see that the uncertainty in predicting outcome applies equally to the prognosis for antisocial conduct in later life.

8 Is there a link with antisocial conduct?

Asperger (1944), in his original paper, recently translated so well by Uta Frith (1991), repeatedly stressed the unfeeling behaviour, the egocentricity and the maliciousness, indeed the 'delight in malice', displayed by some of the children apparently because they could not sense the hurt in others. He instanced obstinate disobedience, inability to conform to quite ordinary social demands, pathological lying and outbursts of fierce fighting in response to the teasing that the children's social gaucheness often evoked from their classmates. Lorna Wing (1981), too, found that a few (4 out of 34) of her more seriously handicapped patients with Asperger's syndrome were antisocial, sometimes in a bizarre way. She ascribed this to their lack of 'two-way social interactions'. Yet, a review of 132 reported cases of Asperger's syndrome, using Wing's strict criteria, and excluding for this reason both Tantam's series and our own, found only three individuals among them who had been violent (Ghaziuddin *et al.*, 1991).

Some of the children I have known revealed fixed feelings of hatred for no identifiable reason: of a sibling, a family pet or even a parent. Others felt themselves to be discriminated against. Yet others made unwarranted accusations of ill-treatment against parents or teachers, which often caused much distress.

This chapter will focus on the antisocial conduct of schizoid children in childhood and adult life compared with that of their matched controls who had also been referred to the clinic as children.

We were particularly concerned to establish how common serious criminal behaviour might be in the later life of schizoid children because newspaper reports of some incomprehensible and apparently motiveless crimes have suggested that their perpetrators were 'loners'. In one such account, a diagnosis of schizoid personality disorder in the perpetrator is reported. This was the case of a young man who murdered his parents. He was 'one of Britain's top graduate mathematicians' and had apparently had a very normal upbringing. He developed a consuming hatred of his parents and, long before the murder, had been preoccupied with fantasies of violence (*The Independent*, 1992).

The Report of the Butler Committee on Mentally Abnormal Offenders (Home Office and Department of Health and Social Security, 1977), set up in the wake of the conviction of Graham Young for murder by poisoning while on conditional release from Broadmoor Hospital, indicated that such rare offenders may long have been preoccupied with and collected poisons or weaponry. Other accounts described the vivid fantasy worlds of such people, their poor capacities for reality testing, and indeed their deviant definitions of reality (Howells, 1978). Moreover, a study of violent recidivists, published some years ago (Kozol *et al.*, 1972), reported these as asocial non-conformists lacking in feeling for other people, often with exclusive personal pursuits, yet resembling non-antisocial original thinkers in some of their personality traits.

There have also been a few accounts of violent patients in secure hospitals who were subsequently diagnosed as having Asperger's syndrome (Mawson *et al.*, 1985; Baron-Cohen, 1988), or who clearly had schizoid features, such as the 'Silent Twins' so vividly described by Marjorie Wallace (1986). These identical twin girls, who were electively mute and engaged in much creative and imaginative writing, were admitted to Broadmoor Special Hospital when they were 18 years old because of fire raising. Apart from their often aggressive relationship with each other, they were solitary and in later life both were diagnosed as suffering from schizophrenia (*The Independent*, 1993).

Seriously delinquent young people in custodial care have also been found to include an excess with schizotypal, paranoid and borderline personality traits, as well as developmental disorders (Hollander and Turner, 1985). Of this particular group of highly delinquent young people most had in addition been exposed to excessive stress and family disorganization, and many were of borderline intelligence. More recently, Coid (1993) studied the personality disorders of seriously psychopathic people confined to special secure hospitals or prison. Many of these very serious offenders had multiple identifiable personality disorders. Among these, borderline personality disorder (according to DSM-III criteria) was the commonest, followed, as was to be expected, by antisocial personality disorder. Offenders with this last disorder were distinguished by an excess of severe family adversity in childhood, such as parental discord, physical or sexual abuse, poverty, periods in care and family delinquency. Paranoid personality disorder was often associated. Schizoid and schizotypal personalities were also found among these psychopathic offenders, but were very much rarer. They tended to be associated with evidence of neuropsychological abnormalities, and in some cases with clear features of Asperger's syndrome and with 'bizarre preoccupations', which later progressed to criminal behaviour (Coid, 1989).

In summary, some unusual criminals *retrospectively* fall into the categories of schizoid, schizotypal or Asperger disorders; but, as we shall see, *prospectively* the number of affected children likely to commit serious criminal actions in later life is very small indeed. The association between serious or unusual crime and schizoid personality may be significant looking backwards, but is very weak looking forwards. And once again, it is not possible to prognosticate for the individual child.

AN APPARENTLY DANGEROUS BOY WHO DID NO HARM

ERIC's parents summoned the police when he was 13 years old because he was threatening to stab his mother with a knife and had also threatened to stab the family dog. He had for some time been telling his parents that if they went to bed he would kill them in the night. The mother reported that sometimes he would softly open their bedroom door at night and that this terrified her. A social worker was called in and she found Eric extremely agitated, angry about the dog, complaining that his parents cared more for the dog than for him, and voicing his fear that, were he to get into a fight, he would not know when to stop and could strangle his opponent. He wanted to go into a home. The social worker found Eric's hatred of the dog to be very fixed indeed and of long standing, noted that Eric smiled queerly to himself at times, and thought he was a 'very strange boy'.

Eric's birth had been uncomplicated. He had been a cuddly baby, an early talker and developmentally normal. But he had always been very determined, disobedient and difficult to control. He had temper tantrums and was extremely aggressive, being asked to leave his nursery school because of his attacks on other children. These symptoms led to his first referral to the child psychiatric clinic when he was not quite 6. At that time his difficulties were attributed to insecurity and poor parent/child interactions, in particular to the mother's all too ready embarrassment by his public non-compliance and her involuntary responses of anger and rejection. But it was noted even then that emotional contact with him was limited, that he engaged in much chatter but was unable to talk seriously about his life or his feelings. He was outspokenly rude to the psychologist, adamant in his refusal to participate in more than the minimum of psychological testing. He was later found to be of average intelligence, but with a very uneven performance on different items of the test.

Now, at 13, Eric was an exceptionally good-looking boy but with an odd, 'knowing', facial expression and a piercing gaze. He said he was clumsy and not 'brainy', but used long words appropriately and revealed abiding interests in dinosaurs, space and science fiction. Eric talked at length about the dog, justifying his reported cruelty to the animal by saying it had ruined his shoes and threatening to 'get the dog the next time'. He accused his parents of always taking the dog's side rather than his. The parents reported on his aggressiveness to the animal and to other children, said he had once threatened to burn the house down, but also mentioned that he never forgot a birthday and was a very good gardener. At school there were no difficulties and he always had a friend.

A behavioural approach to the problem was tried: the father was advised not to reprimand Eric for his hostile mutterings against the parents, reprimands which inevitably led Eric to explode; it was also suggested that the dog might temporarily be sent away. There was some initial success and Eric became kinder to the dog, from whom the family could not part, but further violent outbursts occurred later, Eric threatening that he would kill his father when he grew up, and subsequently once more brandishing a knife at his parents. I was very concerned at his lack of remorse, his callous self-justifications, and I feared for his parents' safety.

Eric was admitted to an assessment centre. While there both he and his parents began to miss each other inordinately and Eric for the first time agreed, as a condition of his returning home, that he would not act threateningly to his parents in future. During his time in the assessment centre, he mixed very poorly with other youngsters and could not appreciate that his immediate revelation that he had tried to knife his father might antagonize the other boys.

A second temporary period in care had to be arranged following a further threatening episode, and during his late teens he once appeared in court on a charge of assault and breach of the peace. But, when he was 24, although he declined to take part in our follow-up study, I heard from his family that he lived in his own flat, was working steadily, visited the parents weekly, and had 'turned out fine'.

CONDUCT DISORDERS IN CHILDHOOD: A RETROSPECTIVE CASE NOTE STUDY

An early case note study (Wolff and Cull, 1986) of 30 schizoid and 30 matched control boys had shown the incidence of childhood antisocial conduct to be the same in the two groups. However, schizoid boys in this sample had engaged in less stealing than the other referred children, and their childhood antisocial conduct was not, as in the controls, related to adversities such as family disruption and socio-economic disadvantage. A subsequent analysis of the childhood records of the schizoid and control boys personally interviewed in adult life, constituting different but overlapping samples, also found similar levels of childhood conduct disorders in both groups, but in these samples schizoid boys stole as often as controls.

Schizoid girls, in contrast, as reported in Chapter Six, did present more often than control girls with pure conduct disorders in childhood (11 out of 33 compared with only 3 among the 33 controls), and also had significantly more conduct disorders recorded throughout their clinic attendances than other referred girls. Indeed, as was to be expected, the control girls, like girls in the general population, were less conduct disordered than control boys. We shall see later that the excessive proneness to antisocial behaviour among schizoid girls continued, and led to greatly increased rates of officially recorded delinquency in their adult lives. It needs to be stressed once more, as was argued in Chapter Six, that this may have been due, at least in part, to a referral artefact. It is possible that withdrawn and solitary behaviour is less socially handicapping for girls than boys, but also that girls who are constitutionally predisposed to schizoid personality traits manifest these in a milder form than boys, so that only those schizoid girls with additional worrying symptoms, such as conduct disorders, are referred to child psychiatric clinics. And, of course, conduct disorder in childhood is well known to be highly predictive of adult delinquency (Robins, 1991).

In the early case note study (Wolff and Cull, 1986) we also looked in more detail at the records of those among the total cohorts of 111 schizoid boys and 34 schizoid girls whose antisocial behaviour had caused particular concern at the time of the referral or had been especially long-lasting. There were 20 such boys and 13 girls. Among the 20 boys, 16 had been physically aggressive or had threatened violence; 13 had stolen; 7 wandered; 2 had engaged in fire raising; 2 were cruel to animals; and 3 became seriously fraudulent later. Eight of these boys had voiced unusual fantasies. Moreover, 5 boys had been suspended from school; 16 had spent long periods away from home in a child psychiatric unit, a special residential school or a children's home, because their aggressive attacks, especially on other children at school, had become unmanageable. Fourteen had appeared at a Scottish children's hearing or in court, and 4 had been in an approved school or assessment centre.

Among the 13 seriously antisocial girls, 9 had been aggressive or threatened violence; 7 had engaged in pathological lying (5 had falsely reported their parents to be cruel to them and 2 had used aliases); 7 wandered; 6 had stolen; 2 had stolen babies from their prams. Among these girls 9 had voiced unusual fantasies. One had been suspended from school; 7 had lived away from home in a child psychiatric unit or a special residential school; 5 had appeared at a children's hearing or at court; and 5 had been in an approved school or assessment centre.

In this case note study it was found that proportionally more girls than boys had been conspicuously antisocial in childhood, and more girls than boys had translated their fantasies into action in the form of pathological lying.

SOME CONSPICUOUSLY ANTISOCIAL SCHIZOID CHILDREN

Two antisocial boys who later became fraudulent

Case 1

JASON presented at the clinic at the age of 10 because of compulsive wandering. He frequently took long train journeys and once caught a plane from Edinburgh to London. He apparently had no difficulty travelling without a ticket. His mind was occupied with ideas of sex and sin. At school his nick name was 'the professor', and he thought they called him 'crazy' because he kept apart from other children. Residential care was the only way in which his dangerous wandering could be contained. He was in a child psychiatry in-patient unit (where at first they put him in a red jacket for greater visibility) and then in a residential school for maladjusted children. Here he adopted the surname of the only friend he had ever made, with whose mother he apparently had a sexual relationship during a school holiday with this family. His most stable years, from 17 to 25 years of age, were as a cook in a private boarding school. But then he became a compulsive gambler and had very large debts. He left this job to study philosophy at a further education college, but lost his grant money through gambling. He never felt really close to anyone, although he had had fleeting homo- and heterosexual experiences. When he consulted me once in later life, he was himself very concerned about his 'personality', worried that he might become 'a psychopath'. He was a very intelligent, appealing and sensitive young man, anxious and solitary. A brother shared some of his personality attributes and his mother, an intelligent woman, had a disabling speech defect, was anxious and excitable and made poor emotional contact with other people. Jason was last seen in court on a charge of fraud, when my evidence in his defence about his unusual personality-development failed to protect him from a prison sentence.

Case 2

ROSS had been a solitary boy with a vivid fantasy life given to aggressive attacks on other children. His talk was garbled and often addressed to no one in particular. Although of average intelligence, he was seriously retarded in reading and spelling. He, too, had spent some years in a boarding school.

At the age of 23 he came to see me with a probation officer while facing charges of fraud. He and an older cousin, both heavy drinkers, had posed as garage proprietors and bought and resold spare vehicle parts without paying for them. Ross used aliases and fictitious autobiographical details to avert trouble. To me he reported several suicide attempts, boredom and depression, but also much stealing, drinking, gambling and serious fighting. He said he cared for no one, not even for his tolerant family. He thought he was a good salesman: 'I've always put it down to my charm. I wrap them round my little finger.' He worried that he might go mad. By the age of 27 he had married a disabled girl and had a child. Social workers supervising the family were concerned about possible physical abuse to the child. Ross denied this, but told me (and I found this hard to believe) that he had been responsible, some time ago, for his cousin falling to his death.

Case 3. An aggressive boy

DAVID presented in early childhood with a severe expressive developmental language delay. He was a loner at school, given to unprovoked attacks on other children in class and in the playground. His family was united and supportive of him. During his primary school years, he was in a special class, where a behavioural approach to his aggressive outbursts worked well, to his own satisfaction. His speech improved greatly and was normal by the time he started secondary school. But he was still educationally retarded, despite normal intelligence, and he remained a loner.

Unfortunately no secondary day school was found suitable for his particular educational needs, and he was sent to a special boarding school. He complained about the lack of structure at this school and the staff failed to heed advice against involving him in exploratory group therapy. Twice, under stress, he made serious attacks on other people at the school, the second leading to a court appearance. At this stage, now 15 years old, David was preoccupied with fantasies of sex and violence. He read avidly about violent crimes and at home he had amassed collections of photographs of a notorious murderer as well as anarchist literature and callous posters, which frightened his parents. Fortunately, after leaving school he was offered a place at a Rudolf Steiner training centre with the gentle, non-intrusive but well-structured and collaborative work orientation that is customary in these settings. David refused to take part in our follow-up study. Although not working, he was then at 21, living in his own flat and visiting his parents weekly. There had been no further trouble.

Case 4. A girl with a transient Munchhausen syndrome

DIANA was repeatedly admitted to hospital in adolescence with false pregnancies. On one of these occasions she was found, wearing a medical student's white coat, examining another patient's ear with an auriscope. The gynaecological unit this girl attended was at the time plagued by a series of small, unexplained fires. Diana gave herself a new name in adolescence, one she was to change again in young adult life when her first child was born. She came from a structurally united but very poor and socially deprived family, and had spent some years in foster care. Both parents were strange people, the mother permanently and manifestly distraught since the death of a child in an accident many years ago.

Diana took part in our follow-up study. Although of only low average abilities, she presented a sophisticated appearance and spoke well, as she had done as a youngster, too. Several of her children had been taken into care, and she was now living with her third partner.

ANTISOCIAL CONDUCT REVEALED IN THE FOLLOW-UP INTERVIEWS

We have seen that both the first and the second follow-up study of schizoid and control young men found no differences between the groups in either delinquent behaviour or excessive drinking. Indeed, at the time of the second follow-up at a mean age of 27 years, non-significantly more control subjects (12 out of 32 as against 9 of the 32 schizoid young men) had had contact with law-enforcing agencies.

Only 17 schizoid girls were personally interviewed, also at a mean age of 27 years. Their rates of self-reported antisocial behaviour and excessive drinking were similar to those of the schizoid young men (8 of the 17 young women had had contact with law-enforcing agencies). And this suggests that they were, in fact, an excessively delinquent group, because usually girls and women are far less anti-social and have fewer drinking problems than boys and men. Unfortunately, no matched control group of girls were followed-up.

At the end of the interviews a primary or secondary diagnosis of antisocial personality disorder according to DSM-III criteria was made for 6 out of 32 schizoid men (compared with 4 out of the 32 controls) and in 3 of the 17 schizoid young women.

A CRIMINAL RECORDS SURVEY

With the help of the Scottish Criminal Records Office a computer search was undertaken for any recorded offences for the total cohorts (described in the last chapter) of 109 schizoid boys and 32 schizoid girls, and of 110 control boys and 32 control girls, all then over the age of 16 years.

Rates of offending

In both schizoid and control groups the proportion of people with any convictions was higher than expected for the general population (32 per cent for schizoid men and 34.5 per cent for control men; 34.5 per cent for schizoid women and 15.5 per cent for control women; comparable population norms for men were 22 per cent and for women 5 per cent) (Wolff, 1992). This is not surprising in groups referred as children to a child psychiatry department, among whom the rates of childhood conduct disorders were, of course, higher than for children in the general population. What was striking was the high rate of criminality in the schizoid women (three times as high as for a comparable group in the general population). The mean numbers of offences recorded for schizoid and control men were 10.8 and 12.2 respectively; but for women they were 4.9 and 1.6 respectively, that is, much higher in the schizoid girls grown-up than in their matched controls.

Moreover, while about a third of male schizoid and control offenders had had one or more custodial sentences, among the women, one-third of schizoids but no controls at all had been in prison. This highlights the severity of antisocial conduct among schizoid girls in later life.

The nature of the offences

No differences were found between the schizoid and control groups in the nature of their offences and, in particular, by the time of the survey (at a mean age of 26 and a half years) no schizoid person had committed any particularly violent crime. However, as we shall see, three years later one of the schizoid young men made repeated newspaper headlines because, at the age of 21, he committed a very serious sexual and physical assault on a housewife.

The age of offending

Farrington and Hawkins (1991) showed that the personal attributes and background of men who persist in criminal behaviour beyond the age of 21 are different from those who engage in more transient youthful crime. We therefore looked at offenders among our schizoid and control groups who had offences recorded only under the age of 21 and those with offences beyond this age. We found no statistical differences between the schizoid and control young men; if anything, there was a trend for more persistent offending within the control group (the numbers of women affected were too small for comparisons to be made).

The correlates of criminality

What was interesting was that the associations between recorded criminality and a variety of other factors were different in the schizoid and control groups.

While the control group showed the expected association with sex, significantly more men than women having been convicted, this was not so in the schizoid group, where equal proportions of men and women had been convicted. In the control group of boys conviction for a criminal offence was significantly associated with a lower childhood IQ (the numbers for the control girls were too small for statistical analysis), but this was not so for schizoid boys or for schizoid girls. Lower socio-economic status of the individual's family of origin was associated with later criminality, but less strongly among schizoid than control boys (the numbers of girls were again too small for statistical analysis). A possible explanation, which needs to be confirmed, is that schizoid children and young people, because of their insensitivity to social cues, are less open to normal socialising processes than other people and conform less in their behaviour to normal sexual and social stereotypes.

ONE AMONG 109 SCHIZOID BOYS COMMITTED A SERIOUS CRIME

JO had gained entry into a woman's house by posing as a Roman Catholic priest. After talking to her for some time he sexually assaulted her after making a severe, unprovoked attack on her with a poker. A few days earlier, wearing a priest's habit, he had obtained a meal and permission to celebrate mass in the Edinburgh cathedral. He was subsequently found to have stolen the elder's purse. He had also instigated an intensive police search in the city for a supposed IRA terrorist, whom he falsely claimed to have known in Ireland and to have met again in Edinburgh. He had had previous convictions for minor fraud and theft as well as for one not very serious sexual assault. As a child his severe oppositional behaviour had caused trouble from the age of 2 and a half years and his aggressive behaviour with other children led to his exclusion from nursery school. He was of superior intelligence, but with severe specific developmental learning difficulties. He had been a charming boy to look at, apparently friendly and outgoing. But he was in fact quite solitary, grossly lacking in social sensitivity and given to unpredictable and incomprehensible outbursts of aggression, which led to repeated exclusions from school. Jo's parents were affectionate and supportive of him and suffered greatly from the consequences of his antisocial conduct. The father, a somewhat withdrawn, mildly schizoid man, always in work and not at all delinquent, had adopted quite fierce methods of controlling his son. Whether this was initially a reaction to Jo's difficulties is not known, nor can we be sure whether it contributed in any way to Jo's own coercive attacks on other people.

This young man was given a finite prison sentence on appeal, having previously been sentenced to life imprisonment in the High Court. His potential future dangerousness was a major issue and could clearly not be accurately forecast.

While Jo was assessed correctly as unlikely to respond to psychiatric treatment, a case could probably have been made for diminished responsibility as a result of his serious and constitutional personality disorder and he might have been more appropriately placed in a special, secure hospital. Of course, this may not have been his wish and would have raised a number of ethical issues, which will be discussed at the end of this book.

THE ANTECEDENTS OF ADULT DELINQUENCY IN REFERRED SCHIZOID AND CONTROL CHILDREN

Our data allowed us to relate the systematically recorded childhood features of 32 schizoid boys and 33 schizoid girls, and of their 65 matched control children, with one measure of adult delinquency derived from the criminal records survey: whether or not there had ever been a conviction (see the Appendix, p. 171). It must be remembered that these groups of children were neither representative of all schizoid referred children (they included all the girls but only about a quarter of the boys), nor of all other referred children (the control groups were chosen to match the schizoid groups for socio-economic background and IQ, and were as a result of both higher social class and higher IQ than referred children as a whole).

In the control group of boys and girls, a conviction after the age of 16 was, not surprisingly, most highly associated with a record of contact with those agencies most involved with delinquent children: social work departments and children's courts or the Scottish Children's Hearings. Manual working-class status of the father was next most highly associated with adult conviction, followed by delinquency in other members of the family, most often a sibling, and by the presence of a conduct disorder in the child him/herself.

Among the schizoid children, there were similar but less strong associations between contacts with social work departments and children's hearing or court, and later convictions. Occupational class of the father did not distinguish between those who were later convicted and those who were not, nor did a family history of delinquency. But, in contrast to the controls, a reliable assessment of the children's overall exposure to emotional or other privations in childhood did. In the schizoid children, as in the controls, childhood conduct disorder was significantly related to later convictions, but, again in contrast to the controls, childhood aggression was even more strongly associated with this. In this schizoid group, mean intelligence was lower for children later convicted but reached significance only on the performance test.

In these groups of psychiatrically referred children (schizoid and control), family disruption or discord, separation experiences, parental ill health and parental personality disorder were not statistically associated with later convictions, nor were specific developmental disorders, educational difficulties or a reliable measure of overall childhood stresses. This is in line with the finding of others (Robins, 1991) that the child's symptoms, rather than his or her life circumstances, are the most predictive indicators of an adult antisocial development.

The one measure that seemed to protect against adult delinquency in our groups was a presentation with pure emotional disorders. This occurred in 20 of the control boys and girls and in 5 of the schizoid children. None of these had any convictions in later life.

One other finding from these groups of schizoid and control children grown-up is noteworthy. While in the control groups there was no association between psychiatric treatment in adult life and adult convictions, among schizoid people this association was marked ($p < 0.01$), more delinquent schizoid people also having had contact with psychiatric services (14 out of 22 compared with 5 out of 16 among the controls).

In summary, the childhood factor most strongly protecting schizoid and control children against adult delinquency was a presentation with a pure emotional disorder. Within the schizoid group aggressive conduct disorder (as well as contact with social work departments or children's courts or panels), low intelligence and a global measure of childhood privation (including lack of adequate parenting, inadequate social and educational stimulation, socio-economic privation) were most highly associated with one or more convictions in later life.

While low socio-economic status of the childhood family was associated with later convictions in the controls, this was not so for the schizoid group, and, again in contrast to the controls, adult schizoid people with convictions were more likely also to have adult psychiatric disorders.

WHAT IS KNOWN ABOUT THE CAUSES OF AN ANTISOCIAL PERSONALITY DEVELOPMENT IN GENERAL?

Antisocial personality disorder is not all of a kind

We need to be clear that the development of an antisocial personality disorder, or sociopathy, comes about as a result of many different, often overlapping, personal attributes and circumstances (Wolff, 1993). *In its most common form*, it arises from aggressive and other antisocial conduct disorders in childhood, whose causes are both constitutionally and environmentally determined. Yet by no means all antisocial children develop antisocial personality disorders in later life. It is only when the childhood conduct disorder starts very early in life, is severe and consists of many different types of antisocial behaviour that the risks for adult antisocial personality are high (Robins, 1991).

Although the multiple and powerful causes of childhood conduct disorders are well established, it needs to be stressed again that *adult antisocial conduct* is related to childhood antisocial behaviour itself, and to its childhood consequences, such as court appearances, rather than to the adverse circumstances that brought the childhood disorder about.

The constitutional factors contributing to the common antisocial *conduct disorders in childhood* are first of all being male; second, having an outgoing temperament with restlessness, impulsivity and overactivity predisposing the child, most often a boy, to respond adversely to early privations and inept child-rearing methods at home, and to educational failure at school; third, educational failure itself may have a constitutional basis in the form of specific developmental delays of language and learning skills.

The experiential adversities most powerfully linked to *childhood conduct disorder* are those associated with poverty and with personality disorders, especially sociopathy, of the parents (Earls, 1994). The more immediate impact on the children is likely to be related to large family size, marital discord, disrupted family relationships, drug and alcohol abuse on the part of the parents and, more immediately still, poor child-rearing practices. The main features of these which have now been identified as promoting an antisocial development in children are inadequate supervision, parents being unaware of where the child is and what he is doing, and coercive and punitive but inconsistent methods of control (Patterson and Dishion, 1988).

In addition, there is an important consequence of being brought up in a punitive way, especially for boys. They tend to believe that other children are hostile towards them even when they are not. This makes affected boys retaliate with aggression, and their conduct disorder escalates (Dodge *et al.*, 1990).

Educational failure, more likely when there has been poor socialization in the early years and when the child is not very able intellectually, can add to the risks of childhood conduct disorder (Wolff, 1993), although educational failure alone does not engender antisocial behaviour. It has also been established that aggressiveness in parents is often transmitted to their children (Huesmann *et al.*, 1984), and that social adversities, such as unemployment, promote such intergenerational continuities.

In rarer cases, pervasive hyperkinesis and associated specific developmental learning difficulties can act as very powerful constitutional determinants for later childhood conduct disorders and delinquency (Taylor *et al.*, 1991) in interaction with adverse child-rearing patterns.

WHAT DISTINGUISHES SCHIZOID ANTISOCIAL CHILDREN?

I shall argue that schizoid personality can be regarded as one of the rarer constitutional predispositions to childhood conduct disorders. What appears to differentiate schizoid from other conduct disordered children is, first, that girls are more often affected; second, that many conduct-disordered schizoid children have not suffered from any particularly adverse life circumstances; and third, that they often have parents who are quite skilled at bringing up children. In addition, the children's oversensitive, sometimes even paranoid, personality can lead some of them, wrongly, to attribute hostile intentions to other children. The often associated specific developmental learning difficulties also contribute to the educational difficulties of affected children, over and above their poor capacities for social integration and conformity at school, and may contribute to the development of childhood conduct disorder in some cases.

In our samples of 32 schizoid boys and 33 schizoid girls and their matched controls for whom systematic childhood data were available, we found that childhood conduct disorder was significantly associated with a reliable overall measure of social deprivation in the schizoid and controls groups ($p < 0.05$) and, in the controls only, also to low socio-economic class ($p < 0.01$). Aggression in childhood was also related to low socio-economic class in the controls ($p < 0.05$) but not in the schizoid children, again suggesting that in schizoid children antisocial behaviour is less dependent on environmental adversity than it is in other disturbed children (see the Appendix, p. 171).

SCHIZOID PERSONALITY AND THE DEVELOPMENT OF MORALITY

One further fundamental way in which schizoid personality traits might promote an antisocial development now needs to be considered.

It is in the second year of life that children are first capable of appreciating what is right and wrong and begin to evaluate their own competence (Kagan, 1981). It is at this stage that they become aware of small flaws or blemishes in everyday objects, and of standards of behaviour, especially of what they themselves can and cannot do. This is the time at which evaluative language first appears, with words like 'good', 'bad', 'dirty', 'nice', 'broke', but also phrases like 'hard do', 'can't', 'fix it'. This discriminatory capacity is central to the development of morality and the sense of what is right and wrong in relation to human interactions. Notions of duty, of 'shoulds' and 'oughts', manifest a little later. A vital ingredient for this earliest development of moral standards is thought to be the capacity for accurate empathy, that is, for being able to put oneself into another person's position and feel with him or her. Even young infants repond emotionally to the expressed feelings of others, but, until a sense of the other as a separate person with his or her own needs and thoughts has developed, again beginning in the second year, empathic responses to other people, such as offering comfort when others are distressed, are not possible. Hoffman (1987) has described the stages of empathic development and how children can best be socialized to act with altruism towards others, avoid doing harm and offer help to those in need. In order to respond to socialization towards altruism, and become a person with a conscience in identification with the role models presented by parents and teachers, children need to be able to feel with and for others but also to have a cognitive understanding of what other people are likely to feel and think (Wolff, 1991a).

Many people with schizoid personality traits, as we have seen, find empathising difficult: they cannot put themselves into other people's shoes. This may make it very difficult for them to appreciate the effects of their own behaviour on others. But, more than this, it may in some affected children be an obstacle to the development of morality and conscience.

In the case of autistic children, grosser deficits in identifying emotional expressions have been discovered by Hobson (1986, 1991), and deficits in appreciating what is in the minds of other people (i.e. a lack of a 'theory of mind') by Baron-Cohen (1989) (see also Chapter Ten). But autistic children, in contrast to schizoid children, are often severely handicapped, lead restricted lives as adults and have little impact on other people apart from their immediate carers. This is not so for the 'loners' described in this book, who lead independent lives in the outside world.

While the majority do in fact manage their interpersonal relationships well, especially if they find warm and appreciative partners, a few (like Ross and Jo, described above) remain severely impaired in their empathic responses to other people and fail to develop a firm sense of morality and a reliable conscience.

CONCLUSIONS

Conduct disorders in childhood are as common in schizoid boys referred to a child psychiatric clinic as in other referred children, and the risk of delinquency in adult life is correspondingly, but not very greatly, increased compared with delinquency rates in the general population.

Schizoid girls, in contrast, are much more often conduct disordered than other referred girls, and in adult life their rates of delinquency are very high indeed compared to the usually very low community rates of female delinquency.

The excess of conduct disorders and later delinquency in schizoid girls may be due in part to referral bias. Schizoid traits may well manifest less obviously in girls than in boys. Moreover, some schizoid traits, such as solitariness, may be socially more acceptable in girls than in boys. For both these reasons fewer girls with symptoms confined to those of schizoid personality are likely to be referred to child psychiatric clinics and only affected girls with other, associated childhood disorders, such as antisocial behaviour, will be seen by clinicians.

The risk for schizoid children of committing serious offences in later life is very low indeed. But, among that small group of people who commit incomprehensible, motiveless but life-endangering crimes, there will be some with clear-cut schizoid, schizotypal or Asperger disorders going back to early childhood (Coid, 1989). Such people need to be identified. In Chapter Eleven I shall argue for special consideration of such offenders both on account of their constitutional disabilities, which include impaired judgement, and because of the particular difficulties of predicting the likelihood of future similarly dangerous behaviour.

Of more practical importance is the recognition that among the many people, men and women, who suffer from much more common social and emotional difficulties and induce suffering in others, for example in marriage relationships and the upbringing of children, there will be a few with schizoid or schizotypal personalities, whose reactions cannot be explained on the basis of their past life experiences or present adversities, but make sense only when their personality make-up is understood. This is an essential basis for helpful interventions and for predicting the possible outcome, for example, in marriage counselling and in child-protection work.

9   Intellectual interests and giftedness

> People respect talent even if they think you are weird.
>
> (Grandin, 1992, p. 122)

This quote comes from an article entitled 'An insider's view of autism' written by a 44-year-old woman with an international career as a designer of livestock equipment. Temple Grandin explains how frustrating it was in her very early years to understand everything that was said to her, but to be unable to speak; she could only scream. She describes vividly her oversensitivity to noise and touch, and the extreme anxiety this caused her. For some years she took small doses of an anti-depressant which helped her overcome her anxieties and also, she believes, improved her sociability, her speech, her ability to make eye contact with other people and her posture. Intelligence tests in childhood had shown that she fell into that rare group of autistic people who are of superior ability, and she herself knew that she was always especially gifted at forming visual representations in her mind. This gift she uses in her work and as a basis for remembering. Temple Grandin wrote: 'I prefer factual, nonfictional reading materials. I have little interest in novels with complicated interpersonal relationships' (p. 123); and 'Almost all my social contacts are with livestock people or people interested in autism' (p. 122). Here she is alluding to her restricted range of interests, and it is this obsessive preoccupation with a particular activity, or narrow range of activities, which characterizes some people with autism and also a proportion of people with schizoid personality characteristics. A very moving encounter with Temple Grandin has recently been described by Oliver Sacks (1995).

This chapter will summarize what has been written about the special giftedness of some people with autism and with Asperger's syndrome, and will describe the gifted children and young people in my own groups of former schizoid patients. A discussion of the associations between exceptional abilities and schizoid or schizotypal personality traits and mental illness will follow.

THE 'SAVANT' PHENOMENON

Extraordinary abilities are sometimes found in people who, overall, function at a mentally handicapped level. This unevenness between different aspects of intelligence contributes to, but cannot alone explain, the 'savant' phenomenon, so carefully studied by Hermelin and O'Connor (Hermelin and O'Connor, 1986; O'Connor and Hermelin, 1988).

These authors suggest that giftedness among people in general, for example in mathematics, music and drawing, while not necessarily tied to general intelligence, usually depends on an overall high intellectual level of outstanding achievements, but that extraordinary feats, for example in calendrical calculations, musical reproduction or artistic products, are performed by some people with autism who function overall at quite a low ability level. In addition to their narrow preoccupation with a special interest, such 'savants' also have outstanding memories, as Temple Grandin appears to have had, and a particularly well-developed capacity for extracting rules and regularities from, for example, the calendar, tonal music and the visual world. 'Savants' are not helped by their special gifts to reproduce atonal music or fragmented, unstructured designs which do not conform to traditional musical or visual rules and structures.

More recently, Pring and Hermelin (1993) have studied savant visual artists. Their talents resembled those of the autistic children and adults who have acquired fame because of their remarkable drawing and painting gifts: Nadia, with her extraordinary horses and horsemen (Selfe, 1985), who lost her ability as she got older and began to speak; Stephen Wiltshire, with his exact and yet totally original and lively architectural drawings of buildings and urban scenes (Wiltshire, 1987; see also Sacks, 1995), whose gift remains; and Richard Wawro (Treffert, 1989), who became somewhat less original although more prolific as he grew older.

Pring and Hermelin point out that both Nadia and Steven Wiltshire produced drawings of remarkable accuracy after only the briefest inspection of their subjects: pictures of horses and horsemen in Nadia's case, real buildings in the case of Steven. Yet, while very detailed and totally accurate, the pictures of both were not like photographic reproductions at all, but highly original works of acknowledged artistic merit executed in an immediately recognizable personal style. Selfe (1977), the psychologist who studied and reported on Nadia, believed that her gift was based on her clear and lasting memories of what she saw, that is, of *percepts* in her mind, which she could then change and transform in her graphic work. Once children have language, they turn what they perceive into *concepts*, which inhibit graphic effort. Children do not normally look at models in order to draw people or objects. They draw what they know rather than what they see.

This theory is not borne out by the experimental study of Pring and Hermelin (1993). They found no difference between artistically gifted savants and artistically gifted normal children in their memory for pictures of objects: both relied more on semantic than structural features, that is on concepts rather than percepts. The accuracy of reproduction was also similar in the two groups. And on a picture-sorting task it was again the semantic nature of the object rather than its shape which determined success in the artistically gifted, for both savants and normal children. The authors argue that artistic giftedness depends both on visual knowledge and semantic organization, and they conclude that savants are no different from other artists in the mental organization underlying their special gift. They differ only in the restriction of competence to their extraordinary abilities.

I have known a number of autistic children, boys and girls, with artistic gifts. One, with a moderately severe learning difficulty, persistent gaze avoidance and barely able to talk, was a brilliant and colourful drawer of trains, buses and whole cityscapes from memory. His products resembled those of Steven Wiltshire and yet they were quite characteristically his own. This boy temporarily lost his urge to draw in his early teens, but then became interested once more and attended art classes to the delight of his teachers. His products, now largely based on photographs of landscapes and buildings he has seen, are a source of much pleasure for himself, his family and their friends. They continue to have considerable artistic merit, but to my eyes they have lost the special spark of genius which I thought I had detected in his childhood work.

The definition of the savant syndrome includes an impaired level of general intelligence. Although many savants reported in the literature were autistic, a number were not. The rarity of autism in the general population and its high prevalence among savants suggests a special predisposition to selective giftedness among autistic people as compared with other people with learning difficulties. Treffert (1989) suggests that almost 10 per cent of autistic people have a special gift. He distinguishes between talented savants whose gifts are greater than expected from their general, usually impaired, level of abilities, and prodigious savants whose gifts are far beyond the range of normal ability. His review of the literature reveals the variety of human abilities in which special gifts are seen: calendrical caculation; music, especially piano playing; lightning calculation and other mathematical feats; art, including painting, drawing and sculpture; mechanical ability; mnemonism; and, very rarely, unusual sensory discrimination. Eidetic imagery, that is unusual memory for the exact visual display seen is common, but Jerome Bruner (as quoted by Treffert, 1989) has suggested that the gift may depend on a failure to forget rather than on enhanced abilities to remember. Literary skills, perhaps not surprisingly in this handicapped and often language-impaired group, are not among the special gifts of savants.

The reason for describing the savant phenomenon among autistic people is that very similar exceptional abilities, but without associated general intellectual impairment, are also seen in schizoid children and adults.

IS GIFTEDNESS ASSOCIATED WITH SCHIZOID/SCHIZOTYPAL PERSONALITY TRAITS?

The genius who survives as such has successfully run the gauntlet of premature death, the inanities of formal education, the social and ethical pressures of his immediate environment, and the more general cultural influences that have given direction and content to the civilization in which he was born.

So wrote L. M. Terman (1970, p. 26), who undertook the biggest long-term study of gifted children. Because people with schizoid disorders are relatively immune to social pressures, one might suppose that those of high intelligence would more often than other intelligent people have original thoughts and creative achievements.

One can look at the possible association between personality traits and giftedness in two ways: are certain traits found to excess among gifted people? and do people with these traits more often than others also have extraordinary abilities?

Possible schizoid/schizotypal traits among gifted people

Ochse (1990) reviewed the literature on creative geniuses. Among their characteristics are an often fanatical and stubborn motivation to pursue their special field of activity and satisfaction coming from the intrinsic aspects of the work itself rather than from public acclaim. He found many geniuses to be characterized by 'aloneness', not due to circumstances but as part of their personality. He comments on the relative rarity of genius in women, despite the fact that family encouragement, especially from fathers, was often recorded in the childhoods of gifted women. He suggests that women have 'greater affiliative tendencies'. It is worth here reminding ourselves that schizoid disorders and Asperger's syndrome are always commoner in men than women.

The extensive literature on the psychology of genius and special giftedness (e.g. Cox, 1926; Juda, 1949; Barron and Harrington, 1981; Albert, 1983; Ochse, 1990; Post, 1994) records the high intelligence and perseverance of gifted people and the highly intelligent and encouraging parents they often had. Abnormalities of personality are in fact rarely recorded, despite the observation, to which we shall return, that mental illnesses are more common in the families of geniuses than in the general population. Terman, however (as reported by Stein and Heinze, 1983), did find highly gifted boys as a group to be less sociable and less interested in competitive games than other children. More of them were regarded as 'queer' or 'different' by their peers. Unusual play interests and imaginary companions were also common.

In addition, a cognitive style known to have a hereditary basis and characterized by 'allusive' thinking with unusual word associations (McConaghy and Clancy, 1968; Tucker *et al.*, 1982) has been found to characterize highly creative people as well as people with a predisposition to schizophrenia. Divergent thinking with prolific and unusual associations accompanied lesser creative gifts, but has also been found in people with schizotypal personality traits (Woody and Claridge, 1977), and in the relatives of schizophrenic patients. We must be clear that such personality traits do not usually amount to personality disorder, but fall within the normal range of personality variation.

Post (1994) found schizotypal, schizoid and paranoid traits, short of those required for a diagnosis of personality *disorder*, to occur in only 6.8 per cent of the 291 world-famous men whose biographies he had read, but, among these, in 20 per cent of the intellectuals, that is philosophers and other eminent thinkers.

All these studies suggest that the personality traits found in people genetically predisposed to schizophrenia may be among the features of a proportion of highly-gifted people.

Is special giftedness a feature of schizoid disorders?

Manfred Bleuler (1978) who, like his father Eugen, devoted his life to the clinical study of schizophrenic patients and their families, regarded a creative inner life as an integral part of the schizoid personality, which he found to excess among the children of his schizophrenic patients. He also thought that the creativity of schizoid people contributed to cultural development.

Treffert (1989) records a man with Asperger disorder and exceptional mathematical ability. Asperger himself (1944) drew attention to his patients' special giftedness and to that of some of their relatives. The mother of one of these children came from a family which included one of the greatest Austrian poets as well as other poets, all of them 'charmingly' eccentric. Another of Asperger's child patients had extraordinary mathematical gifts even in early childhood and grew up to become an eminent theoretical astronomer. As a boy he had totally ignored other people, was motorically clumsy, but had been clearly good at maths from the age of 3, able to calculate cubic roots on school entry (Asperger, 1961).

SCHIZOID CHILDREN WITH SPECIAL GIFTS

Although there were no geniuses among the schizoid children I have known, a number had not only special interests but special gifts. These gifts ranged from electronics, mathematics and music to drawing and painting, and even story writing. This is all the more remarkable because of the specific language-related developmental delays and the communication difficulties that were also common in this group. When the special gift was an artistic one, the style and content, of the drawings in particular, although always unique to the artist, nevertheless resembled those of the autistic children I have known and of the published work of savant artists. Architectural drawings and drawings of roads, railway stations and transport vehicles were especially common, and executed with a remarkable eye for detail even by quite young children (see Figure 1). And it must be said that among schizoid children without special artistic gifts, drain pipes, heating systems and road maps were often favourite, sometimes obsessionally repetitive, subjects for drawing.

Among the 32 schizoid boys and 17 schizoid girls who were personally interviewed in adult life, an impressionistic assessment of special giftedness identified 9 children, all boys, with long-lasting talents. Four had exceptional drawing skills. One drew and crayoned marvellously accurate species of birds, but lost this interest later. One drew and modelled human figures of great liveliness, but again this gift left him without a trace. Another boy had varied artistic talents in childhood, designing a triangular house, for example, and presenting me on one occasion with a circular slide rule he had made from cardboard, which worked very well (he was then 11 years old). This boy became a successful art student and later pursued an arts-related career, but had given up painting. These three boys had all been of

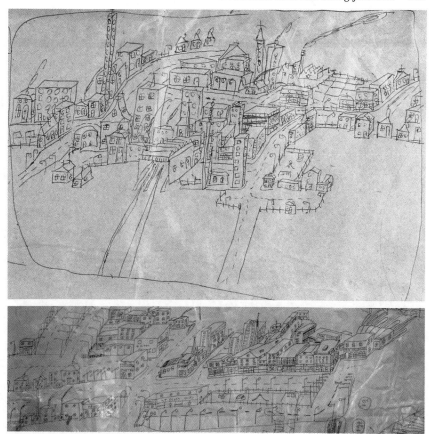

Figure 1 Two of numerous architectural drawings made by a 9-year-old boy with schizoid personality traits

superior intelligence and with normal language development. The fourth (Thomas, described in Chapter Four), of limited abilities and with both delay and deviance of language development, had drawn and crayoned railway trains and architectural themes since middle childhood. He had attended art classes and at follow-up, when in his twenties, he was spending much time copying aeroplanes from magazines with considerable skill and reproducing from memory surprisingly accurate pictures of buildings, mainly in the Georgian style (see Figure 2).

A fifth boy, with a passion for painting and drawing, usually of science-fiction themes, had been of only low average overall abilities and had specific developmental learning difficulties not involving spoken language. His artistic skills were not exceptional. He, too, had gone to art college for a while. He was later unable to sustain a working life, but continued to spend his time at home painting. Another boy, not in the follow-up study, of average abilities and without language impairment, had drawn extraordinarily lively pictures when he was 7 years old, with

Figure 2 Twisborough Old Mill drawn by Thomas in adult life

details that most children never record, such as steam rising from the food his mother served at table (Figure 3(a), (b) and (c)). He continued to draw with some passion, mainly machinery, well into adult life.

Three of the boys had surprising literary skills. One, of high average ability, began to write lively, although very short, thrillers in his late teens and wished he had enough talent to become a writer. Another, of quite limited general ability, presented me with a series of stories in his late teens, which were unexpectedly well written and suggested he had greater powers of concentration and persistence than I had thought. A third, Anthony G, the highly-intelligent boy with a special mathematical gift, had made up stories since the age of 4. In his early twenties he wrote long tales about a macabre invented world, using quite idiosyncratic language. An extract from his writings and his life story as I know it appears in Chapter Four.

The invented world Anthony G created in early childhood, with a special geography, population and language, falls into the category of 'paracosm', also mentioned in Chapter Four and so vividly described by MacKeith and his colleagues (Silvey and MacKeith, 1988; Cohen and MacKeith, 1991). These authors did not record any special literary talents in the 64 adults who gave them details of their childhood experiences. But a number of these people were in childhood described as 'loners', 'solitary', 'less than averagely gregarious', 'odd', 'different'

Figure 3 Pictures by a 7-year-old boy with schizoid personality traits (a) The family at dinner

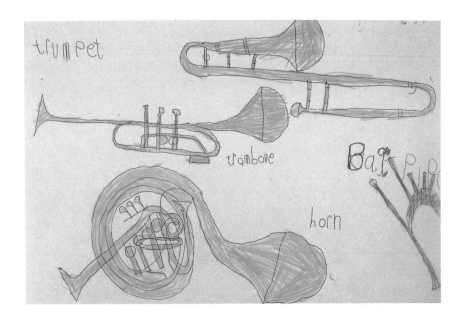

Figure 3 (b) Musical instruments

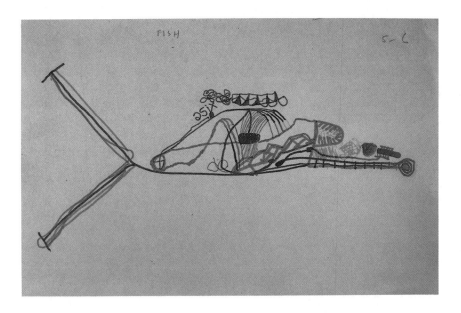

Figure 3 (c) A fish

from other children, slow to learn to read, 'single-minded' or as having a 'one track mind'. It is possible that a small number had schizoid features, but we cannot be sure from the accounts provided.

Two of the schizoid boys in my series were specially gifted at mathematics or electronics. Anthony G (see Chapter Four) was a mathematician who became an astrophysicist. The other boy had made television sets since childhood, his room at home looking like a jungle of electronic equipment. He used his skills in his early working life but not for long.

One boy, Ian, whose story opens this book, had a special musical gift which persisted and determined his career choice.

The gifts of the 32 control boys who were also followed-up were either not 'intellectual' or began to be expressed only in later life: two developed outstanding athletic skills in their late teens and one a talent for art in early adult life, which led him to become an art teacher.

Because we found that most of the children with schizoid disorders had the features of schizotypal personality in adult life, a condition genetically related to schizophrenia, it is important to record not only that gifted people often have gifted relatives, but that an excess of serious mental illness has been found among the relatives of gifted people. Moreover, exceptional giftedness has also been reported among the relatives of schizophrenic patients. This is thought to confer a biological advantage to people with schizotypal traits and perhaps to explain the fact that schizophrenia, often devastating to the individuals affected, persists within a population from one generation to the next (see also Claridge, 1985).

MENTAL ILLNESS AND GIFTEDNESS

Again we can look at this possible relationship in two ways. Are gifted people and their relatives more likely than others to have mental illnesses with a known genetic basis? Is special giftedness found more often among the biological relatives of patients with schizophrenia or major affective illnesses than among relatives of healthy people?

Mental illness among gifted people and their relatives

Adele Juda (1949) examined the physical and mental health of 294 geniuses and their families, admittedly without the scientific rigour that would now be required. Most were entirely healthy and the notion, then current, that intellectual achievement is promoted by psychic distress was clearly incorrect. But there was a much higher incidence of psychosis, both schizophrenia and affective psychosis, among these geniuses and their families than is found in the general population. Schizophrenia tended to occur in the artists; manic-depressive psychosis among the scientists. Eccentrics, or 'schizothymics' as Juda called them, were correspondingly more common among the artists; cyclothymia (or lability of mood) among the scientists.

Karlsson (1968, 1970 and 1974) developed the idea that schizophrenia is in part caused by a gene which is also carried by people with superior intellect or leadership qualities. He surveyed genealogy books, volumes of *Who's Who* and mental hospital records in Iceland. While he was able to discover how many mentally ill patients and their relatives were listed in *Who's Who* (see below), he was less successful in tracing mentally ill people in the families of the apparently very few geniuses which Iceland produces. His data is largely anecdotal (Karlsson, 1974).

More recently, a psychologist and two English scholars recorded the biographies and family histories of eminent writers who became psychotic (Claridge *et al.*, 1990). They chose writers because of the particular abnormalities of language and thinking found in psychotic people. Among the authors they describe and whose diagnosis they make on the basis of the available material, which sometimes included medical records, are Virginia Woolf and Sylvia Plath. What is clear once again is that both schizophrenia and affective psychoses occur in these exceptionally gifted writers. Sadly, the personality features of these authors are not described as fully as their illnesses and no attempts are made to assign personality diagnoses to them.

Yet Post (1994) found psychoses to be very rare among outstandingly creative individuals and to take the form mainly of affective, not schizophrenic, illnesses.

Giftedness associated with mental illness

Heston and Denney (1968) were the first to follow up children who had been permanently separated in infancy from mothers with schizophrenia and compare them with similarly separated children of healthy biological parents. The amount of institutional care was the same for each group, and most children subsequently lived in alternative families. Both groups were interviewed at a mean age of 36. As expected, significantly more children of schizophrenic mothers later developed schizophrenia (5 out of 47 compared with none of 50 controls); their overall IQ was lower than that of the controls; and more were intellectually impaired (4 compared with none). In addition, more of them had been antisocial and more had served prison sentences (11 compared with 2). Among the antisocial offspring of schizophrenic mothers the majority had schizoid disorders (using this term as we have done, in the older sense of 'schizophrenia related'). What is of interest here, however, is that 7 of the 47 children of schizophrenic mothers had significant musical abilities and, among those without any psychosocial impairments, more had special talents and led 'colourful' lives when compared with the control group. They had more creative jobs and more imaginative hobbies, such as painting, music and exploring antique aircraft.

The main basis for believing that giftedness is associated with major mental illnesses comes from Karlsson's (1968 and 1970) pedigree studies of Icelandic families whose complete genealogy could be traced over a number of generations. He studied mental hospital records from which he extracted details about patients' relatives, which he then matched with names appearing in books listing Iceland's eminent people. He found a number of family trees in which both giftedness and schizophrenia occurred in successive generations. The gifts of the individuals he traced consisted of scholarship, political leadership, and financial expertise in association with civic responsibilities. But this excess of eminent individuals was again not confined to the families of schizophrenic patients; it was found also among relatives of patients with manic-depressive psychoses.

We must conclude that special giftedness appears to be associated with both schizophrenia and affective psychoses, but that the evidence does not yet rest on a very firm scientific basis.

A number of eminent scientists, artists and philanthropists, as well as eccentrics and recluses, appear to have personality features congruent with Asperger's original description and with the characteristics of our own schizoid/schizotypal young people. Unfortunately, published accounts rarely give all the information necessary for a confident diagnosis.

CONCLUSIONS

In this chapter I have reviewed the associations of schizoid/schizotypal personality with special giftedness. More schizoid children than expected have special gifts. Their artistic products tend to resemble those of autistic savants; but their musical and mathematical talents are different and a number have literary gifts, which are extremely rare among autistic people.

There is some evidence, not yet firmly based, for an excess of psychotic illnesses among gifted people and their relatives, as well as for an excess of gifted people among the relatives of psychotic patients. The puzzle is that both schizophrenia and affective psychoses appear to be involved. In the case of schizophrenia, which is itself detrimental to creativity, the link with giftedness is likely to be through schizoid/schizotypal traits, which are part of the schizophrenia spectrum – much commoner than the psychosis itself and not at all incompatible with the highest achievements.

10 How can we best understand the condition?

This chapter summarizes what has emerged from the literature and from our own studies in Edinburgh about the nature of schizoid/schizotypal and or Asperger's disorders: how they are best classified diagnostically; how common they are likely to be; their probable genetic basis and relationship to both schizophrenia and childhood autism; and their possible underlying psychological processes.

IN SEARCH OF THE MOST FELICITOUS DIAGNOSTIC LABEL

The widespread current view, as expressed in the most recent edition of the International Classification of Mental and Behavioural Disorders, ICD-10 (WHO, 1992 and 1993; and also in DSM-IV, APA, 1994), is that Asperger's syndrome is among the Pervasive Developmental Disorders of which childhood autism is perhaps the best known. Asperger's syndrome is said to include autistic psychopathy and schizoid disorder of childhood, but is classified separately from schizotypal disorder (in DSM-IV, 'Asperger's disorder' is to be distinguished from schizoid personality disorder). In ICD-10, the term 'Asperger's syndrome' is clearly intended to cover the condition Asperger described (autistic psychopathy of childhood) and the syndrome my colleagues and I have been outlining: schizoid personality of childhood. However, the implication is that schizoid disorder of childhood differs from schizoid personality disorder in adult life, which remains within the personality disorder group of conditions in ICD-10. In this classificatory system personality disorders are described as often beginning in late childhood or adolescence, but as not appropriately diagnosed before the age of 16 or 17. Furthermore, in ICD-10 (although not in the American diagnostic system, DSM-IV) schizotypal disorder is grouped with the schizophrenias, not with the other personality disorders.

Of course, one should be wary of making a diagnosis in childhood that has a poor prognosis, especially when there is uncertainty about the outcome for the individual child and when the outcome is largely determined by the child's ongoing life experiences. This is so especially for the label 'dissocial personality disorder', which includes antisocial or psychopathic personality. Although a high proportion of seriously antisocial children later develop this personality, over half do not, and the risk of loading the dice against a good outcome through the social, cognitive and emotional processes of a self-fulfilling prophesy must be avoided.

It is also important to avoid, if possible, a diagnostic label with ominous overtones. Both the terms schizoid and schizotypal imply a relationship with schizophrenia, a condition which developed very rarely indeed in the later life of the children with whom we are concerned. Yet, as will already be clear, a biological link with this psychotic illness does exist, and it would not be in line with the principles underlying the ICD classifications to give different names to the same conditions merely because they manifest in different age groups.

From the start, it has been my belief that the children I called 'schizoid' were showing in their early years the personality characteristics previously identified as schizoid mainly in adult people. Once I had read Asperger's first paper (1944), I was in no doubt that my children were also exactly like those he had so beautifully described. Like Asperger, I considered the condition to be innate, not due to life experiences, and probably with a genetic cause because so many parents showed similar personality traits. Like Asperger, I found the condition to be very stable over time. Lorna Wing (1981), too, thought Asperger's syndrome *could* be regarded as a form of schizoid personality, but she found this idea unhelpful.

The advent of the new American classificatory systems, DSM-III (APA, 1980) and DSM-IV (APA, 1994), separated the former, more global, diagnostic category of schizoid personality disorder into the subgroups 'schizoid' and 'schizotypal', which, together with 'paranoid' personality, now make up 'cluster A' of the DSM-IV personality disorders. Of these three disorders, schizotypal personality appeared to be most often and most closely related to schizophrenia. But, as indicated in Chapter Two, the evidence for the biological differentiation of these disorders is not very firm and their symptoms often overlap.

In the longest high-risk study, that is a follow-up into middle age of children of mothers with serious schizophrenic illnesses compared with the offspring of normal parents, schizotypal personality was most common among the high-risk subjects and distinguished between the groups most strongly. But paranoid personality also distinguished significantly between the groups, as, to a lesser degree, did schizoid personality, although this disorder was usually found in association with schizotypal personality (Parnas *et al.*, 1993). Among biological relatives of schizophrenic patients too (Kendler *et al.*, 1993), schizotypal personality was the most common personality disorder distinguishing these relatives from those of patients with other psychiatric illnesses and from a psychiatrically healthy control group. But paranoid personality also distinguished the relatives of schizophrenic patients, whereas schizoid personality did not, but was very rare.

Schizotypal personality disorder has been described in children (Nagy and Szatmari, 1986), and children so labelled again closely resemble our group of schizoid children, even to the extent that a very few, although more than expected, developed schizophrenia in later life. Moreover, in adult life the majority of the schizoid children we followed-up, both boys and girls, fulfilled the diagnostic criteria for schizotypal personality disorder.

It would be wrong to call groups of children with a similar clinical picture and a similar outcome by different names. Asperger's group of 'autistic psychopaths', our group of 'schizoid' children and Nagy and Szartmari's children with 'schizo-typal personality disorder' were all, as far as one can tell, clinically similar. They were also quite similar to the small group of children, for whom clinical vignettes were provided, diagnosed as having 'Asperger's syndrome' in a community study in Sweden by Ehlers and Gillberg (1993). These authors used differing but overlapping diagnostic criteria, including those of ICD-10, and criteria derived more directly from those of Lorna Wing (1981, 1992).

Yet the patients Wing diagnosed as having 'Asperger's syndrome', as well as those of her colleague, Digby Tantam (1991), differ in one important way from Asperger's patients and from our own: they were as a group much more seriously handicapped and their outcome in later life was much worse than that both of the children with whom Asperger had kept in touch and of the 'schizoid' children we have systematically followed up.

At the present time, therefore, the term 'Asperger's syndrome', as defined in ICD-10 and as used by Wing, Tantam and also by Frith and her colleagues in their experimental work (1991), seems to imply a condition which may be equivalent to high-functioning autism and which is more serious than that of the children described by both Asperger and ourselves. I have made it clear that within our group of schizoid children some were intellectually gifted and some, even if not of exceptional intelligence, had the characteristic symptoms of schizoid personality only to a mild degree. A minority, usually those of only low average intelligence, were more seriously impaired both in childhood and in adult life and resembled children with Wing's 'Asperger's syndrome'. Only the condition of these more impaired children could realistically be regarded as forming part of an 'autistic continuum'.

While we found continuity of characteristic personality traits in almost all our schizoid children, a number of them did not have these traits in any severe or handicapping form in later life. For this reason, and because their overall outcome was relatively good and their progress over time largely uninfluenced by their life experiences, I do not think they are likely to be harmed by a diagnostic label which suggests a continuity with an adult personality type.

Diagnostic labels, especially in the domains of the developmental disorders of childhood and of the personality disorders, have been altered and regrouped a number of times over the past three decades, and are likely to undergo further transformations. Meanwhile, I suggest the label 'schizoid/Asperger disorder' as being the most appropriate for the full range of children and adults with the characteristic features described in this book, on the understanding that 'schizoid' includes all DSM-IV cluster A personality disorders most particularly, schizotypal disorder.

I suggest further that, despite the very common association with specific developmental disorders, which in our schizoid children, as in all affected children, improved with age, the condition itself should be classified not with the develop-mental but with the personality disorders because, unlike developmental disorders, its characteristics tend to remain stable well into adult life.

THREE SUGGESTED MODIFICATIONS FOR THE CLASSIFICATORY CRITERIA OF SCHIZOID/ASPERGER DISORDERS

The legitimacy of our diagnosis of schizoid/Asperger disorder for the children in our series might be questioned because the ICD-10 criteria for Asperger's syndrome did not fully apply to our groups. Yet all diagnostic classifications are working models and need to be, and indeed are, modified in the light of new findings. In ICD-10 there are four *research diagnostic criteria* (WHO, 1993) for Asperger's syndrome:

1 The absence of clinically-significant general delay in spoken or receptive language or cognitive development, with normal development of adaptive behaviour and curiosity about the environment in the first three years of life, but with delayed motor milestones and clumsiness as a common feature.
2 Qualitative abnormalities of reciprocal social interaction as for autism.
3 Unusually intense, circumscribed interest or restricted, repetitive and stereo-typed patterns of behaviour, interests and activities.
4 The disorder is not attributable to other varieties of pervasive developmental disorder, simple schizophrenia and schizotypal disorder being among those here listed.

The ICD-10 *clinical diagnostic guidelines* are congruent, also exclude schizotypal disorder, but specifically include schizoid disorder of childhood and autistic psychopathy (WHO, 1992).

Although in general, the above criteria 1, 2 and 3 applied in our patients, their features diverged from this definition in two ways. Schizotypal disorder could be diagnosed at follow-up in most of the affected people; and specific developmental language delays were common.

Developmental language delays have previously been described in both schizophrenic and schizotypal children, although never as severe as in early childhood autism (Baltaxe and Simmons, 1992). In our schizoid groups, one girl and one boy had had severe early language delays, which cleared up entirely in both. We saw earlier that some children with developmental dysphasia or semantic and pragmatic language disorders described in the literature (Bishop, 1989; Cantwell *et al.*, 1989; Brook and Bowler, 1993) had the same interpersonal and cognitive difficulties as autistic children or children with Asperger's syndrome. Clearly, the social impairments associated with severe early language delay were also similar to the impairments of our group of children.

Ehlers and Gillberg (1993), in their population survey of Asperger's syndrome, used three sets of slightly different but overlapping diagnostic criteria, including those of ICD-10. However, the exclusion criterion of 'no general delay in language and cognitive development' in the latter would have excluded several of their cases.

I suggest, therefore, that two of the exclusion criteria for the disorder, absence of schizotypal disorder and absence of significant delay in spoken or receptive language, should be omitted from the ICD definition. In addition, because unusual fantasy differentiated significantly between our schizoid and control groups, both in childhood and in adult life, this feature should become one of the positive diagnostic criteria for the condition.

HOW COMMON IS THE DISORDER LIKELY TO BE IN THE GENERAL POPULATION?

A total population study of 7- to 15–16-year-old children, carried out in Gothenburg, gave the prevalence of definite, suspected and possible Asperger's syndrome cases (vignettes for all of which resembled the clinical features of our cases of schizoid/Asperger disorder) as 7.1 per 1,000 children (Ehlers and Gillberg, 1993). To date, this is the only population-prevalence study of this disorder in childhood. It is likely that children with mild and very mild forms of the syndrome, not amounting to a disorder, will have been excluded.

One very crude way of estimating the possible population prevalence in adult life of schizoid/Asperger traits, not necessarily amounting to personality disorder, can be derived from our own research findings. Our young men and women were 26 and a half years old at the time at which a psychiatric records search for schizophrenia was undertaken (see Chapter Seven). Seven cases of schizophrenia were found among 141 subjects then aged over 16 years. The incidence of schizophrenia among this group of people was thus 5 per cent. The estimated population prevalence for schizophrenia by this age is around 0.4 per cent.

By no means all patients with schizophrenia have schizophrenia-related personality traits before their illness. Cutting reviewed the literature on this topic and concluded that about a quarter of schizophrenic patients had had the traits of schizoid personality, in its older wider sense, before the start of their illness (Cutting, 1985). One can then assume that our schizoid/Asperger children who later developed schizophrenia made up 25 per cent of schizophrenic patients of their age in the general population. The 5 per cent (one-twentieth) of our former patients who developed schizophrenia later should thus be equivalent to the 25 per cent of 0.4 per cent, that is, 0.1 per cent, of schizophrenic patients aged 26 and a half years with premorbid schizoid traits. The population prevalence of schizoid/Asperger disorders would thus, very roughly, be 20 times 0.1 per cent, that is 2 per cent of people in the general population. The assumption here is that the risk for later schizophrenia is as great for children and young people with very mild schizoid traits as it is for people with schizoid/Asperger disorder. These theoretical 2 per cent of people would include all those with a personality predisposition to schizophrenia, however mild.

It must be stressed that these calculations are highly speculative, but the resulting prevalence figure is not greatly at variance with Ehler and Gillberg's actual prevalence rate of 0.7 per cent for what must be the more severe forms of this condition, that is, for recognizable cases of Asperger disorder in childhood.

It is worth mentioning, too, that the lifetime prevalence rates of schizotypal personality disorder in the control groups with which biological relatives and offspring of schizophrenic patients have been compared, were 0.4 per cent and 5 per cent respectively (Kendler *et al.*, 1993; Parnas *et al.*, 1993).

And there is a further point. The personality characteristics of schizoid/Asperger disorders can be viewed as either categorical or dimensional. Both possibilities allow for the wide range in severity that our studies revealed: from psychosocial normality to a grossly disabling condition. But the categorical perception of the condition assumes that there is a qualitative cut-off point between people with and without schizoid/Asperger features, compatible with an underlying genetic basis involving only a very few genes. The dimensional view of the condition, in contrast, assumes that it shades into normality, is normally distributed in a population and that its hereditary basis, like that for height and intelligence, is multigenic.

This latter view is held by Claridge (1985), who devised two questionnaires to tap the characteristics of schizotypal and borderline personality. He found that in normal people scores for these questionnaires correlated with some of the psycho-physiological features (sensory-evoked potentials) discovered by other workers to distinguish schizophrenic patients and their biological relatives. Yet, and this was puzzling, such relatives in fact had normal scores on his two questionnaires (Claridge *et al.*, 1983). It is just possible that these questionnaires in fact tap personality features other than those of schizoid/Asperger disorders, because our own schizoid groups at follow-up, both men and women, had absolutely normal scores on Claridge's tests and did not differ at all from the male control group of former child patients who were also tested in adult life.

THE GENETIC BASIS OF SCHIZOID/ASPERGER DISORDER

There have so far been no studies into the genetics of schizoid/Asperger disorders in childhood, perhaps because researchers are still in the process of defining the syndrome and agreeing on its boundaries. The evidence for a genetic basis is at present based entirely on clinical impressions and on descriptions of groups of cases and individual families with affected children. Asperger (1944) found that among the 200 children he had seen over ten years almost all had at least one parent with similar personality traits, and that the fathers were often highly intellectual.

From the case notes of the schizoid/Asperger children I examined systemati-cally, I judged 12 mothers and 7 fathers of 32 boys to have definite schizoid traits (18 mothers and 18 fathers, if mild schizoid traits are included), compared with one mother and no fathers (2 mothers and 3 fathers, if mild traits are included) among the 32 boys in the control group (see Chapter Three). However, among the 33 girls whose case notes were looked at in the same way, I found only one mother and 4 fathers with definite schizoid traits (6 mothers and 10 fathers, if mild traits are included) compared with 2 mothers and 2 fathers (3 mothers and no fathers, if mild traits are included) among the controls. It must be stressed that these were impressionistic assessments only, not backed by systematic interviews or person-ality inventories. Despite this reservation, my findings are congruent with Asperger's and with those of other workers. In Wing's series of 34 cases, for example, 5 of the 16 fathers seen and 2 of 24 mothers were found to have behaviour resembling that of Asperger's syndrome (Wing, 1981). And among Gillberg's 23 cases, about half of the children had one or two parents affected by the same or a similar condition (Gillberg, 1989).

The genetic basis for disorders of the schizophrenia spectrum, which include schizotypal personality disorder (the commonest) but also paranoid and schizoid disorders, but which excludes borderline personality disorder, rests on much firmer ground. Twin and adoption studies as well as controlled long-term follow-up studies of the offspring of schizophrenic mothers have all confirmed the strong genetic relationship of schizophrenia with schizotypal personality, and to a lesser degree also with paranoid and schizoid personality, although the latter is often only found in association with schizotypal disorder (see Chapter Seven). Schizotypal personality disorder also aggregates in families, but, with one exception, most studies have not shown an increase of schizophrenia itself among the biological relatives of people with schizotypal disorders. The reason for this may be that schizotypal personality is a milder and very much commoner condition than schizophrenia and that the biological relatives of schizotypal people will have low rates of schizophrenia, while relatives of the more seriously affected people with schizophrenia will have high rates of both schizophrenia and schizotypy. As a result, much bigger samples are needed to show up an excess of schizophrenia among biological relatives of schizotypal people than to reveal an excess of schizophrenia among relatives of schizophrenic patients (McGuffin and Thapar, 1992).

The genetic link of schizophrenia with schizotypal, and to a lesser extent with paranoid and schizoid personality disorder, is clear. About a quarter of schizophrenic patients have had schizoid or schizotypal personalities before the onset of their illness; but only about 5 per cent of similarly affected youngsters, our schizoid/Asperger children, develop a schizophrenic illness in later life. Among the biological relatives of schizophrenic patients the proportions with schizotypal personality disorder have varied from 5 per cent among all relatives (Kendler *et al.*, 1993) to around 20 per cent for the children of mothers with serious schizophrenia (Parnas *et al.*, 1993).

THE RELATION WITH SCHIZOPHRENIA

Asperger himself believed that the childhood condition he described to be distinct from schizophrenia and that the personality patterns of children who later became schizophrenic are different from those of autistic psychopathy (Asperger, 1961). He found that only one of his 200 children developed this illness in later life (Asperger, 1944). It must be said, however, that his follow-up information was not systematically obtained: we do not know how many of the 200 children he actually saw in later life or at what ages.

Schizophrenia is no longer regarded as a homogeneous condition with the same causes at play in every case. Many schizophrenic patients have been found to have long-standing structural abnormalities of the brain, probably present since before birth. Some of these are thought to be due to environmental causes, such as a viral infection of the mother during pregnancy or trauma to the baby before or during birth. An excess of obstetric complications (O'Callaghan *et al.*, 1992) and of low birth weight (Rifkin *et al.*, 1994) has been reported for schizophrenic patients. It may also be the case that a genetic predisposition increases the vulnerability of the foetus to environmental hazards and to other abnormal genes. Jones and Murray (1991) believe that developmental brain processes have in-built safety margins, so that a serious illness like schizophrenia develops only when several causes operate together; either a number of contributory abnormal genes or abnormal genes together with some organic, environmentally caused, brain injury during foetal life. It must also be stressed again that people who later develop schizophrenia are of lower than expected intelligence (Castle and Murray, 1991), and this was so also in our groups (Wolff, 1992). The question is: is schizoid/Asperger disorder the expression of one of the genetic factors which contribute causally to some cases of schizophrenia?

We saw in Chapter Seven that patients with schizophrenic illnesses have had an excess of schizotypal or schizoid personality disorders before the onset of their illness (Foerster *et al.*, 1991; McCreadie *et al.*, 1994). More recently, childhood information collected in a longitudinal study of a national cohort of children was compared for those few who later developed schizophrenic illnesses and those who did not (Jones *et al.*, 1994). Developmental delays in walking, speech acquisition and educational functioning, as well as solitary play and social anxiety, features quite compatible with the childhood symptoms of our schizoid children, characterized the future schizophrenic patients.

Only about a quarter of schizophrenic patients have had schizoid or schizotypal personality disorders before the onset of their illness. In our follow-up studies we found that around 5 per cent (12 times the expected rate) of schizoid/Asperger children had developed schizophrenia in later life. The risk for the individual affected child is thus very low, but our findings do support the idea that one of the genetic contributors to the causes of a proportion of schizophrenic illnesses is the genetic predisposition to schizoid/Asperger or schizotypal disorder.

Several possible indices or 'markers' for a genetic predisposition to schizophrenia have been identified. Some consist of deviations from normal neurophysiological functions; some of abnormal scores on tests of cognition. Eye-tracking of a moving target is significantly less smooth in schizophrenic patients and in 50 per cent of their first-degree relatives, than in healthy people and has been reported to be abnormal also in patients with schizotypal personality disorder (Muir *et al.*, 1992). Our schizoid boys at follow-up did not differ on this test either from their own controls of other referred children grown-up or from previously tested population controls (Blackwood *et al.*, 1994). Nor did our schizoid patients in adult life differ from controls on a test for attentional abnormalities: P300 latency and amplitude. These are patterns of electrical impulses in the brain evoked by attending to irregular sounds against a background of regularly recurring noises and recorded by electroencephalography (EEG). This test, too, is performed significantly less well by patients with schizophrenia and by a proportion of their biological relatives (Roxborough *et al.*, 1993).

The explanation for the discrepancy in the findings between our former patients and the relatives of schizophrenic patients in these studies may lie in the heterogeneity of schizophrenia: different groups of patients and their relatives may have different predisposing, genetically determined abnormalities. The relatives of schizophrenic patients in some of these studies were not systematically assessed for schizophrenia-related personality disorders, so that we do not know whether those relatives who had abnormal scores on the tests were the same relatives who also had the personality characteristics of schizophrenia spectrum disorders. Moreover, the abnormal electrophysiological responses were found in the relatives of families with more than one schizophrenic patient, and such families will not be representative of all the families of schizophrenics.

In conclusion, while the personality characteristics of our schizoid/Asperger child patients in adult life conformed to those of schizophrenia spectrum disorders, and their risk of later schizophrenia was raised, we do not yet know how similar this group of former patients is in personality characteristics to those relatives of schizophrenic patients who have the neurophysiological deficits associated with schizophrenia.

SCHIZOID/ASPERGER DISORDER AND CHILDHOOD AUTISM

There is no question that the individual features of schizoid personality in childhood resemble those of childhood autism. In both conditions there are qualitative abnormalities of reciprocal social interactions; unusually intense circumscribed interests and repetitive activities; and abnormalities in verbal and non-verbal communication. Moreover, in a few cases of high-functioning autism and of very severe schizoid disorder, it may be difficult to decide which diagnosis is the most appropriate. Among Wing's and Tantam's cases of severe Asperger's syndrome, a high proportion had had the features of childhood autism in the past. But in our own groups of less impaired schizoid children, only a minority had had autistic symptoms in early childhood and never the complete syndrome. What is more, while the features of our children *resembled* those of autism, they were *not the same*. The deficits in social interaction did not markedly affect our children's attachments to their parents, and they usually manifested only on school entry. Peer relationships were the most impaired. Our children's special interest patterns were often sophisticated, quite unlike the repetitive, stereotyped behaviours and utterances of autistic children. And the unusual modes of communication of our former patients were in most cases unlike those of autistic children, that is immediately apparent to everyone but had carefully to be looked for. In addition, our schizoid children were not, like autistic children, deficient in imaginative play capacities. On the contrary, they often engaged in unusual imagination and fantasy.

Yet the concept of an *autistic spectrum* is a valid one. Well-functioning autistic people and severely impaired people with schizoid/Asperger disorder have much in common. But whether this term should be applied to the full range of conditions, from those of severely impaired autistic people to those of perfectly normal, even highly gifted, people with schizoid personality features, is much more problematical. We shall see that the clinical and educational needs of seriously impaired children and adults with these conditions are very different from the needs of those schizoid people, in fact, the majority, who are more mildly affected. For research purposes, too, it seems to me important to differentiate between mildly and severely affected people with schizoid/Asperger disorder, just as it has been rewarding to distinguish between low- and high-functioning autistic people.

Quite apart from the similarities of symptoms in the two conditions, clear genetic links have been established between schizoid/Asperger disorders and childhood autism. A few families have been reported who had both an autistic child and a child with Asperger's autistic psychopathy (van Krevelen, 1963) or in whom both conditions occurred in close relatives (Gillberg, 1991). De Long and Dwyer (1988) found a high incidence of Asperger's syndrome among first and second degree relatives of high-functioning autistic people (68 per cent) compared with autistic people with an IQ less than 70 (6 per cent). These workers also found an increased rate of manic-depressive illness in the first group of families. Piven *et al.* (1990) reported social and cognitive deficits, similar to but milder than those of autistic people, among grown-up siblings of autistic patients.

We ourselves in a blind, controlled study of parents of autistic children and parents of children with other handicaps, found significantly more parents of autistic children to have mild schizoid personality traits and to be more 'intellectual' than the other parents (Wolff *et al.*, 1988; Narayan *et al.*, 1990). As long ago as 1975, Netley *et al.*, admittedly in a non-representative group, found mothers of autistic children more often to have some disorganization of thought processes than mothers of non-autistic children. More recently, Landa *et al.* (1992) found that parents of autistic children more often than parents of controls had atypical social patterns of behaviour, in particular, disinhibited social communication, awkward or inadequate expression of ideas and odd verbal interaction, all features of an abnormal pragmatic language use that resemble some of the symptoms we have defined for schizoid personality. And Piven *et al.* (1994) found parents of autistic children to be more aloof, untactful and unresponsive than parents of children with Down's syndrome. Furthermore, in a controlled population-based study, parents of autistic children were found to have the full picture of Asperger's syndrome more often than parents of normal control children. But the number of parents affected was very small (Gillberg *et al.*, 1992).

Twin studies of autistic children have shown that non-affected identical twins more often than expected have cognitive and social deficits, milder but similar to those of autism itself (Folstein and Rutter, 1988; Bailey *et al.*, 1995).

In a major study of the siblings and other relatives of young people with autism, compared with those of a control group with Down's syndrome, Bolton and his colleagues (1994) again found a considerable excess among the former of what they call 'a lesser variant of autism', in addition to the expected very small excess of childhood autism itself. This 'lesser variant' was present in 12.4–20.4 per cent of the brothers and sisters of autistic people, compared with only between 1.6–3.2 per cent of people with Down's syndrome. It consisted of subtle impairments of social interaction (including lack of friendships and reciprocity, impaired conversation and social disinhibition); of communication (including language delay, articulation disorder, reading retardation and spelling difficulties); together with repetitive stereotyped behaviour (circumscribed interests). While the language problems were usually outgrown, the social difficulties often became more apparent in later in life (see also Rutter, 1992).

The authors clearly think that this 'lesser variant' of autism is quite different from either Asperger's syndrome as defined in ICD-10 (they found just one sibling affected by this in their group), or our schizoid children. Yet, to me, the features listed of this 'lesser variant' of autism seem quite similar to the features of the young people described in this book. Sadly, Bolton and his colleagues give us no illustrative case vignettes and tell us little about the actual life adjustment, difficulties or possible gifts of the affected people they identified. They make the important point that the causes of autism are likely to involve several genes; that not all affected people will have been exposed to the same genetic and other causal influences; and (as a result of their analysis of birth injuries among their groups) that the obstetric abnormalities of autistic children are likely to have been brought about by genetic abnormalities of the foetus itself.

In summary, the evidence is that autism and Asperger's syndrome aggregate in families; that among the biological relatives of autistic children there is an excess of people with mild schizoid features; and also an excess with features (atypical social interactions, communication deficits, and circumscribed interests) similar to but milder than the deficits of autism itself, which some workers have hesitated to label as either 'schizoid' or indicative of Asperger's syndrome.

THE GENETIC IMPLICATIONS OF THE SUGGESTED LINK BETWEEN SCHIZOID/ASPERGER DISORDER AND BOTH AUTISM AND SCHIZOPHRENIA

We have seen that a number of previous studies revealed a genetic association between autism and schizoid/Asperger or allied disorders. Our own work suggests that there is also a link between schizoid/Asperger disorder and schizophrenia. This appears at first sight to go in the face of much evidence that there is no excess of schizophrenia among the biological relatives of autistic people and that autism is not among the psychiatric disorders that characterize relatives of schizophrenic patients.

Yet, in one study of children who developed schizophrenia before puberty, 3 out of 18 had had symptoms of autism in very early childhood (Watkins *et al.*, 1988) and in another 9 out of 35 had developmental abnormalities including isolated symptoms of autism (Russell *et al.*, 1989). Moreover, in a follow-up of 16 high-functioning autistic children, one developed schizophrenia and several had isolated symptoms of this illness or schizotypal personality features in young adult life (Szatmari *et al.*, 1989b). There are other reports of autistic children who later developed schizophrenia (Clarke *et al.*, 1989), although Volkmar and Cohen (1991), in a study of case records of adolescents and adults who had been diagnosed as autistic in early childhood, suggest that the incidence of schizophrenia among autistic people is no greater than that in the population as a whole (see also Werry, 1994).

It seems to me quite possible to reconcile the same genetic factor, manifesting as schizoid/Asperger disorder, as a predisposing cause of both autism and schizophrenia, with the observations that autism and schizophrenia do not segregate in the same families and only very rarely occur in the same patient. We merely have to postulate that for autism as well as for schizophrenia another gene (or genes), different for each condition, is also among the necessary causes. Neither autism nor schizophrenia are likely to be unitary conditions, and for each illness we know that other, non-genetic, causal factors may play a causal part in a proportion of cases. Among these prenatal or birth injury and an IQ below that expected for the individual may feature in schizophrenia, prenatal developmental abnormalities and certain chromosomal and other congenital abnormalities in a minority of autistic children (Bailey, 1993; Bailey *et al.*, 1995).

IS THERE A GENERAL UNDERLYING PSYCHOLOGICAL DEFICIT IN SCHIZOID/ASPERGER DISORDER?

The psychological deficits of autistic people

Two types of psychological deficits have been the focus of recent research into the possible underlying abnormalities of autistic people: an inborn incapacity to recognize and respond to the emotional states of other people; and a failure to develop a 'theory of mind' that is a failure to grasp what goes on in other people's minds, what their likely thoughts and intentions are. Both deficits could account for autistic people's lack of empathy and their difficulties in reciprocal social interactions. Until recently, these two postulated deficits, one a failure of emotional the other of cognitive development, have been discussed as if one had to be the primary deficit, the developmental forerunner of the other. Yet in normal child development, emotional and cognitive advances occur together.

Similar research strategies have been used to explore the two postulated types of psychological deficits (see Hobson, 1986, 1991, 1994; Frith, 1989; Baron-Cohen, 1989). In both sets of studies autistic people were compared on specific tasks with non-autistic people, usually matched for measures of intelligence and/or age. Research into emotional perception and responsiveness, for example, has examined children's capacity to match specific emotions displayed by people on video- or audio-tapes with line drawings of faces expressing a variety of common emotions. Research into 'theory of mind' has used the paradigm of an object seen by the experimental subject and by two doll witnesses to be hidden in one of two containers. Doll number one leaves the room; doll number two then moves the object to the other container; the first doll returns and the question for the experimental subject is: 'Where does doll number one think the object is?'

Most, although not all, autistic children in middle and later childhood, unlike other children over about 4 years of age, believe the first doll thinks the object is hidden where they themselves last saw it, in the second container. They are not able to work out that as doll number one did not see the switch of containers, she would still be looking for the object in its first hiding place. Autistic children tend to attribute their own knowledge to other people, irrespective of the other people's viewpoints and experiences. Frith and her colleagues (Frith *et al.*, 1991) sought to find a single cognitive deficit with its accompanying emotions to explain manifestations of both autism and Asperger's syndrome, which they regard as equivalent to high-functioning autism. The nature of this deficit they believe to be an incapacity to imagine accurately what goes on in other people's minds, associated with an inability to engage in pretend play, or even in playful deceptions. Autistic children cannot lie in a game (Sodian and Frith, 1992), and well-functioning autistic children have difficulties in interpreting non-straightforward actions and stories involving pretence, jokes, lies, irony and figures of speech, in more naturalistic settings (Happé, 1994a). Yet it must be stressed right away that a number of our former patients with schizoid/Asperger disorders had a vivid fantasy life and that some engaged in quite florid pathological lying, in both childhood and adult life, including the assumption of aliases.

Some researchers have recognized that in such a severe and complex disorder as autism there is unlikely to be a single primary deficit. And recently, the apparent theory of mind deficits have been attributed to autistic children's difficulties with information-processing, that is comprehension, rather than to their conceptual impairment (Tager-Flusberg and Sullivan, 1994). Francesca Happé, too, in a recent research review (1994b), is clear that not all cases of autism and Asperger's syndrome show theory of mind deficits. She invokes a second psychological disability, described by Frith: a lack of 'central coherence', that is, a deficit in the capacity, present in normal children after about 10 years of age, to perceive whole configurations rather than part aspects of objects and other experiences. Sally Ozonoff and her colleagues (1991a) take a yet wider view. They found that only a few high functioning autistic people (who included some with Asperger's syndrome) had the kind of theory of mind deficits described above for seriously impaired autistic children, that is, the inability to attribute correct beliefs to others. More widespread were 'second-order theory of mind' deficits, in which the experimental subjects failed to predict what one person thought another person was thinking. In addition, Ozonoff and her colleagues explored 'executive functions', that is, problem-solving abilities (including planning, maintenance of problem-solving set, impulse control, inhibition of irrelevant responses, organized search for solutions and flexibility of thought and action) in high-functioning autistic people. They found selective deficits in this domain, especially in planning efficiency, maintaining required set, and ability to shift set and behaviour appropriately. Their autistic subjects also performed less well than controls on tests of emotional perception and long-term verbal memory.

Are there differences in psychological functioning between people with autism and schizoid/Asperger disorders?

The 23 'high-functioning autistic' subjects in the study just described, ranging in age from 8 to 20 years, in fact included 13 autistic people and 10 with Asperger's syndrome. The researchers found that, not surprisingly, the Asperger group were of higher verbal intelligence and had fewer autistic symptoms than the autism group. An analysis of the similarities and differences in psychological functioning of these two groups showed that both were impaired on emotional perception and on executive function tests, but only the autistic, not the Asperger, group had theory of mind and verbal memory deficits (Ozonoff *et al.*, 1991b).

The emotional deficits of both autistic and schizoid/Asperger children had already been demonstrated some years ago in one of our own studies (Wolff and Barlow, 1978; see also Chapter One), in which we found schizoid children to be even more impaired both in the attribution of emotions and psychological motives to people in photographs and in the use of psychological constructs in describing other people.

In another recent study, the psychological functioning of adults with Asperger's syndrome (of low average mean intelligence) was compared with that of schizophrenic patients and healthy people (Bowler, 1992). Here, too, the Asperger group were found to be as capable as normal controls in solving second order theory of mind problems. Furthermore, in a study of siblings of high-functioning autistic children compared with brothers and sisters of children with hyperactivity, language disorders and other learning difficulties, it was found that the siblings of autistic children were more impaired on tests of executive functioning but not on theory of mind tests ((Ozonoff *et al.*, 1993).

In summary, these findings (together with the symptomatic analyses of first degree relatives of autistic people cited above) suggest, *first*, that there are indeed psychological differences between high-functioning autistic people and people with Asperger's syndrome. In particular, people with Asperger's syndrome do not show the deficits in theory of mind which are so typical even of high-functioning autistic people. On the other hand, they do have the same deficits both in emotional perception and expression, and in executive functioning, that is in planning, working memory and cognitive flexibility, that characterize the autistic group. *Second*, an excess of the biological, non-autistic, relatives of autistic subjects probably have mild clinical features of schizoid/Asperger disorders as well as some of the psychological deficits demonstrated in subjects with Asperger's syndrome.

11 How can we intervene most helpfully?

We shall now move on to consider the treatment needs of those affected children and their parents whose difficulties are serious enough for them to be referred for professional help in childhood, and of that minority of affected adults who become psychiatric patients or who are identified within the criminal justice system.

Here we have as yet no research evidence to guide us. Instead, this chapter is largely based on my clinical experience with schizoid children and adults, and with their parents.

ASPERGER'S ADVOCACY OF AN INDIVIDUALIZED, PROTECTIVE THERAPEUTIC APPROACH

In his original paper, Hans Asperger (1944, 1991) stressed the children's need for individual teaching and for what he called 'affectionate pedagogy'. Because schizoid children of normal intelligence tend to do so well in later life, at least occupationally, while in childhood they are sometimes impossibly difficult to look after at home and school, he advocated a protective environment throughout their childhood. The children's special gifts need to be encouraged and preserved. All educational transactions should be done, he suggests, with the teacher's emotions 'turned off'. Teachers must guard against feeling angry and they should not try to evoke affection from the child. But they need to be in control, even if at times this seems to take the form of allowing the child to 'get away with things', and their instructions to the child should be given in a cool, objective, non-intrusive manner. Often it is better not to direct requests to the child personally, but rather to indicate 'one always has to do such and such' or 'this is how these things are done'. Endless arguments and discussions should be avoided and the children's characteristic negativism circumvented, with humour if this seems appropriate. Affected children may have to be taught in words, and repeatedly, the sort of social rules other children pick up intuitively. But with patience and practice the children's social adaptation and educational progress will improve. An essential ingredient of treatment is for the child's teacher or therapist to convey understanding, genuine affection and real concern for the child.

Asperger himself (see Frith, 1991b) admitted the children to his special in-patient unit in the University Paediatric Clinic of Vienna. This was run on

Heilpaedagogik lines, that is, on a combination of humanistic, educational and therapeutic principles, by a close-knit team of doctors, nurses and teachers. He always recognized the biological basis of the children's difficulties and was respectful of their parents who, he thought, often understood their children exceptionally well.

We shall now consider the clinical and educational interventions best suited to schizoid children within the current framework for health care and educational services.

THE IMPORTANCE OF MAKING THE DIAGNOSIS IN CHILDHOOD

Children with schizoid/Asperger features, who often stand out as 'loners', are rare. Family doctors and teachers in ordinary classes may not be familiar with the syndrome. For this reason, a referral to a child psychiatric clinic or a child psychological department is essential when the affected child has serious social or educational difficulties.

The first step is to make the correct diagnosis. The second helpful intervention is to convey to the affected children and their parents that the children's difficulties stem from their particular personality make-up. If similar traits can be identified in other members of the family this can be reassuring, because it underlines the familial basis of the difficulties. In addition, because affected parents have usually managed their lives quite well, hope for improvement of the child's adjustment in later life can be given a more realistic basis. It is important to make it clear from the outset that the parents are in no way responsible for the difficulties. It also needs to be stressed that the child's basic personality features are not likely to change, and that the family and the school will have to accommodate to his or her special needs. On the other hand, treatment of associated symptoms (such as specific educational delays, aggressive outbursts, stealing, depression or, much more rarely, hyperkinesis and attention difficulties, or delusional experiences) can be very effective.

EFFECTIVE THERAPEUTIC INTERVENTIONS

Support for child and parents

The primary role of the psychiatrist or psychologist who is called upon to help is to provide very long term, even if infrequent, support for the family as they negotiate the child's path through the school years and into further education and a working life.

The main ingredient of an emotionally supportive approach is to understand accurately how the child views himself and his world, to reflect that understanding back to him and, preferably in the child's presence, to convey it to the parents.

The place of psychotherapy

I take the view that interpretative psychotherapy for schizoid children is hazardous, carrying the risk of disintegration of an already fragile personality organization and of the development of psychotic symptoms. Likewise, I would avoid family approaches to diagnosis and treatment that seek to uncover underlying family motives or to change the structure of family relationships. As I indicated at the start of this book, before I recognized the special personality features of schizoid children, I tried to help by using the principles of dynamic psychotherapy with the children, as well as family interventions. Not only were my efforts fruitless; the children's symptoms were sometimes made worse and the morale of the family undermined.

Instead, I found it helpful to put all my efforts into validating the child's often very accurate perceptions of himself and his difficulties, and to working out in detail, together with him and his parents, how these can best be overcome. The aim always was to improve the self-esteem of child and parents, to acknowledge their real difficulties and to preserve hope for the future. Because no rapid changes in the child's functioning can be expected, it is important that the therapist is available in a supportive, non-intrusive way for child and family on a very long-term basis.

Advocacy for the child within the educational system

The second essential therapeutic task is to act as the child's advocate in relation to his or her school and to the school psychological services. As a basis for this a full psychometric assessment is essential. Everyone needs to know how intellectually gifted or, more rarely, how intellectually impaired the child is. Because specific developmental disorders affecting language, reading, spelling, coordination and occasionally mathematics, are so commonly associated, a full assessment of possible educational delays which require remedial teaching is also necessary.

Affected children often find the hurly burly of playtime in a crowded playground intolerable, and may need to be allowed to seek refuge in a quiet place instead. Often they are also helped by being excused from taking part in team games.

If there is severe educational retardation in relation to age and intelligence, or if the child's school behaviour is intolerable because of aggressive outbursts, eccentricities provoking to other children, or other behavioural symptoms such as oppositional behaviour, stealing or school refusal, special schooling may have to be arranged. Day special schooling is preferable, because at least the child can get home and away from group pressures for major parts of his or her life. If no suitable special day school is available, boarding school is an option, but only if the school regime is flexible and the staff fully understand the child's difficulties, the reasons for these, and how best he or she can be helped to tolerate life within a school community.

One mother whose son is now grown up, looked back on her years of clinic attendances and of her son's school difficulties as follows:

He remembers coming and he remembers you as being sympathetic to him. He could never understand why there was a problem. He didn't really enjoy being at school and trying to learn what other people wanted him to learn nor the way they tried to do it. He always wanted to go his own way. He hasn't basically changed. It's just easier when you're not at school. He has a detached appreciation of things. [He's] . . . a non-conformist and if you press [him] too far, you'll disturb him.

He now knows that it [coming to the clinic] helped me to be confident that my analysis of him was reasonably correct. . . . The school always said 'You're encouraging him. We can't go on making exceptions of him.'

This mother was keen to see me at the time of the follow-up,

because [there are] a lot of individuals with basically nothing wrong with them but at the extreme of personality . . . and I wanted to be sure that people knew about such children and could support them and their parents in the face of school advice to insist on conformity, which really makes matters worse.

After a number of changes of school, much unhappiness and considerable behavioural disturbance, the educational psychologists finally arranged for this boy to move to a very small private day school, where he was allowed to follow his own interests. The mother recalled: 'He was fine at . . . school, although educationally it was poor. And he's been much better since he left school.'

While attending ordinary school this boy was unhappy, stole and had occasional aggressive outbursts. These symptoms all disappeared when he entered his small school, where all children had an individually tailored programme.

He left school at 16 with qualifications below those expected for a boy of his intelligence. He took an arduous menial job for a while, but later followed his bent in work which involved design, construction and photography.

The treatment of associated symptoms

We saw in Chapters Three and Six that co-morbidity, that is the presence of other associated child psychiatric disorders, is very common. Often this takes the form of *reactive disorders (such as aggression, stealing, depression, school refusal)* attributable to anxiety-inducing life experiences. Most often these consist of excessive social pressures, such as for conformity at school, which the child is unable to meet. Once the school setting is changed to fit in with what he or she can manage, such symptoms are likely to disappear.

In a sizeable group of schizoid/Asperger children there are, as we saw earlier, *constitutionally based specific developmental delays affecting educational progress.* Remedial teaching is then necessary.

Much more rarely, schizoid children are also *hyperkinetic*, that is overactive and with *attention difficulties*, again on a constitutional basis. Such symptoms often respond to medication, but, again, special small class teaching may also have to be arranged.

We saw in Chapter Seven that very occasionally, in response to anxiety-inducing experiences, schizoid children develop *transient delusional symptoms*. These respond well to small doses of anti-psychotic medication, usually needed only as a temporary measure during such a crisis.

HELPFUL QUALITIES OF THE SCHOOL ENVIRONMENT

Teachers can be most helpful to affected children by recognizing their personality characteristics as innate, unlikely to change and not caused by adverse child-rearing. This at once achieves mutual understanding between teachers and parents, essential for the parents' peace of mind and for the child's progress. It will help teachers to know that they, too, are not at fault if the child's social and learning difficulties fail to respond to their efforts, and that they need not strive to encourage sociability in a solitary child nor press for social conformity at all costs.

The most helpful approach is to understand and tolerate the child's social isolation and eccentricities, not to pressure him to engage in large group activities, to build his curriculum around his own particular interests, and gradually to encourage him to have a go at tasks that go beyond these. Young schizoid children, for example, with special interests in dinosaurs or the firmament, can write essays on their favourite topics, solve mathematical problems relating to these topics, and slowly learn to shift their interests to other aspects of natural history or the planets. If the child has special interests or gifts these can be used to interest and help the other children in the class, thus improving the affected child's status among his or her peers.

Schizoid children may need a legitimate place of retreat within the school building if the social pressures, such as those of the playground, become overwhelming. Only if the schizoid child's behaviour is intolerably antisocial, if, for example, he attacks his classmates aggressively or destroys his own or other children's work, are active interventions within the school setting called for. These should take the form of *a behavioural approach*, whereby appropriate behaviour is systematically followed by praise or even tangible rewards, and antisocial conduct is, as far as possible, ignored (see David, case number 3, in Chapter Eight).

When such efforts fail or if there is a behavioural or emotional crisis with, for example, persistent aggressive outburst, persistent running away, school refusal, depression or suicidal threats, psychiatric hospital admission may have to be arranged.

CHILD PSYCHIATRIC IN-PATIENT TREATMENT

Such an admission at once relieves the pressures on the child, the parents and the teachers, providing respite for them all. In the setting of the very small school classes usual in such units, schizoid children can begin to make a better adaptation to school life. Behavioural treatment methods, social skills training, as well as non-interpretative and non-intrusive psychotherapy can also be helpful in improving peer relationships, especially if the affected child comes to realize the effect he or she is having on others and what social techniques can be used to improve these interactions.

One boy in later life told me: 'I was a troublemaker in the classroom. I was always made out as a troublemaker at school. . . . Schools can't be expected to cater for people like myself, not these days.' He described how much better a small school class suited him because there he found more people like himself. He feels he has few problems nowadays because he has acquired 'the ability to be objective about things. I have no problem seeing two sides of an argument. . . . It's been a conscious process of development.' He attributed a misunderstanding with a landlady shortly after starting work to 'me being thick-skinned, not noticing subtle signs'.

Social skills training in a protective environment is geared to help people become more aware of such 'subtle signs' and to try out novel ways of interacting with others.

One other undoubted benefit of a psychiatric admission is that it allows for a full assessment of the child's social and educational strengths and weaknesses. Sometimes intensive remedial teaching can lead to significant educational gains in a child with specific learning difficulties. In addition, and on the basis of a full assessment, the respite period can be used to find the most appropriate school setting for the child, and to foster helpful relationships between him and his family and his future teachers.

But it must be said that in-patient treatment is not always successful and that, even if it is, the effects may be short lived. For this reason, if the children cannot adapt to ordinary school life, education in a small class is often necessary to reduce the pressures and, if there are no suitable special day schools or small classes available to cater for their social and educational needs, boarding school can be a helpful option.

THE PLACE OF SPECIAL RESIDENTIAL SCHOOLS IN THE EDUCATION AND TREATMENT OF SCHIZOID CHILDREN

The case of David in Chapter Eight illustrates that residential schools with a primarily psychotherapeutic ethos, in which children are encouraged to examine their feelings, motivations and interpersonal relationships in a group setting, can be unsettling for schizoid children, increasing rather than ameliorating their disturbed behaviour. This is so especially if such groups are run in a confrontational style, with high levels of emotional arousal.

Residential homes and schools to which delinquent children may be sent on court orders often insist on a great deal of social conformity, even if they are not run on very strict disciplinarian lines. These residential settings tend to be noisy and there are often quite high levels of fighting and bullying. Team games are an important part of the programme, the children tend to live and work in rather large groups, and opportunities for privacy are rare. Such settings are also not suitable for schizoid children, although, as we saw in Chapters Three and Six, a number of our subjects were so delinquent that they had to appear in court (or its equivalent

Scottish setting: a Children's Hearing) and some were indeed sent to special schools for child offenders.

The most helpful residential settings for very disturbed schizoid children for whom no suitable day school is available are either small boarding schools for children with emotional and behavioural disorders, or schools run by the Rudolf Steiner movement. Both tend to be situated in spacious grounds, where children can safely be on their own at times, away from larger groups. Both cater for a mix of children: some with educational difficulties, some with emotional disorders and withdrawn behaviour, some with antisocial conduct disorders. The levels of violence in such schools tend to be low, dormitories and school classes are small, and there is usually an excellent staff/pupil ratio. Remedial education is part of the school's programme, and in most such schools the staff aim to provide intimate and concerned care and to keep in close touch with parents. Children are helped to improve their social interactions and behaviour by means of non-intrusive, firm but gentle control, and behavioural methods are often used. Another advantage of such schools is that they offer opportunities for a wide range of activities and interests, increasing for example, children's artistic, musical and athletic skills.

Residential schools for children with emotional and behavioural disorders tend to cater for children of all ability levels. Residential Rudolf Steiner schools often specialize in the education of less able children, although they have provided excellent care and schooling for a number of my own schizoid children who were of normal intelligence, but had very severe behavioural disturbances (see, for example, Sandra in Chapters Six and Seven).

Such boarding schools can be a haven for very disturbed children. Within such an accommodating environment their behaviour disorders often melt away, their school attainments improve, their self-esteem increases, they develop their interests, form friendly relationships with at least a few adults and children, and there is continuity of such relationships, because the children tend to stay in these schools for some years.

THE TREATMENT NEEDS OF MORE SERIOUSLY AFFECTED SCHIZOID CHILDREN

A few schizoid children, as we have seen, are more seriously impaired, with all the features Wing (1981) and Tantam (1991) described for 'Asperger's syndrome', and with an early developmental course resembling that of high-functioning autistic children although without all the symptoms required for this diagnosis. These children, while of normal intelligence, tend to be less able intellectually than the schizoid children who, when the school years are at an end, can find their own way in life and cope quite well. The treatment needs of these more seriously impaired children are similar to those of high-functioning autistic children. It is hopeful that in recent years psychiatrists and psychologists have become more alert to the diagnosis of Asperger's syndrome and, in these more seriously affected children, the diagnosis is less likely to be missed than in the milder cases which formed the majority of my own series and which are likely to be more common.

The medical and educational care of the more seriously affected children is improving, and parent organizations concerned with autistic children (such as the National Autistic Society and the Scottish Society for Autistic Children in the United Kingdom) are taking an increasing interest in Asperger's syndrome and its diagnosis and are beginning to offer support services for parents and for affected children. But the fact remains that the needs of these more seriously affected people for a protective environment, both during the school years and in adult life, are still often not recognized and adequate long-term facilities are scarce.

The following case history illustrates that such children and young people often cope well when they find themselves in a congenial, protective environment but can become seriously disturbed when exposed to the pressures of ordinary school life, of work and of work training.

EDWARD was 5 and a half on referral to the child psychiatric clinic. He had apparently been a lively, active and communicative child until the start of school, which coincided with the birth of his brother.

He now became very quiet, made only a single friend at school, a girl, and was most reluctant to go to school. He became restless, withdrawn and also aggressive, screaming and even attacking his mother physically if she opposed him in any way. He developed food fads, eating only tomato soup for a while, and he took his food to eat in the kitchen, away from the rest of the family. He could not stand television.

Edward's birth had been normal. His expressive language development had been retarded although by the age of 3 he had a good vocabulary. He tended to talk to himself, there was occasional echoing of what other people said, he had some persistent slurring of speech and sometimes got muddled up in what he was attempting to say. There was some gaze avoidance. He had been enuretic until he was 4 years old. His intelligence was average, but his writing was clumsy and his arithmetic poor.

The mother, quiet but sociable, likened Edward's personality as he grew up to that of her father who had been 'shell-shocked' in the war. Edward's father was an exceptionally quiet man. He had an older, unmarried, sister, a brilliant but eccentric and tactless woman, who had dominated his childhood.

Edward was fortunate in being placed in a small special primary day school for children with emotional, behavioural and educational difficulties. There he was given remedial help with his work, the small, quiet class suited his personality, and his lack of sociability was not perceived as a handicap. He attended school regularly and his aggressive outbursts and food fads ceased. He also developed an active interest in astronomy, which he pursued into his adult life.

Because he had done so well, he transferred to an ordinary secondary school when the time came, and at first he coped quite well. But at the age of 14 he again became unhappy and his symptoms of school refusal returned: he 'feigned illness' and missed much schooling. In the absence of a suitable alternative, he stayed on at the secondary school, obtaining only meagre school qualifications. At a time of full employment, his social withdrawal and lack of confidence made it impossible for him to face applying for a job. His attendance at an employment aptitude centre was a failure. Because of his extreme sensitivity and what he called his 'shyness', he could not face the crowd there.

Edward was almost 17 at the time of our first follow-up. He had become extremely withdrawn, spending most of his time at home watching television. He had a single friend, whom he rarely saw. He hardly ever went out, and could not even face going to the shops. He was rigid about domestic routines. But he enjoyed reading and writing stories about outer space and astronomy. During the follow-up interview he was very quiet, made little eye contact and had a tongue-clicking tic. The main worry he and his parents expressed was his continuing unemployment. He had made no move to get a job and, if there had been no expectation that he should go to work, he would have been content with his barren life at home.

At a second psychiatric referral shortly after this interview, the psychiatrist found him solitary, lacking in initiative and with some word-finding difficulties. Daily occupational therapy was now arranged for him at the hospital. His work was found to be accurate, methodical, reliable but slow, and he lacked initiative. But his social isolation was seen as his major handicap.

At the time of our second follow-up study, Edward was 25. Apart from a brief secretarial course, which he completed, he had remained at home until he was 20. Fortunately, arrangements were then made by the psychiatric clinic for him to attend a day centre run on Rudolf Steiner principles. This catered for young people with a variety of mild and moderate physical, intellectual and social impairments. The quiet, friendly and respectful atmosphere there suited him well, and his 'shyness' at first presented no problems. He worked well in the bakery and the woodwork shop. Because of his interest in astronomy, visits to the local observatory were arranged for him. However, this work training centre was established to help school-leavers and young people make the transition from school into working life, and attempts were made to encourage Edward to get a job once more, after almost six years without working. He lasted only five weeks in a gardening centre.

At his follow-up interview, Edward was keen to help with our study. There was still some lack of eye contact. He also revealed obsessional symptoms, checking repeatedly, for example, that he had not accidentally hurt his brother some time ago with a snowball. His interest in astronomy had persisted. He used binoculars to watch the stars and had been accused of 'peeping' by a neighbour. He mentioned that for some years he had had occasional paranoid thoughts that other people made disparaging remarks about him. It was unclear whether he had actually heard voices. But his main complaint about himself was that he was too 'shy' and too self-critical. He still had occasional angry outbursts against his mother.

At 28 he was again seen at a psychiatric clinic, because the staff at the Rudolf Steiner centre he was still attending had become worried about his increasing isolation, his occasional rages against other trainees and staff, and about a recent preoccupation with the 'evils' of sex. The possibility of a slow onset of a schizo-phrenic illness was considered, as indeed it had been at the time of our own second follow-up, but Edward's symptoms did not meet the full criteria for this diagnosis.

Clearly, what this young man needed was a setting like the Rudolf Steiner day centre, but one that catered not just for young people in the years after leaving school, but offered a life long haven in which he could do constructive work and make relationships to the limits of his capacities, without the constant anxieties caused by the expectation that he should make a move and find an alternative way of life. His parents would also have welcomed the prospect that, when they were no longer able to provide a home for him, a residential setting in the community where his personality characteristics were understood and accepted would be available for him. These are precisely the facilities that the national organizations for autistic people are providing for those affected by that condition. Severely affected people with Asperger's syndrome need similar provisions, but geared to their usually rather higher intellectual capacities.

SCHIZOID PEOPLE WHO DEVELOP PSYCHIATRIC DISORDERS IN ADULT LIFE

We saw in Chapter Seven that schizoid people in adult life often seek help for a variety of psychological difficulties. These are frequently related to the particular emotional stresses imposed by their personality characteristics in response to what may appear to be quite trivial life events. Depressive illnesses, anxiety states, obsessional symptoms, panic attacks as well as suicidal impulses can lead to a psychiatric referral. When difficulties in intimate relationships, for example with partners or children, become intolerable, help may be sought from marriage counsellors, social workers, or child psychologists and psychiatrists. Treatment approaches then differ in one major respect from the treatment of similar disorders in non-schizoid people: the underlying personality difficulties need to be recognized and taken into account.

This means that the psychiatric and other professional helpers must be familiar with the condition and must get to know the patient really well, understand his or her mode of thinking and reacting, respect the need for privacy and for a non-intrusive therapeutic approach, and have realistic treatment aims. These should not be to remodel the patient's personality but, at least initially, to help him or her, with appropriate medication and/or psychological and social interventions, to regain the level of functioning that existed before the onset of the symptoms which led to the referral. And couples will need help to understand each other's personality make-up.

Current psychiatric hospital arrangements are sometimes not ideal for schizoid people with superadded psychiatric disorders. A supportive therapeutic relationship may need to be on offer for very many years so that if the symptoms return the affected person and his or her family know to whom to turn. To be seen as out-patients by a succession of junior doctors in training, each liable to be puzzled anew by such patients' apparent oddities of reactions, is not helpful. Nor is it appropriate for the psychiatric professionals to expect that intermittent brief interventions will necessarily bear fruit. In some schizoid people, superadded psychiatric symptoms or serious difficulties with family relationships persist for years. This should not lead to therapeutic nihilism and the giving up of hope.

When, as rarely occurs, schizophrenia supervenes on a schizoid personality development, continuity of care from familiar professionals is essential. Jonathan and Kevin, described in Chapter Seven, were greatly helped by consistent psychiatric care over many years from the same consultant team, familiar with the details of their personality functioning and with their family and social circumstances. Some patients, such as Fay, also described in Chapter Seven, are less fortunate and engender such despair in a changing psychiatric staff that, unless their underlying personality disorder is recognized, their lack of response to the treatments offered can lead to their abandonment.

WHEN DELINQUENCY SUPERVENES

We have seen that both in childhood and in later life some schizoid people develop antisocial behaviour. Often, especially in childhood, this can be directly attributed to finding themselves in an environment with which they cannot cope, such as the hurly burly of an ordinary big classroom, or an over-intrusive residential setting. Several of the former patients described in this book have illustrated that in a different environment, more suited to their individual personality needs, these same previously antisocial young people can cope quite well.

But there is a very small minority of schizoid youngsters who are aggressive and very delinquent, whatever their environment, and who cannot escape the ordinary judicial processes and their consequences. Some schizoid youngsters have in fact managed life in what used to be approved schools, while others developed ever more disturbed behaviour: stealing, fire raising, repeated running away. One of my former patients, a very aggressive boy, whose most stable years were spent in a small residential school for emotionally and behaviourally disturbed children, deteriorated when his time at that school came to an end, became increasingly more violent and finally killed himself in a Young Offenders Institution.

I would argue that when delinquent children or adolescents appear in court any suggestion that they may be schizoid needs to be followed up. They may be loners; their offences are strange or incomprehensible; they do not come from a particularly deprived or delinquent family or social background; there is a history of school failure or of a child psychiatric attendance. A psychiatric opinion should then be sought and, if the diagnosis is confirmed, efforts should be made to find a suitable day or residential setting for them. At the present time, the Rudolf Steiner communities may be suitable. The National Autistic Societies, too, may soon open facilities for the care and education of more seriously disturbed people with Asperger's syndrome.

THE PROBLEM OF DANGEROUSNESS

Even more problematical are the isolated cases where a schizoid person has committed a serious violent or sexual offence or arson. Three issues then arise: can the offender be held responsible for the crime? is he or she likely to act dangerously in the future? and, if custody is needed for the protection of society, should prison or a secure hospital be the preferred option?

I take the view that, because their defective empathy and judgement and their idiosyncratic and obsessional preoccupations with weaponry or poisons in some cases, are constitutionally determined, schizoid offenders cannot be held fully responsible for their criminal actions, which often appear motiveless to outsiders. Although not deluded or hallucinating, a number of such offenders have totally irrational views of their criminal behaviour. Yet psychiatrists have for some time been reluctant to support a 'diminished responsibility' plea for offenders who were not actively psychotic when the crime took place.

The prediction of dangerousness is even more problematical (Floud and Young, 1981; Bottoms and Brownswood, 1982; Chiswick, 1993). Too much caution in the release from custody of potentially dangerous people, inevitably means that many who would never commit another violent crime are confined unnecessarily and their human rights infringed. Yet an error in the opposite direction, when a prisoner or patient in a secure hospital is released and reoffends with violence, understandably provokes public outrage and recrimination.

The case of Jo in Chapter Eight illustrates some of the difficulties. Psychiatrists considered him neither psychiatrically ill nor to have diminished responsibility on account of a mental disorder. The appeal judge, correctly according to present-day judicial practice, imposed a medium-term prison sentence. I knew this young man only as a child and am in no position to predict his future behaviour, yet the sentence made me uneasy. I felt concern both for a possible future victim and for Jo himself. It would not help him at all to be allowed to offend again with the inevitable consequence of an even longer prison sentence. I believe that people like Jo need, if at all possible, to be protected from their own criminal impulses.

There is also the question whether offenders with serious personality disorders who have committed a violent crime should be in prison or in a secure hospital. Here, too, practices have changed (see Dell and Smith, 1983; Dell, 1984). In recent years, and more particularly since the Mental Health Act of 1983 with its new treatability clause, compulsory admissions to psychiatric hospitals as well as admissions to secure hospitals, have been increasingly limited to patients with treatable conditions. Offenders with psychotic illnesses are clearly 'mentally ill' and qualify for such an admission as an alternative to imprisonment. The same is no longer true for people with personality disorders, even if these are severe and have a constitutional basis.

Yet, from the point of view of the schizoid offender and possibly even of society at large, prison is not the preferred option. The close proximity with other prisoners under current conditions in Britain's prisons, the noise levels and the rough prison culture are likely to be particularly disorganizing for schizoid people. A patient I encountered in the Scottish secure hospital some years ago brought this home to me.

This young woman, with all the features of schizoid personality, who had not had a psychiatric referral in childhood, was a repeated fire raiser. Following her last arson attack, she was given a substantial prison sentence. She continued to light fires in her cell and now also began to engage in repeated and serious suicidal actions. These led to her transfer to the secure hospital, although she herself had been opposed to this move. When I saw her in the hospital, her suicidal behaviour had ceased, as had her attempts at fire raising. She had been given a room to herself, she liked the nursing staff, avoided other patients, and was writing poetry. But she still felt that she should not be in a psychiatric hospital.

The dilemmas are many. Questions of punishment and 'just deserts' have not been touched on here, nor the rights of offenders who are not 'mentally ill' or treatable to avoid a hospital confinement. Schizoid offenders themselves may not wish to be sent to a secure hospital in place of prison, because this can mean a longer period of confinement. Psychiatrists in turn are reluctant to admit such personality disordered offenders to a psychiatric hospital because they are unlikely to respond to treatment.

The fact that the hospital environment and ethos may suit schizoid delinquents better than prison, and reduce their disturbed behaviour, may not weigh with either the offender or the psychiatrist. Yet the deterrent effect of a prison sentence is likely to be even smaller for schizoid than for other offenders. It is encouraging that a firm plea has now been made for giving people with severe personality disorders just as much access to in-patient services as patients with other diseases. Prison management should not be the mainstay for the treatment of such patients (Gunn, 1992; DoH and HO, 1994). A recent Appeal Court judgement held that the treatability clause is fulfilled so long as hospital treatment is likely to prevent further deterioration (Brahams, 1994).

THE CHILDHOOD PROGNOSIS FOR LATER LIFE

We have seen that, very rarely, schizoid children develop schizophrenia in later life. A very few may become seriously delinquent and, under the present criminal justice arrangements, can often then not be protected from the penal consequences of their actions.

From the perspective of childhood, however, the future of schizoid children looks quite different. Most of them do *not* develop serious psychiatric illnesses and most do *not* become delinquent. In any case, one can never predict such eventualities for an individual child, and even if one could, it is as yet quite unclear what steps could possibly be taken to avoid such an outcome. For these reasons, I think it is important to base the professional prognosis on what is known to happen in the majority of affected children. If things turn out less well than expected, there will be time enough to face that later; anticipatory fear and anxiety are not helpful.

In any case, both Asperger's clinical experiences (1944, 1991) and my own indicate that the future outlook for schizoid children is on the whole good. Once they leave school and escape the inevitable educational pressures for conformity, their social adjustment tends to improve. They can now find their own educational, work and social environment. We saw from our own follow-up studies that, while schizoid personality characteristics tend to persist into adult life and their intimate relationships may remain constricted, the children's later educational and work achievements were comparable to those of other clinic attenders of similar intellectual abilities; as many schizoid young people as their matched controls were able to lead independent lives; many of them were married; and a few displayed exceptional gifts.

One important point needs emphasis. Because of the profound social and educational difficulties which a number of affected children experience during their school lives, their final school qualifications may be considerably lower than their intellectual level would lead one to expect. Some of these able schizoid children will need, and indeed seek out, opportunities for further education in later life when they have outgrown their developmental educational delays and when they can seek education in the more impersonal and less socially intrusive environment of college or university.

JACK had been in constant trouble at his boarding school, although he himself rather liked the life there because he could get away into the country and he enjoyed sports.

He was of superior intelligence but left-handed, less good at visuo-spatial than at verbal tasks and his writing and spelling were poor. He had amassed enormous collections of various found objects. The boarding school was unable to tolerate his awkward, non-conformist behaviour, and after some years his parents had to take him away. Fortunately, his local education authority then arranged for him to attend a very small day school able to cater for his individual needs. His social adjustment improved greatly. He left school at 16 with a number of 'O' levels and took up farm work.

At his follow-up interview Jack said: 'In school I was capable and competent but lazy. It all went into my head but I never committed my thoughts to paper. I used to rather go out swimming than do homework. . . . I was more rebellious. . . . It was a lifelong regret that I didn't conform enough. I failed myself and them [the parents].' Later in the interview he said: 'I'm very happy on my own. I consider myself to be a loner. My idea of fun is not to go to pubs. My wife would prefer to go out more'.

Some years after this interview I heard that, after ten years as a shepherd, Jack had decided to go to university. He obtained his entrance qualifications at a college and is now doing well in the third year of his degree course. He is happy and has made friends.

12 Schizoid personality, pretence and genius: two extraordinary people

In this last chapter I shall describe two exceptional people in the public domain who may have been schizoid. One was a remarkably gifted young woman who gained notoriety because of her flamboyant but false belief that she was of royal descent, and who ended her life as a chronic schizophrenic patient in a psychiatric hospital. The other was a genius: the philosopher Ludwig Wittgenstein.

THE STORY OF OPAL WHITELEY

I first read about this extraordinary woman in an obituary by the television producer, Ian Taylor (Taylor, 1992). A bright-eyed girl looks out from the page and by her side is a photograph of crayoned capital letters, angular and crowded without intervening spaces. At once I was reminded of the artistic products of some autistic and schizoid children I have known. The obituary recounts the childhood of Opal Whiteley, a woodcutter's daughter raised in the lumber camps of Oregon, and her sudden rise to fame in 1920, at the age of 22, at first in America and then in England, as the author of a diary she claimed to have written when she was 6 and 7 years old. The circumstances of this publication were strange. She had approached a Boston publisher, Ellery Sedgwick, with a book she had written on natural history. Sedgwick, not impressed by the work, was intrigued by its author and by her descriptions of her childhood. When he asked whether she had recorded this, she told him of a diary she had written which a jealous sister had torn into a thousand pieces. These she still had, in shoe boxes now stored in Los Angeles. The boxes were sent for and, under the supervision of Sedgwick's mother-in-law, Mrs Walter C. Cabot, who offered her lodgings, Opal Whiteley pieced together the many scraps, mainly of brown wrapping paper and grocery bags, for publication. In the introduction to this work she explained that she was not the child of Mr and Mrs Whiteley, but had been substituted for a child this family had lost. She was really the daughter of Henri d'Orleans, a descendant of Louis Philippe the last king of France, and her true name was Princesse Françoise d'Orleans.

The diary

The diary created a sensation as 'the most complete picture of a child's inner life that can be imagined', according to the *Times Literary Supplement* (Bradburne, 1962); 'Every true lover of children will read it spellbound' (*Daily Telegraph*, quoted by Bradburne, 1962). Opal Whiteley acquired patrons from among the nobility of England and was subsequently entertained as HRH Mlle Françoise de Bourbon-Orleans by the Maharana of Udaipur. She died at the age of 95 in a mental hospital, where she had been for over forty years with a diagnosis of schizophrenia.

Ian Taylor has been most helpful in talking to me and enabling me to see one of the two books that have been written about this remarkable woman. He also put me in touch with a psychiatrist who had looked after her: Dr Philip Evans. The account that now follows is based on this information as well as on Opal Whiteley's writings.

The diary (Whiteley, 1920) starts with an introduction by Viscount Grey of Fallodon, then special ambassador to the League of Nations. He had heard about the diary from Sedgwick, who was an acquaintance. Intrigued, he asked to meet the author. He was totally charmed by her and by the naivety of a child's observations which he found in her writings. He was especially impressed by her 'interest in all natural objects, which is as spontaneous and simple as it is vivid and intense'. He later brought her to England, introduced her to London society and supported her financially until his death in 1933 (Bede, 1954).

Sedgwick's preface to the diary summarizes Opal Whiteley's biography as she told it to him. She was born twenty-one years previously in a place unknown and her royal parents had died before she was 5 years old. She knew only that they loved her. They left her two notebooks, which had been used to educate her and which contained their photographs and scraps of scientific and artistic information in both French and English. These notebooks were taken from her when she was 12. After her parents' death (she refers to them as 'angel parents') she was given by a nurse to an Oregon lumber man's wife who had recently lost her first child. It was after this child, Opal, that our author was named.

The diary itself, initially subtitled 'The Journal of an Understanding Heart', describes her life within her family whom she saw as persecutory. But it mainly records her observations and fantasies about the natural world about her: its animals, vegetation and geological features. She invented names for the animals who were her main friends and companions. Much evidence is recorded in the two books subsequently written about her (Bede, 1954; Bradburne, 1962) that Opal Whiteley was indeed a solitary child preoccupied with her fantasies about animals and trees and knowledgeable in this field far beyond her years; that she amassed vast collections of botanical and geological specimens; and that she intrigued other children with her specialized knowledge of nature.

Yet the diary does not read like the product even of an exceptionally intelligent 7 or 8 year old. It was written in large, spiky printed letters, jumbled up yet regularly aligned, quite unlike the sloping script young children tend to produce on unlined paper. Also, an intelligent child like Opal would have used joined-up writing. Moreover, the grammar has repetitive errors of a kind not made by children. In fact, young children's grammar tends to be very good, while it is their spelling that is defective. In addition, the sophisticated names and concepts which abound in

Figure 4   Opal Whiteley's diary manuscript
Source: Elbert Bede, *Fabulous Opal Whiteley: From Oregon Logging Camp to Princess in India*,
1954, Binsfords & Mort, Oregon.

the diary are quite unlike those children use and, in later years, a number of acrostics have been discovered in the text, spelling out the author's self-declared royal heritage and various aspects of French geography. In the diary she lists ninety different pets, from small rodents to huge fir trees, all with classical names of people long dead, and she describes cathedral services she held for them.

She writes, for example:

> To-day the folks are gone away from the house we do live in. They are gone a little way away, to the ranch-house where the grandpa does live. I sit on our steps and I do print. I like it – this house we do live in being at the edge of the near woods. So many little people do live in the near woods. I do have conversations with them. I found the near woods first day I did go explores.

and:

> By the woodshed is a brook. It goes singing on. Its joy song does sing in my heart. . . . Under the steps lives a toad. He and I . . . we are friends. I have named him. I call him Lucian Horace Ovid Virgil...
>
> And I hear Peter Paul Rubens squealing in the pig-pen. Now I go. We go on explores...
>
> I don't think I'll print more to-night. . . . This is a very wonderful world to live in...
>
> And I do want to talk with William Shakespeare . . . with Elizabeth Barrett Browning in the pasture, and with Peter Paul Rubens and Aphrodite – in the pig-pens...
>
> That baby calf I have named Mathilde Plantagenet. I have named her so for Mathilde that was daughter of Roi Henri I and Mathilde that was daughter of Sainte Marguerite that was Reine d'Ecosse. Mathilde Plantagenet is her name because the name of the man Mathilde did marry, it was Geoffroi Plantagenet.

She reports 'The Mamma' spanking her for wringing out clothes all over the kitchen floor, and writes: 'After I did have many sore feels. . . . I did so try hard to be helps.'

At the end she provides an alphabetical list of the characters in her diary, beginning:

> Adamnan of Iona, a sheep
> Agamemnon Menelaus Dindon, a pet turkey . . .
> Alan of Bretagne, a fir tree . . .
> Alcuin, a sheep . . .
> Aristotle, a pet bat who died of eating too many mosquitoes . . . .

The diary reveals much knowledge of French and Roman Catholic ritual, although the evidence is that she learnt French only after her arrival in Los Angeles when she was about 19 years old.

The apparent enigma

The accounts of Opal Whiteley's life by Bede (1954) and Bradburne (1962) struggle with two apparent problems: whether the diary is genuinely that of a child or whether it is a fake written later in its author's life; and whether Opal Whiteley was really a French princess or an impostor. The idea that she may genuinely but falsely have believed in her royal heritage, and that she may have been only half aware of her fraudulent activities is not considered. This is in contrast to the recent book about Princess Caraboo (Wells, 1994), an uneducated, eccentric but charming country girl with a remarkable memory, who adopted many aliases and briefly lived the life of an exotic princess. It is also in marked contrast to the account by Richard Holmes (1993) of the brilliant, eccentric, but very attractive eighteenth-century poet, Richard Savage. He may or may not have had a schizoid personality. He was often solitary and also, in Samuel Johnson's terms, 'morally incapable of friendship in its true sense' (Homes, 1993, p. 192). But he did have a large circle of friends, as well as numerous sexual relationships. He, too, falsely claimed noble descent and enchanted but gravely exploited his friends and patrons, among the former the young Samuel Johnson, who wrote his biography. Holmes attributes Savage's activities to firmly held false beliefs rather than to deliberate fraud, and it is in this spirit that I think Opal Whiteley's life, too, needs to be appraised.

Opal Whiteley's life before publication of the diary

In 1915, Elbert Bede, the editor of a local Oregon newspaper, heard that a girl from a logging camp, then aged 17, had been elected State President of a youth organization: the Junior Christian Endeavor. He interviewed her and found her very young looking but self-assured, with an 'innocent' personality. She told him of her plans to tell the children of Oregon about God using animals and flowers as illustrative material. She had been a member of the youth organization for four years and had become an outstanding chairman of its committee. Bede describes her as 'vibrant, fluttery, whimsical . . . informed strangely beyond her years, deeply earnest and seriously religious'.

Bede had in fact had a previous encounter with her, when he heard her give a 45-minute talk at the age of only 13, without notes and illustrated with biological and geological specimens, each correctly labelled in both Latin and English.

Subsequently, a school teacher recalled her as 'dreamy, studious . . . very religious' and 'an unusual child and the most intellectual in the school', with a great interest in whatever she was doing. She was said to have had a photographic memory and in church could recite whole pages from the Bible. She was known to have imaginary conversations with birds and animals, she had enormous enthusiasm for botany, and had classified and mounted 'literally hundreds of specimens'. She used queer names for the animals she played with. Other children loved the stories she told them and were much helped by nature studies with her. Her grandmother recalled that even at 6 years of age she had talked like a grown-up.

While always able to attract people, Opal had few if any intimate relationships and none which endured. Bede found that throughout her life she made no deep or lasting relationships, and the associates she did have were often cast aside and apparently forgotten. These included her so called 'foster parents' and also Ellery

OUT OF DOORS

Do you want to know more of the life of the woods and fields?
Would you like to find joy in the everyday things around you?
Hear this Nature Lecture by Miss Opal Whiteley.

Topic _____

Date_____ Time_____

Place _____

Admission 10 Cents

Figure 5 Opal used this picture on a poster publicizing a nature lecture which she gave
while state president of the Junior Christian Endeavor. One of these posters was
discovered thirty-three years later among her effects left at the University of Oregon
Source: Elbert Bede, *Fabulous Opal Whiteley: From Oregon Logging Camp to Princess in India*,
1954, Binsfords & Mort, Oregon.

Sedgwick, the editor who had launched her on the literary scene and introduced her to her chief patron, Viscount Grey of Fallodon. She had great charm but had never had an 'affair of the heart', although in her writings she records her longing for children, including twins.

Her career as president of the Junior Christian Endeavor foundered when she had to address large audiences and temporarily lost both her voice and her hearing. She then decided to write nature books, but thought she needed to know more. She went to Eugene, Oregon, to find work and start a correspondence course in science prior to entering the university there. In the event, the university professors set aside all the entrance rules, offered her a scholarship and admitted her without any preliminary qualifications, declaring that her self-education was far superior to any course she might have taken. They believed she was quite outstanding and would become 'one of the greatest minds Oregon has ever produced'.

Opal embarked on a number of university courses, but took part in no other campus activities and spent her time in the library, the museum and her room, reading and researching far beyond what her courses required. She had amassed 16,000 specimens of flora, butterflies, bugs and rocks, and planned to establish a city museum. She dressed oddly and had many photographs taken of herself in a variety of poses. Her plans to augment her income through work collapsed, as did her aim to join a 'Bible university'. While working very hard for hours at a time, she completed few of her assignments. She left Eugene after 18 months, ostensibly as a temporary measure in order to earn money to produce the nature book on which she was working. In fact, she never returned.

With 100 dollars borrowed from a friend, Opal set off for Los Angeles and arrived penniless; acquaintances took her in. She gave up her original plans and tried to get into Hollywood instead. She sent photographs of herself to a number of famous people, including Douglas Fairbanks, whose reply was preserved. She was socially tactless towards the family who had given her lodgings and towards their friends, and she approached and visited a number of eminent people in Los Angeles, whose names and biographical details she had found in *Who's Who*. Her charm induced many people to help her, but her tactlessness (e. g. calling an elderly gentleman she hardly knew by his first name) ended some of these relationships.

While in Los Angeles Opal ran well-paid outdoor classes for children. One family she lived with is known to have had a library containing French reference books and books about Roman Catholic ritual. During this time, Opal worked 12 to 16 hours a day, often in the city library, at a manuscript no one was allowed to see. This was *The Fairyland Around Us*. Finding no publisher, she herself paid for a small edition of the work to be published. She persuaded a number of eminent educators and scientists to write forewords, and the book included a photograph of herself, barefoot and playing the violin. She sent the book to numerous internationally famous people who wrote admiring comments in a publicity leaflet. These people included the Queens of Belgium and Spain, Lord Curzon and Teddy Roosevelt, two days before his death. It was this book which she took to Sedgwick, the famous Boston publisher in 1919, and it was he who then encouraged her instead to piece together and publish her diary.

Her family and childhood environment

Her childhood environment, according to Bede, offered freedom and tolerance and accepted her as 'a child of eccentric and entertaining genius'. Despite her critical references to 'the mamma' and 'the pappa' in her diary, friends at university recalled her speaking with much affection of both the Whiteley parents, especially her mother.

The publication of her diary had an immense impact and was 'the greatest news story ever' in Oregon itself. Among contemporary local newspaper comments it is stated that, although Opal had lived among the people about her, she had never been one of them but always in a world apart, a world of make-believe. Her disavowed family, the Whiteleys, who absolutely denied the fostering story, had been much respected in their community. Mrs Whiteley had died of cancer three years previously, and was thus spared the pain the diary caused other members of the family. Opal could not bear to witness her mother's decline and left for Eugene at just this time (personal communication from Dr Philip Evans). Shortly before the diary's publication, the family had received a series of anonymous, typed letters supporting Opal's foster parentage and promising silver in lieu of non-payment for her foster care. A parcel of silverware then duly arrived.

All we know about the Whiteley family from Bede (1954) is that Mrs Whiteley was an educated woman and that Mr Whiteley, who was intelligent and indulgent, gave Opal a special room for her specimens and sent her money while she was at university. Dr Evans (personal communication) described the father, a lumberjack, as 'distant and aloof', and the mother, a post-mistress, as 'artistic' and 'a woman of learning' who read poetry and fairy tales to her children. I am not clear about the basis for these descriptions. According to Bede (1954), there had been an aunt, also very imaginative, who developed a mental illness in later life.

Opal Whiteley's life after the diary's publication

Bede (1954) records that after the diary's appearance in book form (it had previously been serialized in a magazine, the *Atlantic Monthly*), Opal developed a persecution complex, believing that Mr Whiteley had withheld information about her early life, that the *Atlantic* had made a deliberate printing error, and had arranged for her to be followed and watched. She broke with the *Atlantic*, forfeiting substantial royalties, and also with her lawyer, and finally left Boston for a Catholic community in Oxford.

Elizabeth Sutton, who wrote children's books under the name of E. S. Bradburne, made a radio broadcast in 1958 about two child diarists, one of whom was Opal. She was then approached by a woman who was convinced that Opal Whiteley was 'the little person we knew in Hampstead as "the little princess"'. At that time, probably in the 1940s, she had been found in a Catholic chapel, hungry but speaking with a cultured voice, by an acquaintance of this woman, who thereupon arranged for her to come for supper once a week. Opal Whiteley told her she was a Princess of the House of Orleans, but the parish priest thought she was an American, deluded about her origins. She spent her meagre income on French history books from Sotheby's and her tiny Hampstead flat was stacked from floor to ceiling with books and magazines (Bradburne, 1962).

Bradburne fills in some of the details (Ian Taylor has many more) of the intervening years. In the 1920s, with financial help from the Duchess of Chartres who accepted Opal's self-declared heritage, and with a special passport arranged for her by Lord Grey of Fallodon (Bede, 1954) usually reserved for exiled royalty, Opal went to India, ostensibly to research her royal father's journeys of exploration in that part of the world. *The Times* (Society Page, 1924) reported : 'Miss Opal Whiteley, granddaughter of the Maharana of Udaipur, has left London for India' (Bradburne, 1962). In India an Oregon woman who had known her in youth was astonished to see Opal Whiteley driving in an open carriage in a ceremonial procession to proclaim her as a Hindu princess.

In 1929–30 a series of articles appeared in *The Queen* entitled 'A sun-king in the city of the sun-rise' by Princess Françoise Marie de Bourbon-Orleans, describing her life at the palace of the Maharana of Udaipur, the legends surrounding this family, its religious festivals and cultural traditions and its architecture. The articles are lavishly illustrated with photographs taken by the author (de Bourbon-Orleans, 1929, 1930). The series was 'to be continued', but ends abruptly. The content is moderately arresting and there is nothing odd about the style of writing, although there are occasional flights into poetic expression, such as: 'Seen from this distance the royal palace rises like some legendary citadel which you would never expect to find real'.

In 1936, the *Evening Standard* reported that a niece of the pretender to the French throne had applied for British naturalization. Bradburne reports that many members of the British nobility accepted her story; that the French Royal family considered her to be an impostor; and that most people who knew her found her touching, and felt unable to dismiss her as a fraud, and extended great kindness to her, believing that 'she may not know the truth of her own story herself . . . the whole thing may be some extraordinary delusion' (Lord Huntington, quoted by Bradburne, 1962).

At the time of the coronation of Edward VIII, a friend, the daughter of the Earl of Acton, took Opal to the country for her own safety. The fear was that she might create a public scene because of the delusion she then had of having been secretly betrothed to the Prince of Wales as a child (Ian Taylor, personal communication).

Opal's last published article (de Bourbon-Orleans, 1940), again in *The Queen*, called 'The greatest hoax in history', curiously, concerns the massive deception practised by the debauched Potemkin on Catherine the Great. Opal Whiteley begins her account with great aplomb: 'Catherine the Great, Empress of Russia, never lost her capacity to fall in love. But even those later, bizarre amours which scandalized Europe were really nothing but variations on the theme of her indestructible attachment to one man: Gregory Potemkin.' She was clearly still a gifted writer.

Dr Evans (personal communication) believes Opal Whiteley lived for a time in France and in Italy, but that from the 1940s she was in London as a ward of the city, receiving an allowance she mainly spent on books. She could be seen in

Figure 6 Opal, at about 18, ready to take a nature study class
Source: Elbert Bede, *Fabulous Opal Whiteley: From Oregon Logging Camp to Princess in India,*
1954, Binsfords & Mort, Oregon.

Hampstead, pushing a pram full of books, shouting abuse at children in the streets. It seems that she became increasingly dirty and unable to care for herself and that neighbours thought she was mad. She was admitted to a psychiatric hospital under certificate in 1946, at the age of 48, with a diagnosis of 'classical chronic, paranoid schizophrenia' (Evans, personal communication). Her belief in her royal descent was seen as a chronic delusion.

Elizabeth Bradburne visited Opal Whiteley in hospital some time after 1958 and the psychiatrist introduced her as 'the Princess'. Bradburne (1962) describes her as looking rather like Queen Victoria, small, rotund, around 60 years old, with grey hair and very large soft brown eyes. They spoke for an hour and Opal Whiteley revealed a prodigious memory for the details of every crowned head in Europe.

Bede's book (1954) contains many photographs of Opal from childhood to adult life. She greatly resembles her younger sister, Pearl. In every picture she looks touching, sensitive, and immensely appealing, especially in one, used to advertise a nature lecture while she was president of the Junior Christian Endeavor, in which she is seen holding a butterfly in each hand and with more butterflies in her hair and on one shoulder.

This unique and sad story of a formidably intelligent but solitary child, with a number of exclusive special interests (in natural history, religion and the French nobility) and an extraordinarily vivid fantasy life, amounting to fantastic beliefs, illustrates both the association of schizoid personality with exceptional giftedness and the rare phenomenon of a gradual progression from a schizoid/schizotypal personality disorder to a chronic psychotic state. The great German phenomenologist, Karl Jaspers (quoted by Roberts, 1992), assigned delusional systems to the domain of creativity. Delusional fantasies are thought to be a form of wish-fulfilment and to persist so stubbornly through fear of the pain that would result from re-entry into the real, diminished world (Roberts, 1992).

Opal Whiteley exerted enormous appeal on all who knew her, despite her social disinhibitions and occasional tactlessless. Even the photographs of her in the books about her life are extraordinarily affecting. What is also striking is that, although her gifts were prodigious and she worked hard and with immense persistence, few of her endeavours were successfully concluded.

GENIUS AND SCHIZOID PERSONALITY: THE PHILOSOPHER LUDWIG WITTGENSTEIN

An example of a universally recognized genius who was also schizoid is the great twentieth-century philosopher, Ludwig Wittgenstein. His abnormal personality can in no way be regarded as the most important aspect of his productive life, nor as the explanation of his genius. His extraordinary gifts extended at various times of his life beyond philosophy to engineering, aeronautics, sculpture, architecture, medical research and music (he played the clarinet and could whistle whole concertos) (Malcolm, 1984). His literary style, especially in German, is a model of beauty, clarity and simplicity; and he himself knew that one of his great gifts was to find the similes and metaphors that perfectly expressed his thoughts. As a small boy he constructed a sewing machine which aroused much admiration and he retained a life-long fascination for machinery.

The account which follows cannot do justice to a strange life and a marvellous intelligence. It is based on Wittgenstein's *Secret Diaries 1914–1916* (1991); on David Pinsent's diary and a series of letters to and from Wittgenstein (von Wright, 1990); on Fania Pascal's memoir (1979); on A. J. Ayer's brief biography, which precedes his discussion of Wittgenstein's work (1985); on Norman Malcolm's memoir (1984); on a biographical sketch by G. H. von Wright (1982); on McGuinness' biography of his early years (1988); but especially on the splendidly sensitive account of Wittgenstein's life and work by Ray Monk (1991).

An outline of his life

Wittgenstein was born in 1889, the youngest of a very wealthy and cultured Austrian family. Both parents were musically gifted and Brahms was a family friend (Malcolm, 1984). The father, an engineer described as of great intelligence, willpower and dominance, was a leading figure in the iron and steel industry. Sadly, there are no detailed accounts of his personality, except that he had been a rebellious son who tried to leave home at the age of 11 and at 17 was expelled from school for writing an essay denying the immortality of the soul (Monk, 1991, p. 6). There were four brothers and three sisters. One brother, who lost an arm in the First World War, nevertheless pursued a career as an eminent concert pianist. Three brothers committed suicide in young adult life. Little seems to be known about their lives and personalities (Ayer, 1985). It is unclear whether there really was a nephew, Paul, who had a severe manic-depressive illness or whether he was purely a novelist's creation (Bernhard, 1982).

Wittgenstein did not speak till he was 4 years old and he had a spelling problem, traces of which remained throughout his life. He was educated at home up to 14, then at school until 17. He did poorly at school, which he greatly disliked, and was thought to have practical rather than intellectual gifts. For this reason he transferred to a technical college in Berlin to study engineering. Here he was befriended by a professor and his wife, who corresponded with him and were clearly very fond of him for over thirty years. The wife was for some time very hurt by his apparent disregard for their affection (Wittgenstein, 1991). He then went to Manchester as a research student in engineering and also undertook experiments in kite flying. His aeronautics research is said to have led to the construction of a jet-reaction propeller aircraft (Malcolm, 1984).

There Wittgenstein came across the work of Bertrand Russell and that of the Austrian philosopher, Frege, and in 1912 he went to Trinity college, Cambridge, as a research student in Philosophy. Here he made one of his few close friendships, with a brilliant undergraduate two years younger than himself, David Pinsent (Pinsent, 1990), who studied first mathematics and then law and was killed in a flying accident during the First World War. They shared an interest in music, and Pinsent was one of the few people at that time to understand Wittgenstein's

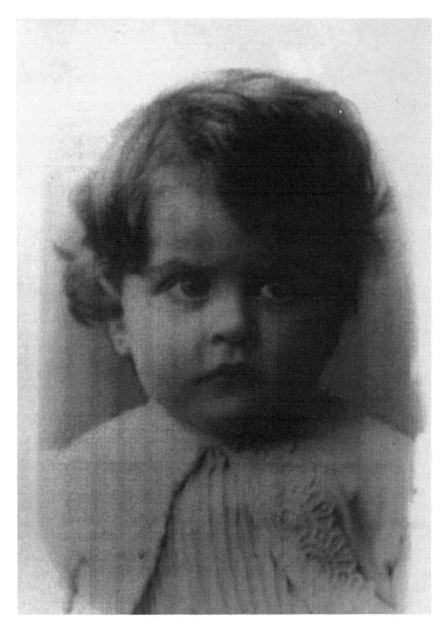

Figure 7   The infant Ludwig Wittgenstein
Source: Ray Monk, *Ludwig Wittgenstein: the Duty of Genius*, 1990, Jonathan Cape, London.
Reprinted with permission of The Free Press, a division of Simon & Schuster Inc.

philosophical ideas in the way he intended. Although Pinsent was unaware of this, Wittgenstein was in love with him (Monk, 1991).

During his early Cambridge years, Wittgenstein lived extravagantly, paying for joint holidays with Pinsent to Iceland and Norway. He was also generous, making regular anonymous gifts to a number of scholars and artists. He did not appreciate his election to the elite society, the Cambridge Apostles, just as later as a Fellow he rarely dined in college. In 1913, he went to Norway to live as a recluse in a seaside hut he had built for himself in order to work better. He learnt Norwegian.

At the outbreak of the First World War he volunteered for the Austrian army. He was asked to train as an officer, fought on the Eastern front and won a number of medals for bravery. Finally, he was taken prisoner of war in Italy. He worked on his philosophy throughout the war, and at the end of the war he sent the manuscript for his *Tractatus Logico-Philosophicus*, which he had carried in his rucksack, to Russell who arranged for its publication. During the war he also kept a diary, partly in code. He read Tolstoy and the Gospels and, while never a believer, became a religious person.

After his father's death, Wittgenstein inherited a great fortune, but gave it all away, not to the poor, whom he thought it might corrupt, but to his family who, being so rich already, would not be harmed (Ayer, 1985). Henceforth, he lived most frugally, deckchairs being among the sparse furnishings in his Cambridge rooms in later years.

In 1918, thinking that he had said all there was to be said about philosophy, Wittgenstein took up teacher training and then taught for six years in rural elementary schools in lower Austria. His solicitous sisters tried to help by sending food parcels to him, but he returned them all unopened. The villagers thought he was 'strange' and took him for an eccentric aristocrat. They could not understand why such a man should live among the poor when he showed so little sympathy for their way of life (Monk, 1991, p. 194). He found the local inn too noisy and slept in the school kitchen.

There was constant friction with the children's parents and his fellow teachers. He gave extra tuition to the intelligent children whom he wished to enter for higher school education and, while some of the children appreciated this, Wittgenstein was oblivious of their parents' need to have them help on the farms and of the financial implications of his plans for such poor children. He also boxed the children's ears and pulled their hair when they failed to grasp algebra, and the girls especially resented this. Finally, after hitting a rather dull and delicate boy on the head, he panicked when the boy collapsed. The family brought a court case against Wittgenstein, which he won because, to his own later shame and regret, he lied about the extent of his physical punishments. He then resigned from his post (Monk, 1991). In the same year (1926) he published a German dictionary which he had compiled with the active help of the children, for use in rural Austrian elementary schools.

Years later, to the consternation of some of the families, he returned to the district to apologize in person to the children for his harshness to them in former times.

For a while Wittgenstein worked as a gardener's assistant in a monastery. He then returned to his family in Vienna and, together with an architect friend, designed and supervised the building of a house for his sister. This large, stark building in the Bauhaus style, uncarpeted and with bare electric light bulbs, but with meticulously designed and fashioned doors, windows and radiators, suited his sister admirably, and is now part of the Bulgarian embassy. During this time in Vienna he took part in regular meetings with other philosophers. He also fell in love with a woman, Marguerite Respinger, much younger than himself and not intellectual, of whose head he made a sculpture. His relationship with her lasted for some years, during which she did not at all perceive that he intended to marry her. When she did, however, she ended the relationship. Wittgenstein had had a platonic, childless marriage in mind.

With Maynard Keynes' help, he returned to Cambridge in 1929. Keynes wrote to his wife: 'Well, God has arrived. I met him on the 5.15 train.' Keynes wondered how he would cope and vowed he would not let Wittgenstein talk to him 'for more than two to three hours a day' (Monk, 1991, p. 255). Wittgenstein was awarded a PhD and a Fellowship at Trinity College.

A brilliant mathematics student, Francis Skinner, half his age, now fell in love with him and they had a sexual relationship, which troubled Wittgenstein, who at that time thought sex was incompatible with love. Wittgenstein advised this gifted young man to abandon academic life and become a factory mechanic, advice quite similar to that he had given other promising students to disastrous effect. Skinner died in his early twenties and his mother never forgave Wittgenstein for his influence on her son. Wittgenstein himself was full of remorse for not sufficiently returning Skinner's love.

At this time Wittgenstein prepared 'a confession' for his family and closest friends, consisting of what others thought of as quite trivial matters, such as not revealing that he had once had sex with a woman, and that he was not *one-* but *three*-quarters Jewish. He embarrassed some of his friends by loudly reciting his sins while sitting with them in a Lyon's cafe.

In 1935, he again went to Norway, where he worked on his second major philosophical treatise for two years before returning to Cambridge. With Keynes' help he obtained a lectureship and also became a British citizen. In 1939 he was elected to the Cambridge chair of Philosophy. He now made a close, non-sexual friendship with a post-graduate American student, Norman Malcolm, whose kindness and warmth supported Wittgenstein, especially during his last years.

During the Second World War, he worked as a medical orderly in Guy's hospital and then as a researcher in a clinical laboratory in Newcastle. No one there knew he was a university professor (Ayer, 1985). At Guy's one of his jobs was to deliver medicines from the pharmacy to the wards. This he would do, but he also advised the patients not to take them.

After the war he returned to Cambridge. He now had a second love affair with a very much younger man, a medical student, this time without the ambivalence of such relationships in the past. He gained what was for him a new insight: 'It is

Figure 8 The house Wittgenstein designed for his sister
Source: Photograph by Sean Hudson.

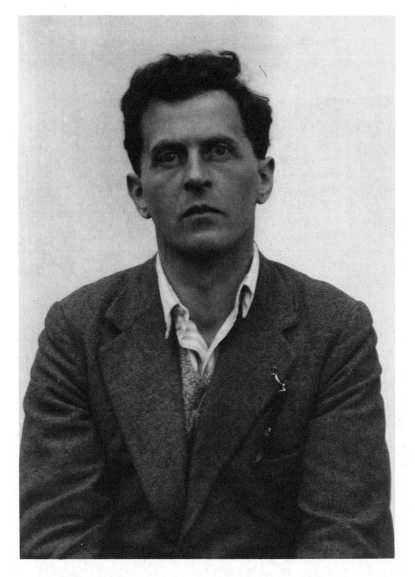

Figure 9 Ludwig Wittgenstein aged 40
Source: With the permission of the Master and Fellows of Trinity College Cambridge.

the mark of a *true* love that one thinks of what the *other* person suffers. For he suffers too, is also a poor devil' (Monk, 1991, p. 491). He was 57.

In 1947, he resigned his chair to live and work in seclusion once more, this time on the Irish coast. Here his immediate neighbours shunned him because they considered him to be mad, and they forbade him to walk on their land because they thought he would frighten their sheep (Monk, 1991, p. 525).

Wittgenstein now began to be ill and he died of cancer in the home of friends in 1951.

Wittgenstein's personality

From his school days onwards, Wittgenstein was in constant strife with other people and found it particularly hard, if not impossible, to tolerate the working classes. Yet repeatedly, in the army during the First World War, as a rural elementary school teacher, and to a lesser extent as a hospital orderly in the Second World War, he sought out this kind of milieu. While in the army, he thought the baseness of the other men frightful and preferred to do night work to escape their company. He felt himself 'wounded' by the crudeness of his surroundings.

As the quotation at the start of this book makes clear, he wonderfully described his difficulty in making sense of other people (Wittgenstein, 1991, p. 18): it was as if he were listening to a Chinese without being able to speak his language.

Many examples of his own over-sensitivity and his insensitivity to the feelings and needs of others are recorded. Pinsent (von Wright, 1990) comments on his extreme sensitivity and fussiness. He would, for example, give his Cambridge visitors tea from chemical beakers because he found ordinary crockery too ugly. On their joint holidays he could not bear the company of other tourists. On one occasion Pinsent, to be polite, joined another traveller in his compartment for a smoke, Wittgenstein would not go and was then in a terrible state, refusing to talk to his friend for some time. Pinsent desperately tried to avoid friction on their holidays and wrote: 'he is so different from other people – he is if anything a bit mad . . . one has to deal with him differently – superficially at any rate' (von Wright, 1990, pp. 56–57). And: 'He is a chaotic person. I have to be frightfully careful and tolerant when he gets these sulky fits . . . in his acute sensitiveness . . . [he] thinks the most awful things of me when he is sulky' (p. 64). Yet these sulky states also greatly distressed Wittgenstein himself, and he repeatedly accused himself of doing other people harm.

Fania Pascal (1979), who taught Wittgenstein Russian, described him as small, with a keen look as of a bird in flight; stern and forbidding yet naive; unaware that he cast a spell and held others in thrall with his talk; elusive and surrounding his comings and goings with mystery. She wrote:

> I could never look on his ability to find out the weak spots of another human being and hit out hard as anything but a flaw. The knowledge that he was at the same time a man of great purity and innocence cannot alter my feeling.
>
> (Pascal, 1979)

His social inappropriateness and disregard for the needs of others were also described by Russell (Ayer, 1985). He would arrive in Russell's rooms at midnight to talk, would walk to and fro and announce that he would commit suicide when he left; so Russell did not like to turn him out. After some hours of silence, Russell asked him was he thinking of logic or his sins?, Wittgenstein replied: 'both', and fell silent again. He dominated most philosophical discussions, apparently oblivious to the fatigue at times engendered in others.

Leonard Woolf, at a later period, was appalled at his rudeness to Maynard Keynes' wife. Yet Wittgenstein himself was so shocked at the Bloomsbury set's frank discussion of sex in the presence of ladies that he walked out (Monk, 1991, p. 256).

Touchingly, quotations from a diary written by Anthony Ryle, then 14 years old and later to become an eminent doctor and psychotherapist, when Wittgenstein stayed with his family during the war, vividly reveal this aspect of his personality: 'Wink is awful strange . . . he's an impossible person everytime you say anything he says "No No, that's not the point." It probably isn't his point, but it is ours. A tiring person to listen to' (Monk, 1991, p. 434).

Wittgenstein's own awareness of his difficulties in following social conventions is indicated by his asking Pinsent to dictate to him letters he had to write out of duty, for example in response to invitations. He was also often tactless, giving other people full details of their shortcomings as he saw them. He dressed oddly for his day, never wearing tie or hat. Many thought he was withdrawn, mysterious, inaccessible, eccentric, even mad. Von Wright (Malcolm, 1984) describes him as a most uncommon man who probably lived on the borders of mental illness, a fear of which was with him throughout his life. Malcolm (1984) found him suspicious of other people's motives and both precipitous and often erroneous in his judgements.

Monk (1991, pp. 428 and 586) comments on his indifference to the feelings of others, and suggests Wittgenstein may have preferred to be in love with someone not in love with him, because the relationship could then be conducted 'safely, in the splendid isolation of his own feelings'. His perception of a relationship was often quite different from that of the other person. When he invited Marguerite to join him for two weeks in Norway, he arranged for her to lodge elsewhere and saw very little of her. He left a Bible in her room. Monk's detailed biography suggests that, while he did fall in love several times, and passionately, his actual sex life was meagre.

His inappropriate social behaviour and his odd mode of dress were often remarked. In the lodgings he shared in Newcastle during the Second World War, the other residents liked to be quiet and read their papers over breakfast, but he would go to join them, bright and talkative. Yet he insisted on having his dinner served in his room and would not be sociable in the evening.

Wittgenstein was naive in relation to Hitler's ideas, his rise to power and the possible dangers to his own family in Austria. He was also for many years an admirer of Otto Weininger's book, *Sex and Character* (1906). Weininger, a Jew, despised women and developed the notions that the feminine elements of human nature as well as Judaism were inimical to human achievement; and that sex and love were incompatible. He, too, may have had a schizoid personality disorder, and he committed suicide at the age of 23. When Wittgenstein recommended his book to his students, they thought it was bizarre.

In later life Wittgenstein described himself as unable to *give* affection, but with a great need *for* affection: 'I am cold and wrapped up in myself' (Monk, 1991, p. 387). Many of his relationships were brief and ended in distance because of what others saw as his egocentricity coupled with exceptional moral rigour (Wittgenstein, 1991). He thought all relationships should be absolutely serious. He lived in constant conflict between his longings for affection and his wish to go his way alone.

Pinsent found him too fervent at times (e.g. when he commented on how 'splendidly' he and Pinsent had got on) and too cool at others. At the end of their first holiday together (von Wright, 1990, p. 65) Wittgenstein told him he had enjoyed it 'as much as it is possible for two people to do, who are nothing to each other'. Pinsent comments: 'I certainly enjoyed it more than that.'

Wittgenstein had recurrent episodes of depression in which remorse and self-castigation filled his inner world. In his youth he thought of suicide daily and his diary written during the First World War (1991) is full of his unhappiness, his shortcomings, and appeals to God ('God help me. . . . God hear me and give me peace. Amen . . . God make me a better person'), despite his disdain for 'transcendental rubbish' (pp. 68, 72).

Although so deadly serious, he had a great liking for American movies and detective magazines, and his letters to Malcolm (1984) have a curiously schoolboyish tone. When visiting Malcolm and his wife in the USA, she offered him rye bread and cheese for his first lunch with them. He liked this so much that he ate nothing else throughout his stay. Another mildly unconventional act was that, when mortally ill and cared for by Mrs Bevan, the wife of his GP, in their home, she bade good night to him one evening before going out, he inspected her appearance and with a pair of scissors cut the buttons off her coat because they offended him. She agreed this was an improvement (Malcolm, 1984). Every evening at 6 o'clock, he and Mrs Bevan would go to the local pub and order two ports. She would drink hers and he, with much amusement, would pour his into the Aspidistra (Monk, 1991, p. 577). These incidents are perhaps in line with what von Wright described as the overwhelming charm of his imaginative powers and the gaiety of his conversation.

Although often depressed and pessimistic, Wittgenstein wrote: 'Die Freude an meinen Gedanken ist die Freude an meinem eigenen seltsamen Leben' ('The joy my thoughts give me is the joy at my own strange life'); and his last words, when told his friends were coming to see him the next day, were: 'Tell them I've had a wonderful life' (Malcolm, 1984).

CONCLUSION

In a number of exceptionally gifted and creative people in the public domain – scientists, artists, writers and philosophers – schizoid traits can be recognized. This recognition can help us to make sense of their personalities and their lives. Very occasionally we find extraordinary people whose fantasies are expressed not in literary products alone, but are acted out in real life to the puzzlement and consternation of their families and friends. Some, like the poet Richard Savage (Holmes, 1993), may have been sociable and possibly not schizoid at all; others, like Opal Whiteley, clearly had a schizoid personality disorder.

The features of the people described in this book have long baffled doctors, psychologists, and indeed the families affected. Schizoid personality traits are most troublesome during the school years of gregariousness and conformity. Affected youngsters are then seen by others and identify themselves as 'loners'. But, once school is over, the majority manage to find a more congenial way of life and cope well with work and often also with their family relationships. Only a few of those who had childhood difficulties have, as we saw, a less happy outcome. It is likely that schizoid and schizotypal personality traits are not at all uncommon in the general population and that they find expression in a variety of ways. In intellectually gifted people, as this last chapter suggests, they occasionally contribute to unique and original achievements.

Appendix

(IQ differences are based on analyses of variance. All other statistics are based on Chi-square calculations for dichotomized variables.)

1 THE CHILDHOOD ANTECEDENTS OF PSYCHIATRIC MORBIDITY IN ADULT LIFE: STATISTICALLY SIGNIFICANT ASSOCIATIONS BETWEEN CHILDHOOD VARIABLES AND LATER PSYCHIATRIC HOSPITAL CONTACT

	Schizoid Boys and Girls (N = 65)	*Control Boys and Girls* (N = 65)
Best measured IQ (lower in those with hospital contact)	NS	Trend (P < 0.05)
	(N = 62)	(N = 41)
Evidence of cerebral dysfunction	NS	P < 0.05
Any childhood conduct disorder	NS	P < 0.05
Aggressive behaviour	NS	P < 0.01
Fantasies of violence	P < 0.05	NS
Overall rating of childhood privations	P < 0.05	NS
Duration of clinic contact (longer)	NS	P < 0.05

2 THE CHILDHOOD ANTECEDENTS OF CRIMINALITY IN ADULT LIFE: STATISTICALLY SIGNIFICANT ASSOCIATIONS BETWEEN CHILDHOOD VARIABLES AND ANY CONVICTIONS AFTER 16 YEARS OF AGE

	Schizoid Boys and Girls (N = 65)	*Control Boys and Girls* (N = 65)
WISC performance IQ (lower in those with convictions)	P < 0.05	NS
	(N tested = 57)	(N tested = 31)
Manual occupation of father	NS	P < 0.01
Any childhood conduct disorder	P < 0.05	P < 0.05
Aggressive behaviour	P < 0.01	NS
Overall rating of socio-cultural deprivation	P < 0.05	NS
Overall childhood privations	P < 0.05	NS

Family history of delinquency	NS	$P < 0.01$
Any social-work contact	$P < 0.01$	$P < 0.001$
Ever at court or at a Children's Hearing	$P < 0.05$	$P < 0.001$
Duration of clinic contact (longer in those convicted)	$P < 0.05$	NS

3 ASSOCIATION BETWEEN PSYCHIATRIC HOSPITAL CONTACT (PHA) AND ANY CONVICTION (C) IN ADULT LIFE

	Schizoid Group			*Control Group*		
	C–	C+	Total	C–	C+	Total
PHA–	32	8	40	41	11	52
PHA+	11	14	25	8	5	13
Total	43	22	65	49	16	65

Chi-square = 7.370, d.f.=1   Chi-square = 0.876, d.f.=1

$P < 0.01$ NS

References

Albert, R. S. (ed.) (1983) *Genius and Eminence: The Social Psychology of Creativity and Exceptional Achievement*. Oxford: Pergamon.

Alvarez, A. (1992) *Live Company: Psychoanalytic Psychotherapy with Autistic, Borderline, Deprived and Abused Children*. London: Routledge.

American Psychiatric Association (1980) *Diagnostic and Statistical Manual of Mental Disorders* (3rd edn). Washington, DC: APA.

American Psychiatric Association (1987) *Diagnostic and Statistical Manual of Mental Disorders* (3rd edn, revised). Washington, DC:APA.

American Psychiatric Association (1994) *Diagnostic and Statistical Manual of Mental Disorders* (4th edn). Washington, DC: APA.

Asendorpf, J. B. (1993) Abnormal shyness in children. *Journal of Child Psychology and Psychiatry, 34*, 1069–1081.

Asperger, H. (1944) Die Autistischen Psychopathen im Kindesalter. *Archiv für Psychiatrie und Nervenkrankheiten, 117*, 76–136.

Asperger, H. (1961) *Heilpaedagogik* (3rd edn). Vienna: Springer, p. 200; pp. 200–205.

Asperger, H. (1979) Problems of infantile autism. *Communication, 13*, 45–52.

Asperger, H. (1991) 'Autistic psychopathy' in childhood, trans. U. Frith. In U. Frith (ed.) *Autism and Asperger Syndrome*. Cambridge: Cambridge University Press, pp. 37–92.

Ayer, A. J. (1985) *Wittgenstein*. London: Weidenfeld & Nicolson.

Bailey, A. J. (1993) Editorial: The biology of autism. *Psychological Medicine, 23*, 7–11.

Bailey, A. *et al.* (1995) Autism as a strongly genetic disorder: evidence from a British twin study. *Psychological Medicine, 25*, 63–77.

Baltaxe, C. and Simmons, J. Q. (1992) A comparison of language issues in high functioning autism and related disorders with onset in childhood and adolescence. In E. Schopler and G. B. Mesibov (eds) *High Functioning Individuals with Autism*. New York: Plenum, pp. 201–225.

Baron, M., Asnis, L. and Gruen, R. (1981) The schedule for schizotypal personalities (SSP): a diagnostic interview for schizotypal features. *Psychiatry Research, 4*, 213–228.

Baron, M., Gruen, R., Asnis, L. and Kane, J. (1983) Familial relatedness of schizophrenia and schizotypal states. *American Journal of Psychiatry, 140*, 1437–1442.

Baron-Cohen, S. (1988) An assessment of violence in a young man with Asperger's syndrome. *Journal of Child Psychology and Psychiatry, 29*, 351–360.

Baron-Cohen, S. (1989) The autistic child's theory of mind: a case of specific developmental delay. *Journal of Child Psychology and Psychiatry, 30*, 285–298.

Barron, F. and Harrington, D. M. (1981) Creativity, intelligence and personality. *Annual Review of Psychology, 32*, 439–476.

Battaglia, M., Gasperini, M., Scinto, G., Scherillo, P., Diaferia, G. and Bellodi, L. (1991) Psychiatric disorders in the relatives of schizotypal subjects. *Schizophrenia Bulletin, 17*, 659–665.

Bede, E. (1954) *Fabulous Opal Whiteley: From Logging Camp to Princess of India.* Portland, Oregon: Binfords & Mort.

Berelowitz, M. and Tarnopolsky, A. (1993) The validity of borderline personality disorder: an updated review of recent research. In P. Tyrer and G. Stein (eds) *Personality Disorder Reviewed.* London: Gaskell, Royal College of Psychiatrists, pp. 90–112.

Bernhard, T. (1982) *Wittgenstein's Neffe: Eine Freundschaft.* Frankfurt am Main: Suhrkamp Verlag.

Bishop, D. V. M. (1989) Autism, Asperger's syndrome and semantic-pragmatic disorder: where are the boundaries? *British Journal of Disorders of Communication, 24,* 107–121.

Blackwood, D. H. R., Muir, W. J., Roxborough, H. M., Walker, M. T., Townshend, R., Glabus, N. and Wolff, S. (1994) 'Schizoid' personality in childhood: Auditory P300 and eye tracking responses at follow-up in adult life. *Journal of Autism and Developmental Disorders, 24,* 487–500.

Bleuler, E. (1930) *Lehrbuch der Psychiatrie* (5th edn). Berlin: Springer, p. 287.

Bleuler, E. (1950) *Dementia Praecox or the Group of Schizophrenias,* trans. J. Zinkin (first pub. 1911). New York: International University Press.

Bleuler, M. (1954) Letter in *American Journal of Psychiatry, 111,* 382–383.

Bleuler, M. (1978) *The Schizophrenic Disorders.* New Haven and London: Yale University Press, p. 434.

Bolton, P. and Rutter, M. (1990) Genetic influences in autism. *International Review of Psychiatry, 2,* 67–80.

Bolton, P., Macdonald, H., Pickles, A., Rios, P., Goode, S., Crowson, M., Bailey, A. and Rutter, M. (1994) A case-control family history study of autism. *Journal of Child Psychology and Psychiatry, 35,* 877–900.

Bottoms, A. E. and Brownsword, R. (1982) The dangerousness debate after the Floud Report. *British Journal of Criminology, 22,* 229–254.

de Bourbon-Orleans, F. M. (1929) A sun-king in the city of the sun-rise. *The Queen,* November 27, pp. 40–41, 74; December 4, p. 18; December 18, pp. 12–13; December 25, p. 12.

de Bourbon-Orleans, F. M. (1930) A sun-king in the city of the sun-rise. *The Queen,* January 1, pp. 16–17; January 8, pp. 17–18; January 15, pp. 14–15; January 22, pp. 13–14; January 29, pp. 28–29.

de Bourbon-Orleans, F. M. (1940) The greatest hoax in history. *The Queen,* October 9, pp. 12 and 31.

Bowler, D. M. (1992) 'Theory of mind' in Asperger's syndrome. *Journal of Child Psychology and Psychiatry, 33,* 877–893.

Bradburne, E. S. (1962) *Opal Whiteley: The Unsolved Mystery.* London: Putnam.

Brahams, D. (1994) 'Treatability' and discharge of psychopaths. *Lancet, 343,* 847.

Brook, S. L. and Bowler, D. M. (1993) Autism by another name? Pragmatic impairments in children. *Journal of Autism and Developmental Disorders, 22,* 61–81.

Cannon, T. D. and Mednick, S. A. (1993) The Schizophrenia high-risk project in Copenhagen: three decades of progress. *Acta Psychiatrica Scandinavica,* Supp. 370, *87,* 33–47.

Cantwell, D. P., Baker, L., Rutter, M. *et al.* (1989) Infantile autism and developmental receptive dysphasia: a comparative follow-up into middle childhood. *Journal of Autism and Developmental Disorders, 19,* 19–31.

Castle, D. J. and Murray, R. M. (1991) Editorial: The neurodevelopmental basis of sex differences in schizophrenia. *Psychological Medicine, 21,* 565–575.

Chick, J. (1978) *Schizoid Personality in Childhood: A Follow-up Study.* M. Phil. Thesis, University of Edinburgh.

Chick, J., Waterhouse, L. and Wolff, S. (1979) Psychological construing in schizoid children grown-up. *British Journal of Psychiatry, 135,* 425–430.

Chiswick, D. (1993) Forensic psychiatry. In R. E. Kendell and A. K. Zealley (eds) *Companion to Psychiatric Studies* (5th edn). Edinburgh: Churchill Livingstone, pp. 793–816.

Claridge, G. (1985) *Origins of Mental Illness: Temperament, Deviance and Disorder.* Oxford: Basil Blackwell.

Claridge, G., Robinson, D. L. and Birchall, P. (1983) Characteristics of schizophrenics' and neurotics' relatives. *Personality and Individual Differences, 4*, 651–664.

Claridge, G., Pryor, R. and Watkins, G. (1990) *Sounds from the Bell Jar: Ten Psychotic Authors.* London: Macmillan.

Clarke, D. J., Littlejohn, C. S., Corbett, J. A. and Joseph, S. (1989) Pervasive developmental disorders and psychoses in adult life. *British Journal of Psychiatry, 155*, 692–699.

Cohen, D. J., Paul, R. and Volkmar, F. R. (1986) Issues in the classification of pervasive developmental disorders: towards DSM-IV. *Journal of the American Academy of Child Psychiatry, 25*, 213–220.

Cohen, D. and MacKeith, S. A. (1991) *The Development of Imagination.* London: Routledge.

Coid, J. (1989) Psychopathic disorders. *Current Opinion in Psychiatry, 2*, 750–756.

Coid, J. W. (1992) DSM-III diagnosis in criminal psychopaths: a way forward. *Criminal Behaviour and Mental Health, 2*, 78–94.

Coid, J. (1993) Psychopathic disorder. In P. Tyrer and G. Stein (eds) *Personality Disorder Reviewed.* London: Gaskell, Royal College of Psychiatrists, pp. 113–164.

Cox, C. M. (1926) *Genetic Studies of Genius. Vol II. The Early Mental Traits of Three Hundred Geniuses.* Stanford, Connecticut: Stanford University Press.

Cull, A., Chick, J. and Wolff, S. (1984) A consensual validation of schizoid personality in childhood and adult life. *British Journal of Psychiatry, 144*, 646–648.

Cutting, J. (1985) *The Psychology of Schizophrenia.* London: Churchill Livingstone.

Dell, S. (1984) *Murder into Manslaughter: The Diminished Responsibility Debate in Practice.* Maudsley Monograph No. 27, Oxford: Oxford University Press.

Dell, S. and Smith, A. (1983) Changes in the sentencing of diminished responsibility homicides. *British Journal of Psychiatry, 142*, 20–34.

Department of Health and Home Office (1994) *Report of the Working Group on Psychopathic Disorder*, Chairman John Reed. London: DoH.

Dodge, K. A., Bates, J. E. and Pettit, G. S. (1990) Mechanisms in the cycle of violence. *Science, 250*, 1678–1683.

Done, D. J., Johnstone, E. C., Frith, C. D., Golding, J. and Shepherd, P. M. (1991) Complications of pregnancy and delivery in relation to psychosis in adult life: data from the British perinatal mortality survey sample. *British Medical Journal, 302*, 1576–1580.

Earls, F. (1994) Oppositional-defiant and conduct disorders. In M. Rutter, E. Taylor and L. Hersov (eds) *Child and Adolescent Psychiatry: Modern Approaches* (3rd edn). Oxford: Blackwell, pp. 308–329.

Eggers. C. (1978) Cause and prognosis of childhood schizophrenia. *Journal of Autism and Childhood Schizophrenia, 8*, 21–35.

Ehlers, S. and Gillberg, C. (1993) The epidemiology of Asperger syndrome: a total population study. *Journal of Child Psychology and Psychiatry, 34*, 1327–1350.

Ekstein, R. and Wallerstein, J. (1956) Observations on the psychotherapy of borderline and psychotic children. *Psychoanalytic Study of the Child , 11*, 37–46.

Eldar, S., Bleich, A., Apler, A. and Tyrano, S. (1985) Elective mutism – an atypical antecedent of schizophrenia. *Journal of Adolescence, 8*, 289–292.

Essen-Moeller, E. (1946) The concept of schizoidia. *Monatschrift für Psychiatrie und Neurologie, 112*, 258–271, S. Karger AG, Basel.

Farrington, D. P. and Hawkins, J. D. (1991) Predicting participation, early onset and later persistence in officially recorded offending. *Criminal Behaviour and Mental Health, 1*, 1–33.

Fenton, W. S. and McGlashan, T. H. (1989) Risk of schizophrenia in character disordered patients. *American Journal of Psychiatry, 146*, 1280–1284.

Fine, J., Bartolucci, G., Ginsberg, G. and Szatmari, P. (1991) The use of intonation to communicate in pervasive developmental disorders. *Journal of Child Psychology and Psychiatry*, *32*, 771–782.

Fish, B., Marcus, J., Hans, S. L., Auerbach, J. G. and Perdue, S. (1992) Infants at risk for schizophrenia: sequelae of a genetic neurointegrative defect – a review and replication analysis of pandysmaturation in the Jerusalem infant development study. *Archives of General Psychiatry*, *49*, 221–235.

Floud, J. and Young, W. (1981) *Dangerousness and Criminal Justice*. London: Heinemann.

Foerster, A., Lewis, S. W., Owen, M. J. and Murray, R. M. (1991) Premorbid adjustment and personality in psychosis: effects of sex and diagnosis. *British Journal of Psychiatry*, *158*, 171–176.

Folstein, S. and Rutter, M. (1988) Autism: Familial aggregation and genetic implications. *Journal of Autism and Developmental Disorders*, *18*, 297–331.

Frances, A. (1985) Validating schizotypal personality disorders: problems with the schizophrenic connection. *Schizophrenia Bulletin*, *11*, 595–597.

Freud, A. (1946) *The Ego and the Mechanisms of Defence*. London: The Hogarth Press.

Frith, U. (1989) *Autism: Explaining the Enigma*. Oxford: Blackwell.

Frith, U. (ed.) (1991a) *Autism and Asperger Syndrome*. Cambridge: Cambridge University Press, pp. 37–92.

Frith, U. (1991b) Asperger and his syndrome. In U. Frith (ed.) *Autism and Asperger Syndrome*. Cambridge: Cambridge University Press, pp. 1–36.

Frith, U., Morton, J. and Leslie, A. M. (1991) The cognitive basis of a biological disorder: autism. *TINS*, *14*, 433–437.

van der Gaag, J. R. (1993) *Multiplex Development Disorder: An Exploration of Borderlines on the Autistic Spectrum*. M. D. Thesis, University of Utrecht.

Geleert, E. R. (1958) Borderline states in childhood and adolescence. *Psychoanalytic Study of the Child*, *13*, 279–295.

Ghaziuddin, M., Tsai, L. and Ghaziuddin, N. (1991) Brief report: violence in Asperger's syndrome. *Journal of Autism and Developmental Disorders*, *21*, 349–354.

Gillberg, C. (1989) Asperger syndrome in 23 Swedish children. *Developmental Medicine and Child Neurology*, *31*, 520–531.

Gillberg, C. (1990) Autism and pervasive developmental disorders. *Journal of Child Psychology and Psychiatry,* *31*, 99–119.

Gillberg, C. (1991) Clinical and neurobiological aspects of Asperger syndrome in six family studies. In U. Frith (ed.) *Autism and Asperger Syndrome*. Cambridge: Cambridge University Press, pp. 122–146.

Gillberg, C., Gillberg, I. C. and Steffenburg, S. (1992) Siblings and parents of children with autism: a controlled study. *Developmental Medicine and Child Neurology*, *34*, 389–398.

Goldenson, R. M. (ed.) (1984) *Longman's Dictionary of Psychology and Psychiatry*. London: Longman.

Goldstein, J. M. (1992) Gender and schizophrenia: a summary of findings. *Schizophrenia Monitor*, *2*, 1–4.

Grandin, T. (1992) An inside view of autism. In E. Schopler and G. B. Mesibov (eds) *High-Functioning Autism*. New York: Plenum, pp. 105–126.

Gunderson, J. G., Kolb, J. E. and Austin, V. (1981) The diagnostic interview for borderline patients. *American Journal of Psychiatry*, *138*, 896–903.

Gunn, J. (1992) Personality disorders and forensic psychiatry. *Criminal Behaviour and Mental Health*, *2*, 202–211.

Happé, F. G. E. (1994a) An advanced test of theory of mind: understanding of story characters' thoughts and feelings by able autistic, mentally handicapped, and normal children. *Journal of Autism and Developmental Disorders*, *24*, 129–154.

Happé, Francesca (1994b) *Autism: An Introduction to Psychological Theory*. London: UCL Press.

Harrington, R. (1993) *Depressive Disorder in Childhood and Adolescence*. Chichester: Wiley.

Hermelin, B. (1978) Images and language. In M. Rutter and E. Schopler (eds) *Autism: A Reappraisal of Concepts and Treatment*. New York: Plenum.

Hermelin, B. and O'Connor, N. (1970) *Psychological Experiments with Autistic Children*. Oxford: Pergamon.

Hermelin, B. and O'Connor, N. (1986) Annotation: low intelligence and special abilities. *Journal of Child Psychology and Psychiatry, 29*, 391–396.

Heston, L. and Denney, D. (1968) Interaction between early life experience and biological factors in schizophrenia. In D. Rosenthal and S. Kety (eds) *The Transmission of Schizophrenia*. Oxford: Pergamon, pp. 363–376.

Hobson, R. P. (1986) The autistic child's appraisal of expressions of emotion. *Journal of Child Psychology and Psychiatry, 27*, 321–342.

Hobson, R. P. (1991) Methodological issues for experiments on autistic individuals' perception and understanding of emotion. *Journal of Child Psychology and Psychiatry, 32*, 1135–1158.

Hobson, R. P. (1994) On developing a mind. *British Journal of Psychiatry, 165*, 577–581.

Hoffman, M. L. (1987) The contribution of empathy to justice and moral judgement. In N. Eisenberg and J. Strayer (eds) *Empathy and its Development*. New York: Cambridge University Press, pp. 47–80.

Hollander, H. E. and Turner, F. D. (1985) Characteristics of incarcerated delinquents: relationship between developmental disorders, environmental and family factors, and patterns of offence and recidivism. *Journal of the American Academy of Child and Adolescent Psychiatry, 24*, 221–226.

Holmes, R. (1993) *Dr Johnson and Mr Savage*. London: Hodder & Stoughton.

Home Office and Department of Health and Social Security (1975) *Report of the Committee on Mentally Abnormal Offenders*. London: HMSO.

Home Office (1989) *Statistical Bulletin*, Issue 32/89. London: Home Office, Statistical Department.

Howells, K. (1978) The meaning of poisoning to a person diagnosed as a psychopath. *Medicine, Science and the Law, 8*, 179–184.

Huesmann, L. R., Eron, L. D., Lefkowitz, M. M. *et al.* (1984) Stability of aggression over time and generations. *Developmental Psychology, 20*, 1120–1134.

The Independent (1992) 21 October, p. 8.

The Independent (1993) 12 March, p. 2.

Jaspers, K. (1963) *General Psychopathology*, trans. J. Hoenig and M. Hamilton. Manchester: Manchester University Press, pp. 328 and 447.

Jenkins, R. L. (1968) The varieties of children's behavior problems and family dynamics. *American Journal of Psychiatry, 124*, 1440–1445.

Jenkins, R. L. and Glickman, S. (1946) The schizoid child. *American Journal of Orthopsychiatry, 16*, 255–261.

Jones, P. and Murray, R. (1991) Aberrant neurodevelopment as the expression of the schizophrenia genotype. In P. McGuffin and R. Murray (eds) *The New Genetics of Mental Illness*. Oxford: Butterworth-Heinemann, pp. 112–129.

Jones, P., Rodgers, B., Murray, R. and Marmot, M. (1994) Child developmental risk factors for adult schizophrenia in the British 1946 birth cohort. *Lancet, 344*, 1398–1402.

Juda, A. (1949) The relationship between highest mental capacity and psychic abnormalities. *American Journal of Psychiatry, 106*, 296–307.

Kagan, J. (1981) *The Second Year: The Emergence of Self-Awareness*. Cambridge, MA: Harvard University Press.

Kanner, L. (1943) Autistic disturbances of affective contact. *The Nervous Child, 2*, 217–250.

Karlsson, J. L. (1968) Genealogic studies of schizophrenia. In D. Rosenthal and S. Kety (eds) *The Transmission of Schizophrenia*. Oxford: Pergamon, pp. 85–94.

Karlsson, J. L. (1970) Genetic association of giftedness, creativity and schizophrenia. *Hereditas, 66*, 177–181.

Karlsson, L. J. (1974) Inheritance of schizophrenia. *Acta Psychiatrica Scandinavica*, Supp. No. 247.

Kendler, K. S. and Gruenberg, A. M. (1984) An independent analysis of the Danish adoption study of schizophrenia. *Archives of General Psychiatry*, *41*, 555–564.

Kendler, K. S., McGuire, M., Gruenberg, A. M., O'Hare, A., Spellman, M. and Walsh, D. (1993) The Roscommon family study: III. Schizophrenia-related personality disorders in relatives. *Archives of General Psychiatry*, *50*, 781–788.

Kolvin, I. and Fundudis, T. (1981) Elective mute children: psychological development and background factors. *Journal of Child Psychology and Psychiatry*, *22*, 219–232.

Kolvin, I., Barrett, M. L., Bhate, S. R., Berney, T. P., Famuyiwa, O., Fundudis, T. and Tyrer, S. (1991) The Newcastle child depression project: diagnosis and classification of depression. *British Journal of Psychiatry*, *159* (Supp. l. 11), 9–21.

Kozol, E., Boucher, R. J. and Garofalo, R. F. (1972) The diagnosis and treatment of dangerousness. *Crime and Delinquency*, *18*, 371–392.

Kraepelin, E. (1919) *Dementia Praecox and Paraphrenia*, trans. R. M. Barclay. Edinburgh: Livingstone.

Kretschmer, E. (1925) *Physique and Character: An Investigation of the Nature of Constitution and of the Theory of Temperament*, trans. W. J. H. Sprott. London: Kegan Paul, Trench & Trubner.

Krevelen, D. Arn. van (1963) On the relationship between early infantile autism and autistic psychopathy. *Acta Paedopsychiatrica*, *30*, 303–323.

Landa, R., Piven, J., Wzorek, M. M., Gayle, J. O., Chase, G. A. and Folstein, S. E. (1992) Social language use in parents of autistic individuals. *Psychological Medicine*, *22*, 245–254.

de Long, G. R. and Dwyer, J. T. (1988) Correlation of family history with specific autistic subgroups: Asperger's syndrome and bipolar affective disease. *Journal of Autism and Developmental Disorders*, *18*, 593–600.

McConaghy, N. and Clancy, M. (1968) Familial relationships of allusive thinking in university students and their parents. *British Journal of Psychiatry*, *114*, 1079–1083.

McCreadie, R. G., Connolly, M. A., Williamson, D. J., Athawes, R. W. B. and Tilak-Singh, D. (1994). The Nithsdale Schizophrenia Surveys XII. 'Neurodevelopmental' schizophrenia: a search for clinical correlates and putative aetiological factors. *British Journal of Psychiatry, 165*, 340–346.

McCrimmon, D. J., Cleghorn, J. M., Asarnow, R. F. and Asteffy, R. (1980) Children at risk of schizophrenia. *Archives of General Psychiatry*, *37*, 671–674.

McGuffin, P. and Thapar, A. (1992) The genetics of personality disorder. *British Journal of Psychiatry*, *160*, 12–23.

McGuinness, B. (1988) *Wittgenstein – A Life: Young Ludwig*. London: Duckworth.

McLennan, J. D., Lord, C. and Schopler, E. (1993) Sex differences in higher functioning people with autism. *Journal of Autism and Developmental Disorders*, *23*, 217–227.

Mahler, M. S., Ross, J. R. and De Fries, Z. (1949) Clinical studies in benign and malignant cases of childhood psychoses. *American Journal of Orthopsychiatry*, *19*, 295–305.

Malcolm, N. (1984) *Ludwig Wittgenstein: A Memoir* (2nd edn). Oxford: Oxford University Press.

Mawson, D., Grounds, A. and Tantam, D. (1985) Violence and Asperger's syndrome: a case study. *British Journal of Psychiatry*, *147*, 566–569.

Monk, R. (1991) *Ludwig Wittgenstein: The Duty of Genius*. London: Vintage.

Mouridsen, S. E., Rich, B. and Isager, T. (1993) Brief report: Parental age in infantile autism, autistic-like conditions, and borderline childhood psychosis. *Journal of Autism and Developmental Disorders*, *23*, 387–396.

Muir, W. J., St Clair, D. M., Blackwood, D. H. R., Roxborough, H. M. and Marshall, I. (1992) Eye-tracking dysfunction in affective psychoses and schizophrenia. *Psychological Medicine*, *22*, 573–580.

Munk-Jorgensen, P., Kastrup, M. and Mortensen, P. B. (1993) The Danish psychiatric register as a tool in epidemiology. *Acta Psychiatrica Scandinavica*, Supp. 370, *87*, 27–32.

Nagy, J. and Szatmari, P. (1986) A chart review of schizotypal personality disorders in children. *Journal of Autism and Developmental Disorders*, *16*, 351–367.

Nannarello, J. J. (1953) Schizoid. *Journal of Nervous and Mental Diseases*, *118*, 237–249.

Narayan, S., Moyes, B. and Wolff, S. (1990) Family characteristics of autistic children: a further report. *Journal of Autism and Developmental Disorders*, *20*, 523–535.

Netley, C., Lockyer, L. and Greenbaum, G. H. C. (1975) Parental characteristics in relation to diagnosis and neurological status in childhood psychosis. *British Journal of Psychiatry*, *127*, 440–444.

O'Callaghan, E., Gibson, T., Colohan, H. A., Walshe, D. G., Larkin, C. and Waddington, J. L. (1992) Risk of schizophrenia in adults born after obstetric complications and their association with early onset of illness: a controlled study. *British Medical Journal, 305*, 1256–1259.

Ochse, R. (1990) *Before the Gates of Excellence*. Cambridge: Cambridge University Press.

O'Connor, N. and Hermelin, B. (1988) Annotation: low intelligence and special abilities. *Journal of Child Psychology and Psychiatry*, *29*, 391–396.

Offord, D. (1974) School performance of adult schizophrenics, their siblings and agemates. *British Journal of Psychiatry*, *125*, 12–19.

Ozonoff, S., Pennington, B. F. and Rogers, S. J. (1991a) Executive function deficits in high-functioning autistic individuals: relationship to theory of mind. *Journal of Child Psychology and Psychiatry*, *32*, 1081–1105.

Ozonoff, S., Pennington, B. F. and Rogers, S. J. (1991b) Asperger's syndrome: evidence of an empirical distinction from high-functioning autism. *Journal of Child Psychology and Psychiatry*, *32*, 1107–1122.

Ozonoff, S., Rogers, S. J., Farnham, J. M. and Pennington, B. F. (1993) Can standard measures identify subclinical markers of autism? *Journal of Autism and Developmental Disorders*, *23*, 429–441.

Parnas, J., Cannon, T. D., Jacobsen, B., Schulsinger, H., Schulsinger, F. and Mednick, S. A. (1993) Lifetime DSM-III-R diagnostic outcomes in the offspring of schizophrenic mothers: results from the Copenhagen high-risk study. *Archives of General Psychiatry*, *50*, 707–714.

Pascal, F. (1979) Wittgenstein: a personal memoir. In C. G. Luckhardt (ed.) *Wittgenstein: Sources and Perspectives*. Hassocks, Sussex: The Harvester Press, pp. 23–60.

Patterson, G. R. and Dishion, T. J. (1988) Multilevel family process models: traits, interactions and relationships. In R. A. Hinde and J. Stevenson-Hinde (eds) *Relationships Within Families: Mutual Influences*. Oxford: Clarendon Press, pp. 283–310.

Petti, T. A. and Ricardo, M. V. (1990) Borderline disorders of childhood: An overview. *Journal of the American Academy of Child and Adolescent Psychiatry*, *29*, 327–337.

Piven, J., Gayle, J., Chase, G., Fink, B., Landa, R., Wzorek, M. and Folstein, S. (1990) A family history study of neuropsychiatric disorders in the adult siblings of autistic individuals. *Journal of the American Academy of Child and Adolescent Psychiatry*, *29*, 177–184.

Piven, J., Wzorek, M., Landa, R., Lainhart, J., Bolyon, P., Chase, G. A. and Folstein, S. (1994) Personality characteristics of parents of autistic individuals. *Psychological Medicine*, *24*, 783–795.

Post, F. (1994) Creativity and psychopathology: a study of 291 world-famous men. *British Journal of Psychiatry*, *165*, 22–34.

Pring, S. and Hermelin, B. (1993) Bottle, tulip and wineglass: semantic and structural picture processing by savant artists. *Journal of Child Psychology and Psychiatry*, *34*, 1365–1385.

Rado, S. (1954) Dynamics and classification of disordered behavior. *American Journal of Psychiatry*, *110*, 406–416.

Rifkin, L., Lewis, S., Jones, P., Toone, B. and Murray, R. (1994) Low birth weight and schizophrenia. *British Journal of Psychiatry, 165*, 357–362.

Roberts, G. (1992) Review Article: The origins of delusion. *British Journal of Psychiatry*, *161*, 298–308.

Robins, L. N. (1966) *Deviant Children Grown-Up: A Sociological and Psychiatric Study of Sociopathic Personality*. Baltimore: Williams and Wilkins.

Robins, L. N. (1991) Conduct disorder. *Annual Review, Journal of Child Psychology and Psychiatry*, *32*, 193–212.

Roxborough, H., Muir, W. J., Blackwood, D. H. R., Walker, M. T. and Blackburn, I. M. (1993) Neuropsychological and P300 abnormalities in schizophrenics and their relatives. *Psychological Medicine*, *23*, 305–314.

Rumsey, J. M., Rapoport, J. L. and Screery, W. R. (1985) Autistic children as adults: psychiatric, social and behavioral outcomes. *Journal of the American Academy of Child Psychiatry*, *24*, 465–473.

Russell, A. T., Bott, L. and Sammons, C. (1989) The phenomenology of schizophrenia occurring in childhood. *Journal of the American Academy of Child and Adolescent Psychiatry*, *28*, 399–407.

Rutter, M. (1992) Nature, nurture and psychopathology: a new look at an old topic. In B. Tizard and V. Varma (eds) *Vulnerability and Resilience: A Festschrift for Ann and Alan Clarke*. London: Jessica Kingsley, pp. 21–38.

Rutter, M. and Mawhood, L. (1991) The long-term psychosocial sequelae of specific developmental disorders of speech and language. In M. Rutter and P. Casaer (eds) *Biological Risk Factors for Psychosocial Disorders*. Cambridge: Cambridge University Press, pp. 233–259.

Rutter, M. and Schopler, E. (1989) Autism and pervasive developmental disorders: concepts and diagnostic issues. *Journal of Autism and Developmental Disorders*, *17*, 159–186.

Rutter, M. and Schopler, E. (1992) Classification of pervasive developmental disorders: some concepts and practical considerations. *Journal of Autism and Developmental Disorders*, *22*, 459–482.

Rutter, M., Tizard, J. and Whitmore, L. (1971) *Health, Education and Behaviour*. London: Longman.

Sacks, O. (1995) *An Anthropologist on Mars*. London: Picador, pp. 233–282; pp. 179–232.

Scheerer, M., Rothmann, E. and Goldstein, K. (1945) A case of 'idiot savant': an experimental study of personality organization. *Psychological Monographs*, *58*, 1–85.

Selfe, L. (1977). *Nadia: A Case of Extraordinary Drawing Ability in an Autistic Child*. London: Academic Press.

Selfe, L. (1985) *Anomalous Drawing Development: Some Clinical Studies*. Cambridge: Cambridge University Press.

Siever, L. J., Silverman, J. M., Thomas, B. H., Klar, H., Coccaro, E., Keefe, K. L., Pinkham, L., Rinaldi, P., Mohs, R. C. and Davis, K. L. (1990) Increased morbid risk for schizophrenia-related disorders in relatives of schizotypal personality disordered patients. *Archives of General Psychiatry*, *47*, 634–640.

Silvey, R. and MacKeith, S. (1988) The paracosm: a special form of fantasy. In D. C. Morrison (ed.) *Organizing Early Experience: Imagination and Cognition in Childhood*. Amityville, New York: Baywood Publishing, pp. 173–197.

Singer, M. B. (1960) Fantasies of a borderline patient. *Psychoanalytic Study of the Child*, *15*, 310–356.

Sodian, B. and Frith, U. (1992) Deception and sabotage in autistic, retarded and normal children. *Journal of Autism and Developmental Disorders*, *33*, 591–605.

Ssucharewa, G. E. (1926) Die Schizoiden Psychopathien im Kindesalter. *Monatschrift für Psychiatrie und Neurologie*, *60*, 235–261.

Stein, M. I. and Heinze, S. J. (1983) A summary of Terman's genetic studies of genius. In R. S. Albert (ed.) *Genius and Eminence: The Social Psychology of Creativity and Exceptional Achievement*. Oxford: Pergamon, pp. 75–84.

Szatmari, P., Bartolucci, G. and Bremner, R. (1989a) Asperger's syndrome and autism:

Comparisons on early history and outcome. *Developmental Medicine and Child Neurology, 31,* 709–720.

Szatmari, P., Bartolucci, G., Bremner, R., Bond, S. and Rich, S. (1989b) A follow-up study of high-functioning autistic children. *Journal of Autism and Developmental Disorders, 19,* 213–225.

Tager-Flusberg, H. and Sullivan, K. (1994) A second look at second-order belief attribution in autism. *Journal of Autism and Developmental Disorders, 24,* 577–586.

Tantam, D. (1986) *Eccentricity and Autism.* PhD Thesis, University of London.

Tantam, D. (1988a) Lifelong eccentricity and social isolation I: psychiatric, social and forensic aspects. *British Journal of Psychiatry, 153,* 777–782.

Tantam, D. (1988b) Lifelong eccentricity and social isolation II: Asperger's syndrome or schizoid personality disorder? *British Journal of Psychiatry, 153,* 783–791.

Tantam, D. (1991) Asperger's syndrome in adulthood. In U. Frith (ed.) *Autism and Asperger Syndrome.* Cambridge: Cambridge University Press, pp. 147–183.

Tarnopolsky, A. and Berelowitz, M. (1987) Borderline personality: a review of recent research. *British Journal of Psychiatry, 151,* 724–734.

Taylor, E., Sandberg, S., Thorley, G. and Giles, S. (1991) *The Epidemiology of Childhood Hyperactivity.* Maudsley Monograph No. 33. Oxford: Oxford University Press.

Taylor, I. (1992) Obituary: Opal Whiteley. *The Independent,* 24 February, p. 16.

Terman, L. M. (1970) Psychological approaches to the biography of genius. In P. E. Vernon (ed.) *Creativity.* Harmondsworth: Penguin Books, pp. 25–42.

Tienari, P., Kaleva, M., Lahti, I., Laeksy, K., Moring, J., Naarala, M., Sorri, A., Wahlberg, K. E. and Wynne, L. (1991) Adoption studies on schizophrenia. In C. Eggers (ed.) *Schizophrenia and Youth: Etiology and Therapeutic Consequences.* Berlin: Springer, pp. 42–51.

Treffert, D. A. (1989) *Extraordinary People: Understanding 'Idiot Savants'.* New York: Harper and Row.

Tsai, L. Y. (1992) Diagnostic issues in high-functioning autism. In E. Schopler and G. B. Mesibov (eds) *High-Functioning Individuals with Autism.* New York: Plenum, pp. 11–40.

Tucker, P. K., Rothwell, S. J., Armstrong, M. S. and McConaghy, N. (1982) Creativity, divergent and allusive thinking in students and visual artists. *Psychological Medicine, 12,* 835–841.

Tyrer, P. and Ferguson, B. (1988) Development of the concept of abnormal personality. In P. Tyrer (ed.) *Personality Disorders: Diagnosis, Management and Course.* London: Wright, pp. 1–11.

Varma, S. L. and Sharma, I. (1993) Psychiatric morbidity in the first degree relatives of schizophrenic patients. *British Journal of Psychiatry, 162,* 672–678.

Volkmar, F. R. and Cohen, D. J. (1991) Comorbid association of autism and schizophrenia. *American Journal of Psychiatry, 12,* 1705–1708.

Volkmar, F. R., Cicchetti, D. V., Bregman, J. and Cohen, D. J. (1992) Three diagnostic systems for autism: DSM-III, DSM-III-R, and ICD-10. *Journal of Autism and Developmental Disorders, 22,* 483–492.

von Wright, G. H. (1982) *Wittgenstein.* Oxford: Basil Blackwell.

von Wright, G. H. (ed.) (1990) *Pinsent, D. H.: A Portrait of Wittgenstein as a Young Man.* Oxford: Blackwell.

Wallace, M. (1986) *The Silent Twins.* Harmondsworth, Middlesex: Penguin.

Watkins, J. M., Asarnow, R. F. and Tanguay, P. E. (1988) Symptom development in childhood onset schizophrenia. *Journal of Child Psychology and Psychiatry, 29,* 865–878.

Weil, A. (1953) Certain severe disturbances of ego development in childhood. *Psychoanalytic Study of the Child, 8,* 271–287.

Weininger, O. (1906) *Sex and Character,* transl. from the 6th German edn. London: William Heinemann.

Wells, J. (1994) *Princess Caraboo: Her True Story.* London: Pan Books.

Werry, J. S. (1992a) Child psychiatric disorders: are they classifiable? *British Journal of Psychiatry*, *161*, 472–480.

Werry, J. S. (1992b) Child and adolescent (early onset) schizophrenia: a review in light of DSM-III-R. *Journal of Autism and Developmental Disorders*, *22*, 601–624.

Werry, J. S. (1994) Long term outcome of pervasive developmental, psychotic and allied disorders. In L. Hechtman (ed.) *Do they Outgrow it? Longterm Outcome of Childhood Disorders*. Washington, D. C. : American Psychiatric Press.

Whiteley, O. (1920) *The Diary of Opal Whiteley*. London: G. P. Putnam & Sons.

Wiltshire, S. (1987) *Drawings*. London: J. M. Dent & Sons.

Wing, L. (1981) Asperger's syndrome: a clinical account. *Psychological Medicine*, *11*, 115–129.

Wing, L. (1991) The relationship between Asperger's syndrome and Kanner's autism. In U. Frith (ed.) *Autism and Asperger Syndrome*. Cambridge: Cambridge University Press, pp. 93–121.

Wing, L. (1992) Manifestations of social problems in high-functioning autistic people. In E. Schopler and G. B. Mesibov (eds) *High-Functioning People with Autism*. New York: Plenum, pp. 129–142.

Wittgenstein, L. (1991) *Geheime Tagebücher 1914–1916*, ed. W. Baum. Vienna: Turin and Kant.

Wolff, S. (1964) Schizoid personality disorder in childhood. Unpublished paper read at the Sixth International Congress of Psychotherapy, London, August, 1964.

Wolff, S. (1984) Schizoid personality. In J. Wortis (ed.) *Mental Retardation and Developmental Disabilities, Vol. 13*. New York: Plenum, pp. 81–103.

Wolff, S. (1989) *Childhood and Human Nature: The Development of Personality*. London: Routledge.

Wolff, S. (1991a) Moral development. In M. Lewis (ed.) *Child and Adolescent Psychiatry: A Comprehensive Textbook*. Baltimore: Wiley, pp. 187–194.

Wolff, S. (1991b) 'Schizoid' personality in childhood and adult life I: the vagaries of diagnostic labelling. *British Journal of Psychiatry*, *159*, 615–620.

Wolff, S. (1991c) 'Schizoid' personality in childhood and adult life III: the childhood picture. *British Journal of Psychiatry*, *159*, 629–635.

Wolff, S. (1992) Psychiatric morbidity and criminality in 'schizoid' children grown-up: a records survey. *European Child and Adolescent Psychiatry*, *1*, 214–221.

Wolff, S. (1993) Personality disorder in childhood. In P. Tyrer and G. Stein (eds) *Personality Disorder Reviewed*. London: Gaskell, Royal College of Psychiatrists, pp. 64–89.

Wolff, S. and Barlow, A. (1979) Schizoid personality in childhood: a comparative study of schizoid, autistic and normal children. *Journal of Child Psychology and Psychiatry*, *19*, 175–180.

Wolff, S. and Chick, J. (1980) Schizoid personality in childhood: a controlled follow-up study. *Psychological Medicine*, *10*, 85–100.

Wolff, S. and Cull, A. (1986) 'Schizoid' personality and antisocial conduct: a retrospective case note study. *Psychological Medicine*, *16*, 677–687.

Wolff, S. and McGuire, R. J. (1995) Schizoid personality in girls: a follow-up study – What are the links with Asperger's syndrome? *Journal for Child Psychology and Psychiatry* (in press).

Wolff, S., Narayan, S. and Moyes, B. (1988) Personality characteristics of parents of autistic children: a controlled study. *Journal of Child Psychology and Psychiatry*, *29*, 143–153.

Wolff, S., Townshend, R., McGuire, R. J. and Weeks, D. J. (1991) 'Schizoid' personality in childhood and adult life II: adult adjustment and the continuity with schizotypal personality disorder. *British Journal of Psychiatry*, *159*, 620–629.

Woody, E. and Claridge, G. (1977) Psychoticism and creativity. *British Journal of Social and Clinical Psychology*, *16*, 241–248.

World Health Organization (1992) *ICD: The ICD-10 Classification of Mental and Behavioural Disorders – Clinical Descriptions and Diagnostic Guidelines*. Geneva: WHO.

World Health Organization (1993) *ICD-10: The ICD-10 Classification of Mental and Behavioural Disorders – Diagnostic Criteria for Research*. Geneva: WHO.

Zeitlin, H. (1986) *The Natural History of Psychiatric Disorder in Children: A Study of Individuals Known to Have Attended Both Child and Adult Psychiatric Departments of the Same Hospital*. Maudsley Monographs, 29. Oxford: Oxford University Press.

Zeitlin, H. (1991) Childhood development and schizophrenia. In C. Eggers (ed.) *Schizophrenia and Youth: Etiology and Therapeutic Consequences*. Berlin: Springer, pp. 66–77.

Name index

Subject index

adoption studies: of genetics of schizophrenia 16, 87, 128

advocacy: for affected children 138–139

affect: detached 16

affective psychosis: in creative people 120–121; in eminent writers 120; in families of geniuses 119, 120; *see also* manic-depressive illness .

age of onset: of Asperger's autistic psychopathy 20; of 'borderline' states in childhood 24; of schizoid personality of childhood 5, 19

age of referral of schizoid children 4, 31, 67

alcohol problems (excessive drinking): in schizoid men at follow-up 54, 60, 80, 102; in schizoid women 72, 102

aliases: use of 63, 100, 101, 102, 134

allusive thinking 113

animals: special attachment to 6, 7, 25, 76–77, 78

antisocial behaviour: and borderline personality disorder 25; in childhood, risk for later delinquency 55; in childhood of schizoid boys 33; in childhood of schizoid children 96, 100–102, 107; in childhood of schizoid girls 100; and family adversity 99; at follow-up in men 54–55; at follow-up in schizoid men and women 72, 96, 102; *see also* conduct disorder, criminality

antisocial personality disorder 97; diagnosis of 122; general causes of 106–107; in schizoid people at follow-up 102; *see also* psychopathy

associations: odd 40

Asperger's autistic psychopathy of childhood 20–24, 44; compared with infantile autism 23–24; and eminence 121; familial incidence of 22, 127; family aggregation with autism 131–132; relationship to schizophrenia 20, 22, 87, 128; sex incidence of 22; similarity to schizoid and schizotypal personality in childhood 124; treatment for 136–137

Asperger's disorder in DSM-IV 28, 122; and criminality 109; and giftedness 114

Asperger's syndrome 16, 26–28, 35, 113; affected parents 127–128; and childhood autism 130; as classified in ICD-X 28, 122, 125–126; co-morbidity in 66; as a form of schizoid personality 26; and giftedness 110, 114; as a pervasive developmental disorder 26, 122; prevalence of 126; psychological functioning in 133–135; and schizophrenia 26, 86; social adjustment in later life 52, 72; treatment for 142–143; in violent offenders 97

associated symptoms: treatment for 139–140

attachments to parents: of autistic and schizoid/Asperger children 130

autism: and artistic giftedness 112; characteristics of parents of autistic children 131, 135; characteristics of siblings of autistic children 36, 131–132, 135; as classified in DSM-III, DSM-IV and ICD-10 18, 28; comparative study of schizoid and autistic children 10–11; early childhood autism 13; genetic links with schizoid/Asperger disorder 131–133; and giftedness 110, 114; and later schizophrenia 132–133; 'lesser variant' of 131–132; associated with savant